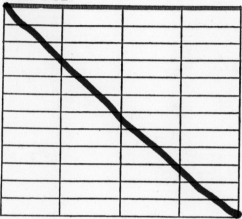

The Art of Media Instruction

The Art of Media Instruction

BY DON GILLIS

CRESCENDO BOOK PUBLICATIONS

Dallas, Texas

The Art of Media Instruction

BY DON GILLIS

Copyright © 1973

CRESCENDO BOOK PUBLICATIONS
Dallas, Texas

Library of Congress Catalog Card Number: **73-85869**

Printed in the United States of America

DEDICATION

This book is respectfully dedicated to Radio Station WBAP, Fort Worth, Texas, which provided my first experience as a professional performer, arranger, writer and director in media; to NBC for extending those experiences through almost 17 years of staff and free-lance broadcasting activity in production and writing; and to Dallas Baptist College, whose pioneer efforts in media instruction provided a valuable laboratory and observation post from which to project the ideas contained in this book. And while it is respectfully dedicated to those just mentioned, it is affectionately dedicated to Barbara, my wife, who lent me ears and opinions as this manuscript emerged from scrawled handwriting into print.

Don Gillis
Columbia, S. C.
August, 1973

ACKNOWLEDGMENTS

To acknowledge the many whose helpful hands contributed to this book would require pages equal to the book itself. Three persons in particular I would remember for special assistance: Jerry Plemons, Specialist, Audio Visual Communications at American Airlines, Dallas, Texas, for his chapter on "Television Photography"; Carol Ann Mills, member of the Library Staff of the University of Texas at Dallas, for her Appendix, "Resources in Media Instruction"; and Robert R. McEmber, Manager, Operations Training-Training Techniques at Eastern Airlines in Miami, Fla., for his many valuable suggestions on TV production and his guidance through flight simulation

FOREWORD

Every elementary school child soon learns that "action words" come in at least three basic varieties—past, present and future. In no time at all, he discovers that the modern counterparts of Dick and Jane ran yesterday, run today and will run tomorrow. The point of concern is not that Dick and Jane are still running in an age of moon walks, but that the schools in which they run in the present are more like the past than the future. The real challenge, as Alvin Toffler reminds· us in *Future Shock*, is to shift the schools from the past tense to the future tense.

This is not to imply that contemporary schools are not changing, because they are undergoing constant and significant changes. The crucial point, however, is that they are changing too often without a clear goal that change is to accomplish, without the adequate involvement of the people—students and teachers—to be affected by the changes and without the basic skills necessary to implement the changes effectively. Consequently, changes in our schools often may bring confusion, disenchantment and a reversion to the comfort of the known past. No area in education has been more characteristic of these phenomena than media and technology.

In elementary and secondary schools over the past two decades, the pendulum has swung periodically from a mood of panacea to disenchantment. Unfortunately, thousands of dollars of media materials and equipment bought with government assistance when technology was seen as the answer to all educational ills gather dust in school closets during the extended periods of teacher apathy.

Most college and university faculties have come through the periodic instructional technology uprisings untouched. For the most part, teaching on the college level remains an anachronism. In the few instances where media have made a significant impact in how learning takes place in colleges, the changes have been slow and painful, resisted tenaciously by most faculty in the trenches of committee rooms and faculty lounges.

The publication of this important book by Don Gillis coincides with an upswing in the belief that media have a role to play in education. The successes of *Sesame Street* and similar television ventures have been instrumental in creating the optimism of the moment. A resurgence of interest in instructional media and technology by major foundations and governmental agencies may pave the way for more substantial and permanent gains to be made with this swing of the pendulum. In short, this is a book whose time has come.

Don Gillis is a Renaissance man living in the twentieth century. He is greater than any label you want to hang on him—composer, conductor, musician, teacher, writer, artist, director, producer, manager, humorist, counselor, friend, learner and worshipper. He is all these at once with a warmth, a genuineness and a wit that are unique. It is important to know these things about Don Gillis in order to understand the far-reaching significance of what he has to say in this book.

Don Gillis has long known and practiced what educators, foundation staffers and governmental report writers are only now discovering—that media provide the opportunities for education to move into the future tense. He has known and demonstrated, too, that media for educational purposes cannot be isolated from the context of the media arts, e.g. music, art, drama, dance, etc., and hope to be effective. His life has prepared him, perhaps more uniquely than anyone else in education today, to write this book putting it all together.

This is a book that should be read by academic deans and curriculum planners who are concerned about substantive educational change. It is a book that should be read by teachers who want to call forth curiosity and creativity from their students through the touch, the sights and sounds of the media arts. It is a reference work and a training guide for librarians, school media specialists and others whose work supports the classroom teacher. And, finally, it is a book that should be read by young people who want to be teachers—teachers that teach in the future tense.

Ralph C. Atkinson, Jr.
Vice-President of Ottawa University
Ottawa, Kansas

TABLE OF CONTENTS

CHAPTER I

WHAT MEDIA CAN DO FOR YOU THAT
YOU CAN'T DO FOR YOURSELF...

"Everything in the world is inside your mind—even secrets!"
(Julie Gillis, age 3½)

Why she said it, I'm not sure. But she did say it one day, running into my arms with a joy that happens only when little ones discover something for themselves. She said it, gave me a hug, and went on her way—content that she had done her part by sharing her discovery with me.

And she had, for she was *self* as media, using self to transmit something to me through words, gestures, facial expressions, body action and much inner excitement as the thought came from inside her mind into mine. And having done her part, she went on her way, leaving me to continue the transmission of not only her thought, but of the situational condition in which the thought was projected. So she was media, and now I am media, and as readers of this word you are media. She knew it, I knew it and now you know it. She was neither mechanistic nor electronic. She, I and you—we're human media.

Perhaps I should have entitled this chapter "What can you do for yourself that you don't do for yourself without media?" Maybe it would be better as "What media can do for others through you—if you would let it." Regardless of its title, in this chapter our discussion is going to range far and wide about you as the user and the maker of media and that great group of tools which comprise the transmittive devices commonly called "hardware." This hardware, whatever it is, and you represent the fullest meaning of the word: *media.*

13

The list of tools we use to transmit to or receive from others is endless. It consists of television, chalk, computers, bulletin boards, radio, ball-point pens, servo-systems, crayons, etc. Make a list for yourself sometime and include the wide variety of all print media and all art. Then add such items as signal flags and satellites, typewriters and cameras, phonographs and audio-video tapes, maps, charts, slide projectors and telephones, motion pictures and teletypes. Your list of things which can be used to allow self to extend self beyond self will grow to staggering lengths.

When you have finished your list (if you can), you might draw up a similar list of transmittive agents by which you may transmit thoughts to others. That list, also, would be tremendous. You, as a member of the human species, are richly endowed to communicate a multiplicity of thoughts from your being even without language. You, as transmittive agent and receiver of transmitted information, plus the long list of physical properties which may be used to help you receive and transmit all that you may wish or desire, are media.

Our objective in this chapter (as indeed it is in the entire book) is a simple one: by showing you the potential of the tools, we hope you will use them in a creative procedure, exactly as the composer uses notes, the artist uses paints and the novelist, poet or playwright uses words. When you get right down to the basics, the tools of media are the instruments by which you may express creativity. You as a member of the human family ARE creative. Your own creative potential, directed within the tool-function potential of media instruments, can—when properly used—become ART. For education, whose responsibility in dealing with the development of the human mind is so awesome, nothing less than those values achieved in the perfect blending of physical-emotional-spiritual materials defined as art should be considered worthy of our efforts.

Think of all the people who have used media tools to create! The "word people," for instance—those whose idea-power and expressive-power were sufficient to be assimilated into "oneness" or word-power—are still with us as live beings, ageless

14

heroes of the knowledge world. Those whose words were put into manuscript and print media captured the nowness of their minds so that they are still actively available to us. All created imaginatively within the tool-power they had—not for themselves, but for others. Were this not true, they would have merely created transiently (by thinking) and let it go at that. So with tools, creative potential and desire to share, they wrote their plays, scientific discoveries, chronicles of history, commentaries on society and their philosophies, poems, novels, instructional manuals and dreamings. These were all motivated by self but accomplished through media tools.

Composers, painters, sculptors, inventors and architects all created with the variety of tools available to them in order to achieve self-expression. They individually selected, from their available tools, the media which each believed would enable him to be locked in to some form of permanence. Those who combined the materials and the ideas best are remembered in relative degrees of greatness. Those who did it least (or not at all) are forgotten. Some of them combined the endowment of creative potential with the best available materials to emerge as artists whose products have remained as evidence of their artistry.

It is not exaggeration to think that one of you may be the Mozart or da Vinci of Media Arts by creating—through our media tools—just as they created with theirs. The creative artist of our times generally has not been active with media potential (in the conglomerate sense of the word) to the extent that the Media Arts needs him to be. He, like many of you, has not yet realized the full potential available to him to take the real arts and utilize them within the technology of the electronic media in the "altogether of" as a creative process. But you, with the purposefulness of needing to communicate in order to consumate your fullest living drive, will accept the new potential of being a creative artist in the new technology—not only for now, but so your artistry may endure beyond your own lifetime. Ours is the first age in which teachers, other than those who have been immortalized for their writings, sayings or

15

students, have enjoyed such an opportunity for immortality as that which presents itself now through the Media Arts.

So first of all, media is going to help you become a creative artist within media itself. With that lofty goal in mind, let us define the scope of the media tools and categorize them in specific function for use in instructional media. But before we do that, let's make a list of the things which media tools can do for you that you cannot do for yourself to provide the basis for our discussion:

a) Extend the sensory capacity of the eye and ear to receive inputs otherwise unobtainable.
b) Increase the power of the individual to have his voice heard and his actions seen at distances far beyond his human capacity to do so.
c) Provide experience otherwise unavailable and unobtainable.
d) Enable the is of events to be captured to become the permanently happening.
e) Provide a mind-to-mind relationship between you and your viewer-listener with a capacity to input with intensity otherwise unavailable.
f) Extend your ability to teach without the necessity of time and place factors being involved.
g) Allow you to deliver educational materials for repeated performance.

In these seven areas of advantage (plus that of art potential), a wide variety of media tools is required. Some of them are quite simple—such as pencil and chalk; some are extremely sophisticated—such as servo-systems and television cameras. Most of the tools require hands-on operation (an individual plus equipment). Devices which are operated even by remote control are still, at one point or another, hands-on in their need for human factors to set them into operation. Typewriters, for example, would be classified loosely under a general heading of "mechanistic," although a typewriter designed to be automated might be classified as mechanical-plus-servo-system. In all cases, persons—rather than person—are involved for we always

16

find one person using the work of many other persons to expand his own ability to be more than self in *any* effort.

"Media," meaning "instruments for use," then, convey ideas and information from self to other selves and things. The word is symbolically multi-meaning. When used in media instruction, it may be defined as "devices (hardware) plus materials to be conveyed (software) plus use and user." For the more specific definition "media" will refer to those mechanistic and electronic devices which are capable of producing and retrieving materials on a more or less permanent basis rather than those products which are transient in their endurance and retrievable potential.

An example of this may be seen in my telling you verbally (orally only) of a film I had in mind to make. Your concept of my speaking would be a transient or of the moment perception. If you were to see that film after I had made it, the product would be retrievable for viewing as often as you desired. If I were to write my ideas on a chalkboard and you were to read the words before they were erased, the transitory element would be involved. If you had video taped the session where I had written my ideas on the chalkboard, the video tape itself would be a product permitting you to have access (by retrieval) to my ideas at whatever time you wanted to view them.

So the element of retrievability is important to us in our ultimate definition of media in instruction. Print materials obviously fit into this retrievable category. A book as well as a microfilm or microfiche are media representing print materials. Both are retrievable, but one utilizes a static form whereas the other, utilizing a static size, employs magnification to change the rigidity of the extremely small photographic prints and make them appear book page size (or in some instances ever larger). A television camera focused on the microfiche screen could capture the image, electronically re-record it and project its image on a large screen to magnify the letters to enormous sizes. Thus the print media takes on a three-way potential: the book itself, a microphotography involvement of the book and the use of the microphotography reader on TV. In all three instances the material is retrievable.

Photography, in all of its forms, plays a major role in our media definition. The devices used in reproducing photographic products also play a major role. These devices include projectors, screens, slides and film as well as their use in the television studio to be transferred to video tape.

A picture taken by a photographer in Leningrad may appear in your newspaper on the same day the picture was taken. It was transmitted via radio, its components broken down into particles which could be transmitted by the radio wave, then re-assembled electronically to be a picture appearing in your newspaper. The newspaper picture is a representation of the one which was made by the photographer. The picture made by the photographer was a representation of the subject being photographed. Sometime take a powerful magnifying lens and look at a newspaper photograph. You will find that its components are individual particles which together form the whole representatively.

The retrievable devices enabling us to hear stored sound (recordings, tapes, motion picture sound tracks), along with the devices used in their reproduction, are also very important to our media definition. Their involvement in media has a parallel course to that of photography.

Perhaps the term "mass media," generally construed to mean "public media" (all items available to the society), overwhelms us in the largeness of its capability and availability to transmit and receive. It thus takes on an understood-but-non-definable rigid-mobility in its connotation. We could enclose the capability-availability factor into terms such as "private media," but that would limit one of the values of instructional media which, however privately designated for specific usage, nonetheless has potential mass media aspects in its use beyond the campus.

Mass media function on a generalized delivery philosophy: all who will participate, may. This leads us to believe that we must use the term "instructional media" and define the scope of it to mean "media used instructionally by self plus devices (mechanistic or electronic) to create a product to be used by another or others for the purpose of being instructed publicly or privately."

Many teachers reject the instructional media approach because it demands a change. Whereas they are comfortable in an environment of known capability performance (the traditional classroom), they are uncomfortable in any new situation where there are more unknown than known capabilities. All of us reflect negatively to unknowns, particularly if they have the capacity to affect us personally. The traditional is our comfort-womb, and the non-traditional looms suspiciously in our minds as potential threat.

We can make the transition easily if we think of the media tools which we already use on a daily basis. Media tools, such as the telephone, have already been allowed into our comfort zone. The telephone functions to allow your voice to be heard "X" distances and allows your ear to hear voices from "X" distances. We call up voices located in different place-zones, accepting the use of this mind-to-mind medium as a natural privilege accorded to us as members of a progressive society.

Already in existence is the picture-phone, a device which will provide us not only with voice information, but with picture information as well. And already there is resistance to the general idea of invasion of our home-comfort privacy by allowing a picture of self to be seen by anyone who dials our number. It conjures up a picture of sensitivity toward the possibility of having our public image destroyed if people see us as we are at home. But it has a cutoff switch as does all media, and we'll get used to it anyway once we use it. The phrase "once we use it" is a powerful hint to all who now stay away from media because of their strangeness to them.

Beyond the element of personal media contact and a few gimmicks such as "information," "weather," "time," and maybe "dial-a-prayer," not much use has been made of the telephone on any organized basis to disseminate instructional material. We do not have (but could have) "dial-an-instructional-unit" formats in which audio-tape feeds of instructional materials could be offered for home study. The telephone is widely used in live TV educational situations where ETV exists in network form. This allows a student to talk directly with the teacher. Dallas Baptist College planned its Learning Center facility to include this instructional service via telephone with a dial-access retrieval capability for home use, and there will be other such systems set up to operate from campus centers which will provide to students a chance to go to school without ever leaving their own homes or phonebooths!

I am sure that the same idea will ultimately prevail with the picture phone or with circuitry which will be connected to one's personal TV set to enable the student to "dial up" retrievable media packages via telephone cable. Such systems are already a part of installations within campus Learning Centers (and immediate campus buildings) for either audio or video reception. Distributed on a more widely retrievable potential, a student body might well be drawn from among those who are currently unable to leave home, job or institution to come to a campus. These will ultimately have an opportunity to go to school at a time and place more directly related to their own needs.

So a teacher uses telephone media freely. There is nothing uncomfortable about that. He uses print media, surviving that effort in comfort. He also uses radio, TV and recordings to be entertained and informed.

Why then should he hesitate to use media tools more generally as a part of his normal teaching procedure? In his use of telephone, radio, TV and recordings he is not required to have much knowledge of the function of the tools in order to use them. And so he is comfortable in the easy-to-perform access to that media which it pleases him to use for his own benefit. He needs to extend his range of effort to use media for the benefit of others. The tools used in media instruction are not so complicated that they cannot be accomplished.

Our reluctance to do so, particularly if we are already teachers, is based on the feeling that having established ourselves as teachers and having prepared to teach within the

20

traditional, we privately resent having any more learning-necessity imposed upon us.

There is also a reluctance to move out of the traditional presentation modes. We have an established and successful way of doing things within a classroom. We have been slowly but reluctantly adapting our procedures to use the normal audio-visual equipment of various projectors, turntables and tape recorders—but only for classroom usage. This has been difficult, for the design of the usual classroom is not always perfect for showing slides and screening movies. And even if it were, an extra effort is involved in securing materials, setting up equipment (which often doesn't function right) and integrating these materials within a methodology largely devoted to lecture.

To use instructional media in the broadest sense of being created creatively (in the arts sense), the classroom methodology must undergo drastic revision. Our classroom has to become the production studio—an entirely different arena. And since this is true, the new teaching procedures (while they may also take into account potential use within the classroom) must first realize that the new viewpoint of the student has been reduced in size to earphones and TV screen, rather than to groups of students with a structured classroom situation. But media, even as really old as they already are, are still considered by many as "new-fangled" ideas. They are often approached with all of the wisdom and openness of mind that says: "If the Lord had wanted us to use media when we teach, He would have said so in the Good Book."

As teachers, there is scarcely one among us who does not know how to operate a simple camera, and most of us along the way have had to take at least one course in which the use of standard audio-visual items such as filmstrip, filmloop and overhead projectors was taught. Even items such as phonographs and cassette tape recorders have been demonstrated to and used by each of us. While we may be helpless if something goes wrong, we at least know how to turn the equipment on and off and use it passably well. It is no giant step from knowing how to operate equipment to begin thinking creatively with it. Once we get over feeling imposed upon because working with media is a time-consuming job, we can begin to realize the power of their abilities and our attitudes will change. So first, as Meredith Willson so aptly put it in *The Music Man*, "You have to know the territory"—and the territory for you is the hardware.

Hardware is that collection of tools which enable us to create in methodology that which is retrievable by a user at any given point beyond the making of the product. Software is the content "represented by creativity" in the materials used to "capture the moment" with retrievable and re-creative capability. Function plus capability of tools plus materials plus retrievability plus human involvement in content equals potential of use by human involvement plus reproductive tools. Both of these terms "hardware" and "software" are absurd words aesthetically, but their consistent usage is so widespread that it would be difficult to change them—even though they equate the ultra-sophistication of technological miracles with nuts and bolts and ideas as scrambled brains, all mushy and jello-like!

Our attempt to arrive at a hard and fast definition of media reminds me of the effort involved in trying to pick up mercury between our fingers, so elusive is the definition capability. But whether or not we can be precise about it, we all have a concept of media as the physical tools used by us to convey non-physical information mind-to-mind or mind-to-thing.

Whatever else media is, then, it is fundamentally transmittive, a carrier agent, a transportive mechanism, an energy force of conveyance. The resources available as content include all of those availably retrievable items which are compatible to the tools we select to use: in short, all of those things which have to do with the stimulus of the senses, principally the primary senses of the eye and ear. There are some media, of course, which employ touch, taste and smell, but not enough of them (yet) to include in a generalized meaning of the word relating to content.

22

So then, media is that which is representative of real in its conveying energy force as it translates real into simulation of real to be used *as* real after the transmitting process has been effected. Real (real things, real words, real sound, real color, real people) is conveyed in unreal state (simulation) by means of energy forces (static and fluid) on their way to becoming a simulation of reality to be used as real by something or somebody.

Media is self-plus and we may both transmit and receive through it, consciously and unconsciously, willingly and unwillingly. Perhaps our understanding of it would be clear if we defined it simply as "the energy-force of X-factor used in the process of mind-to-mind relationship which, by using real as its true-base, changes it to simulation of the real during the transmission process to be used as real in whatever form is generated."

In our discussion I have referred to the arts as media and to the gadgetry of transmissive force as media, and I have referred to the combination of gadgetry, the process of using it, and the product of its use as Media Arts. For me, media is the totality of communication, irrespective of the form it takes or what it takes to produce the form. In a later chapter we will talk about symbolism being the true language of communication and will attempt to equate the process of creativity through symbolistic procedure (as used by the arts) with that same process by which we may produce art through media. But before we use print media (as now) to move you from interest to lassitude, we'll stop defining and start transmitting thoughts more directly related to the title of this introductory chapter. We will, however, keep in mind always that it is the retrievable aspect of whatever media we discuss that is significant to our writing of *The Art of Media Instruction.*

We, as selves—of ourselves—occupying the time-place realm of being, are able to occupy only one space and one time at a time. We can be here or there, but not both. We *are* now, we *were* then, and we *may be* in the future. And in each of the time-place conditions, only the moment of being is actually real, for what *was* is past and what *will be* has not yet happened. I emphasize this only to cause you to be aware that the past is experience used and its experience force is now memory. Memory is a sense which of itself retains the real in simulated energy force. Some forms of media are similar to memory in that they retain the energy forces related to the experience.

In those media areas in which the materials used (physical materials such as tape, recordings, photographs) have enduring energy force themselves (a marble statue as opposed to a sand castle built at the seashore at low tide), a certain permanence of the energy force of experience will prevail. Print media may burn or disintegrate with time, but the faces chipped out on Mount Rushmore may last indefinitely, even beyond the time of communicative potential in a future age to which they mean nothing more than faces chipped from stone. A motion picture may crumble to bits, a phonograph record or magnetic tape may be devoured by fungus growth, a statue may erode into shapelessness, a painting on plaster may be in imbalance with the elements of paint being destroyed by the elements in the plaster, or a knowledge-filled mind may die. The elements of media, then, are an important factor in the transmittive effectiveness with respect to their enduring qualities.

Although we are immutably bound to time and place physically, it is not so mentally. Our minds may travel far and wide at superhuman speeds as we move from experience-event in time or experience-place in space. In both instances, the mind moves at the speed of light simulatively. The mind moves, the body stays—the energy force is experience.

With exterior forces produced by media, the simulated energy force of experience can be vastly strengthened. Beyond our personal capacity to see and hear, the magnifying power of intensity provided by optics and sonic systems now enable our own personal eyes to see farther in all directions and our own personal ears to hear from everywhere.

The telescope and the microscope or even our own eyeglasses make it possible for our eyes to see far more than our own personal eye can ever see. With electronic microscopes, we can see that which appears to be solid and inert *actually* being not-solid at all. And what looks to be dead and lifeless with our own eyes is so "life-filled" with energized forces that our minds, conditioned as they are by human sensory limitation, can scarcely comprehend it all. With additional media beyond the electronic microscope itself, we may see photographs or video tape of what is now available only for the eye to see through the microscope lens. Having made the initial photography (in any form), we may then magnify what we see to powers thousands of times greater than even that which we may see through the microscope with our personal eye. So media can give us power upon power to extend the sensory capacity of our eyes infinitely.

We may go into a meadow and, using all personal physical force, shout as loudly as we can. Our sound is heard through our limited efforts, but we may take a media gadget, a hand-carried amplifier-speaker-microphone, and to the extent of the amplifying energy inherent within the device, our voice (now real and yet simulated at the same moment) is powerful enough to move much farther away from us. If we add a transmitting factor of greater strength (radio), our meadow-shouting effort may now be heard in Bombay, Rome, Tokyo and New York simultaneously. Through media force, we have power upon power to extend the capacity of self to be transmitted everywhere.

This also is true for our ears—remember those voices we heard coming from the moon? In another age we might have been sent to Bedlam for claiming such a thing. But now, accustomed as we are to hearing (and seeing) events from the far ends of the earth as they *are happening*, our ears are like some mammoth sensors attuned to the universe.

Just as we imagined the possibility of the meadow experience growing from just us to potential world communicators and receivers, so we may also imagine our possibility as retrievable instructors, increasing the scope of our influence beyond the numbers contained within the combined classroom

25

attendance of our lifetime. This too may be effected at any given time or place.

What would be the total number of students a teacher may instruct in fifty years of classroom activity? Five thousand? Ten thousand? A hundred thousand? Perhaps it would be difficult to add up the total, but let's say he had 500 students each year for 50 years. The total would be 25,000.

In *one* performance of *one* media unit, translated within the studio into retrievable materials, we could teach that total number, either on a one-to-one basis or in throngs, EACH TIME we taught with media—and not within our structured classrooms, but everywhere and anywhere. As teachers we have not begun to comprehend the numerical vastness of audiences that tune in to hear radio and television. It totals millions of simultaneously listening-viewing individuals. And while I do not project mass-million audiences for each of us *merely* as a result of our using media, the potential to reach such mass audiences *is* there to be achieved.

Such an experience is not unattainable. I personally have experienced broadcast and telecast situations where the audience totaled millions. In addition to presiding as producer-director, I have been commentator and panelist on many other occasions and have conducted symphony orchestras on occasions where the mass live audience (plus other vast audiences reached through delayed broadcasts to the armed forces and overseas stations) reached millions. I have also made recordings that have been heard via radio by added multi-millions of people. To have had those numbers in a single gathering of people would have required a classroom so huge that it couldn't be built. So I speak from the experience of having had it happen to me—and the joy of knowing that one energy expenditure will service millions is an incentive to keep on trying to create that which will be wanted to be used. This was through electronic media, but I have also known the joy of the print media in publications of my music, articles and books. So—it has done for me. This media thing we're talking about, with its pages receiving printed pictures of my thoughts and its

26

lightwaves and soundwaves electronically in motion, is time consuming, but its rewards are boundless. That's what all print media is in a sense, for the lightwaves and soundwaves are themselves tiny picture-symbols of energy forces in motion. Man, in his ingenuity, has probed the previously unknown to be able to define these energy impulses into translatable pictures (simulation) of the real in both sight and sound. Not only has he done that, but he has learned to use the energy force of the symbolization to excite (as energy itself) other devices so as to cause them to simulate the original forces. We call these "happenings" radio, TV, photography and recording. In their mechanistic-electronic performance of transmission, we use the term "recording" to indicate or identify the miracle of stopping the "now" experience at the moment of its happening.

So media not only allows us to extend self to the X-power as it *is* happening, but it also enables us to retain it *as* it happened. Thus, through media we extend self in stopped-time-place. Of course, it is only the simulation of the realness of the experience, but then so is the memory of experience only a simulation of it. The difference is that the energy of a recalled simulative experience is always present (within the limitations of the enduring quality of the materials used) to be re-simulated as we re-hear and re-see. And the stimulae themselves retain the full strength of energy force in media, while the mind itself (confronted as it is with millions of sensory inputs) has a tendency to sort out and keep those stimulae which seem necessary for conscious use, consigning the rest of them to the custody of the unconscious mind.

We, under certain conditions (hypnosis is the classic example), may retrieve these stimulae and return them to the conscious mind, reliving them as of the moment "real" and at the same moment viewing them as conscious spectator of past events. However, except under extraordinary circumstances, we do not allow such stimulae to be retrieved. Media, on the other hand, allows us to escape the bondage of time-place in experience, and, even more, it provides access to stiumlae providing reactivation of these stimulae, irrespective of time-place in which we choose to retrieve the simulated experience.

So through media we not only have the capability of providing the mind with the power to re-travel its own real experience (simulatively—by seeing it again and again), but we may travel faster and further than our own physical bodies would have been able to do in order to provide us with the real experience.

We, as members of the human species, possess (or are possessed transiently by) an energy force we name "spirit." Spirit and mind are interrelated but are not the same thing. The spiritual plane is universal, the composite of all matter and thought. The physical state is in and of the world in our own time-place displacement factor. It is the spirit involved in what we define as natural law which enables the codification of light and sound elements (as symbols) to be observed physically and used for the purpose of television, radio, photography and recording media.

This phenomenon of capturing now through representative energy forces is observable throughout history in communicative objects, things, beings and ideas as expressed by words, paintings, monuments, statues, music, numbers, etc., generated as expression of spirituality codified. The self-generative creative forces found a way to be expressed in a permanence observable by others than self, and so language (in all of the connotative meaning of the word) was produced from void.

If we define "spirit" as nothing more than "selflessness within self," unfettered by time-place limitation, independent of life force for existence yet responding to life force both within and without the body, we may better understand the eternal—both prior to life existence and afterward.

Earlier we spoke of servo-systems as a media tool. Let's talk about them for a moment and see that we as teachers are somewhat like servo-systems. They are made up to perform certain limited-but-specific things by a designated fashion in order to fulfill the objective to cause performance. We train to teach within a subject area and fulfill the objective of training by teaching to cause performance in others. Servo-systems, however, are only electronic devices of a highly

28

complex nature and perform *only* their stated, predetermined objectives. In other words, they perform in *only* a specific way in order to cause *only* specified performance.

A guided missile designed to find a target is supplied with an electronic brain which transmits signals (messages) to various components within itself to do specific tasks. All of these components are designed to function on a scale varying from zero to one hundred per cent of efficiency. The performance of all individual acts depends on and relates to the efficiency of all other components. The missile may also be given the capacity to receive exterior information and translate it into values which cause predetermined responses by the electronic brain to act by redirecting messages to its components to function on a different efficiency scale. This permits the missile to perform a variety of activities in response to the new environmental conditions affecting it. Within certain limitations it has judgment or choice capability, but only that which is predetermined for it. At no time may the electronic brain extend its designated capacity beyond its designated capacity. It may not, of itself, solve a problem for which an answer has not been supplied. We are told that the development of such servo-systems is modeled, to one degree or another, after our own cerebral brain-neural systems. Ours, of course, are infinitely more complicated and have the capacity to find answers not yet supplied through a species endowment we call "reasoning."

The use of this illustration is obvious I think: servo-systems are designed to perform specific functions to "cause" other specific functions to perform designated tasks. As teachers, we decided on a specific objective: to teach. The objective of teaching is to cause others to perform. We carry this objective principle into every element of our teaching as methodology in ways to teach. We, in our personal, super-sophisticated human servo-systems, have infinite capability ourselves to change in response to changing exterior forces. We reason, and by reasoning we may redirect our systems to respond. Our systems, too, are set up to function on a scale of zero to one hundred per cent. Someday we may learn to use them to their maximum potential constantly.

29

Media gives us this small parable to enable us to see ourselves in terms of our capabilities and our potential in the use of our capabilities. The more we know, the better we can perform—but only within the objective we set for ourselves. Within the objective of teaching, the more specific the objective built into our "transmittive" for delivering messages which cause performance in others, the more effective we are as teachers, and they, as students.

It is a peculiar truism in life that the more that is shared, the more we have for ourselves. Learning is one of those cardinal elements such as love and understanding which, when given away, grows larger within the giver. Thus, if through retrievable media we are able to give more to more people, we will still have what we had—plus that which we have given away. It is, in a sense, related to the theory of "particles-plus" (which we will discuss later). You—a particle of teaching energy—plus the student (a particle of learning energy) do not equal two—you equal three: you, him and the new one related to the product created by your performance in him. This extends infinitely, not only between you and him, but also with him and others.

Media, then, numerically extend our capability to release our "one-plus-one-equals-three-plus" to a "one-plus-one-equals-X-power." That fact alone should convince us of media's ability to transform us from a known physical limitation factor to an infinite force factor in our media capability of being accessible to share, instantly retrievable any time and any place to anybody or everybody.

Media is the energy force of transmission on whatever plane it functions—spiritual, mental, physical and eternal. With it in its present intensification, we may "miracalize" our mental potential. However—at least so far—we are not able to use it much with taste, touch and smell senses. We still must rely on the transitive association to do that in formal media. We also receive such sensory stimulation (in sight and sound) associatively, but do not need to rely upon this media as we do the other senses. We may say "candy," but the reading of the

30

word or the sound of it does not transmit the real energy force in word media of actual simulation from taste or smell or touch. We may simulate it to a high degree of realness in sight, but without the associative force brought to the experience by the other senses we are limited in what we can actually do with it through media. Some media attempt to bring scents to pages, or touch (in varied simulative-actual ways), but few have attempted taste transmission.

In other forms of media (not normally related to educative function, yet which *are* educative) we have codified scents and tastes into compounds such as flavors and perfumes, recognizing the potency of such and such scents and flavors in stimulating (through the memory sense) the real. These, as well as the actual, become very subtle factors in human relationship, carrying—as they do—great potential not only for sensory stimulus, but stimulae to trigger emotional and spiritual responses as well. We have even found a stop-action mechanism in some flavors and smells through quick-freezing. We know how (as evidenced by many TV commercials) to create the sensation of taste, smell and touch by intensifying color and using presentational techniques which cause the viewer to salivate at the sight of succulent food displays. Sight combined with words can induce associative concepts related to taste and smell. While we are yet unable to transmit these sensory capabilities except associatively in media, even that potential is greater through electronic instrumentation than it is in mere print media. But it may still happen—although I can imagine that if it does, the cutoff switch on TV sets may become a vital factor in determining whether or not we choose to accept these inputs into our living room.

We have codified energy forces scientifically (as in medicine) to provide instruction to body forces to act as directed by the more powerful entering energy forces, and certain natural laws (having been codified) are observable in their action-reaction potential as they pertain to medicine and body function. This is media translated into pure action-reaction: strength of input force versus strength of reacting force. We

31

must assume that there is an intelligence that responds to stimulae without the need for previous experience in order to generate responsive action. It is also true that some physicians prescribe placebos (sugar pills) which are accepted by patients as real, thus enabling a reaction to simulation which, in some instances, is as effective as the real.

Scientists are now at work testing the potential in synthesizing energy forces to be used instead of "real experience" in the direct transmission of knowledge from one brain to another. That is the transference of knowledge to knowledge apart from the learning process itself. They are, however, a long way from their goal, but I have no doubt that it will be accomplished when some observable (but not yet seen) natural law's components in symbolism will be capsulized for use as we now use sight and sound pictures symbolized by photography and recording.

As to our potential in being able to capture time future before it happens, either simulatively or real, we tend to believe it to be improbable except for special provisions made in simulated events called "prophecy" or "precognition." However, we may involve the law of probabilities as we ourselves predict (based on known factors) with relative accuracy what *will* happen "if." In education we simulate a predicable future state of being *if* certain step-by-step actions are taken. It may be possible someday—since we can now simulate experience in "time was" and "time is" media—to also simulate the experience of "time will be." We do this now with a force we call "imagination" and share imagination with others through media. It is probable that in the Media Arts, as in other arts, that the creator will be able to predict the results of his products which result because of creative experiences. However, he will not (as in the arts) be able to predict with any accuracy the use of his product.

Will media ever be developed to the point where our five senses can be caused to have a real experience instead of a simulated one? In one sense (that of sight) it has already happened, enabling certain blind people to envision through television devices. By directing the stimulae provided by the camera to the receptors themselves (within the optic nerve centers), vision is provided in a sort of senior-grade media miracle. Such potential with receptors of the other senses awaits development—and, if it happens, it may be that the school of the future will be a couch upon which we lie permissively to allow predetermined experience to be ours, not as simulation of experience but as real. It may be done with a knowledge capsule or with an entirely new language called "compression," in which a whole lifetime of knowledge could be contained within an instant of stimulae. Or, perhaps more logically, the knowledge dosage administered would be in one of those time-delayed capsules in which the input energy would be released a bit at a time. Come to think of it, this is about what we have now in our current educational system. Perhaps media will be the agent activated to release the energy more quickly and more intensely to allow knowledge transfer to be affected with a greater degree of input acceptance as needed. One should not be too skeptical about such potential in media, for such a force factor was implanted within the life force of the species which enables it to grow, manufacture new blood cells and activate portions of itself *as needed*. All this occurs within the intelligence source which now governs our instant-to-instant progression through what we call life.

There is still one other unexplored area in which media is powerfully involved. This is the feeling area of the human species. It is actually an indefinable area although we generally call it "the emotions." Within media it is possible to direct predetermined reaction to those stimulae which provoke response in feeling, and with the greater intensity of media, it may be done more quickly and, of course, more subtly than can be accomplished with the real. We shall discuss more of this in the chapter called "Symbolism: the Language of the Media Arts." We mention it here to cause you to be aware of the added potency media has in enabling you to transfer your thoughts to others.

Lest you think you have wandered into some strange science-fiction novel by mistake, let us withdraw from probabilities and conjectures and return to the reality of now plus your potential in the future by re-asking the question expressed in the title of this chapter: What can media do for you that you cannot do for yourself? We have made a limited exploration of the possibilities of media and have made ourselves aware of the obvious while hinting at the future's possibility. We have concentrated on two words: "simulative" and "real" as we discussed experience as an energy force. We have even involved the "spiritual" in our discussion. Perhaps we can say that media is to the mind as the electronics of sight are to the more powerful eye and to the more powerful ear in the electronics of sound. Both are extensions of human physical potential. We as individuals are largely the product of all media sources and, therefore, as individuals we are ourselves "power potential" to be media for others.

We are like the man who knows he has but to push a button to activate forces which will activate other forces which, by their action, activate still other forces until the final force is unmeasurable by human standards. We, as educators, are provided with that super-activating power *if* we press the button to release the accumulated knowledge of the ages contained in the mass-mind of the universe.

Generations ago there was a fixed knowledge-mass (changing but slowly with passing years) accessible to limited numbers of people within the world population. With the coming of new technologies and the vast increase of population, the ratio of knowledge-mass to its accessible retrieval has not perceptibly changed because the knowledge-mass has increased at a greater volume than the accessibility of the population to it. In short, there is more information available per person than present technology (for all of its miracles) can deliver to any one person. Therefore, our future society will either need to find a way in which a greater ratio of world knowledge can be transmitted within shorter time spans to each individual or, reluctantly, allocate to groups of individuals certain specified knowledge areas *only*. This would make the totality of human mind-function become servant to some mystical, giant human-computer group to function as input to the whole of knowledge rather than being a part of the whole of knowledge. It has almost come to that point now where specialists in one small portion of knowledge areas are musts as a part of team efforts of creativity. It is a more potent threat than we now realize, unless other ways can be found to deliver more knowledge more quickly and effectively to more people. At the moment, media (however much in infancy) enables us to do this, and more techniques are being developed.

In my home I have over a thousand books, five or six hundred phonograph recordings and well over a thousand tapes. The combined information from this body of media materials would require several thousand hours of my time to receive their potential input. In addition, I have television, radios, subscribe to several magazines, own a group of paintings and drawings and have a reasonably-sized collection of 35mm. slides, films and video tapes. My problem is not having access to this stored knowledge but having time to use it and still function as a working member of society. How this dilemma will be solved, I do not know. I only know it must be solved by education itself to enable our society to continue to be functional.

So what media can really do for us that we cannot do for ourselves is to give us a sense of responsible action in its use, to be more concerned with the time factor required in the learning process and to attempt to develop methodology which will enable us to give students the advantage of the accessibility within a time period compatible with their needs to be members of society. It may well call for a restructuring of educational procedures in which the elements of time and place no longer become fundamental to the transmission of learning philosophy. In the meantime, we who now have the ability to be the predeterminate agent of experience through media designed either to serve one or great groups of ones must accept the awesome responsibility of any creator in its use. But however great the awesome responsibility of its use, it is more awesome to think of our responsibility for NOT using its powers.

With it we have a capability to use its potential as an ART form, stimulated by the potential of each device coupled with the potential of creative self to generate—as the artist does—new products of enduring capability caused by the perfection of mind-spirit plus desire to share self with others for the purpose of those needing instruction to be instructed. With media you can increase your power to let your voice and your actions be heard and seen at distances beyond your natural ability. You can receive and help experiences to be received which would otherwise be unavailable and unobtainable. You can capture the now of events as they happen and store them in retrievable fashion to be used by others without need to relate to time or place for their use. You can provide a mind-to-mind (or group) relationship between you and others in numerical relationships of unknown quantities. You can extend the sensory capacities of your eyes and ears. You, by envisioning yourself as super-media, can combine your use of as input and your utilization of in creating to extend self beyond self to unimagined limits.

In media instruction the teacher is the creative artist, the spiritual-mental tour guide into the infinity of potential. With it we are power factors of—if actually unknown—predictable potential. We know already that without it we limit ourselves unnecessarily by hanging on to the past with a tenacity that is unseeming to our roles as teachers.

Let me project a truth that is self-evident: "Nothing of itself happens by itself except nothing." Apply to this your relationship with media and you must answer the question: "What am I going to do about it?" Nothing? Or shall we "speak" the void into reality with the creative X-factor called media to create a universe of our own? It is my question—but it is your answer!

CHAPTER II

THE MEDIA ARTS

To the time-honored list of music, the graphic arts, creative writing, dance and drama now come the Media Arts—new and ever-changing in their electronic capabilities, ever-dependent upon the parent arts for their existence. Yet, oddly enough, the one factor they possess in addition to their unique quality of assimilation of all of art's ingredients is their capability to transmit an idea to millions at a time instantly, freeing all other arts from their static position within gallery, printed page, concert hall and theater. In their capability to transmit ideas they cause all of the other arts to assume a fluid state, now making it possible for the Media Arts themselves to become a creative art by combining those arts into the electronics of reproduction. Thus, without question, since the arts themselves are (of themselves) agents of the communication process, their combination within the framework of the media potential now makes possible a form of communication transcending any previous capability achieved in prior centuries. This is so in both instructional and arts creativity.

The Media Arts of themselves, then, become communicative without necessity of language (in the case of music, dance and Fine Arts) and thus remove the language barriers (in these instances) and, because of the characteristics of media, time and space barriers as well. In the hands of a skilled artisan who is fully aware of media's capabilities, the Media Arts in actuality become a new and dynamic form of creative artistry—the product of which is art itself.

As I speak of the Media Arts, my mind is occupied largely with television and less with the other obvious categories of

37

media (although I will admit to a strong inclination toward the audio arts as a powerful force). I speak also of television as an instructional vehicle rather than one of entertainment. This is in order to make clear that, while we will use all of the elemental production characteristics of television, its function will be for mind quickening and absorbtion of content rather than for pure entertainment. I would also include photography because it is, of itself, a Media Art capable of unique powers of artistic self-expression. Since it, along with all of the other arts, can be so easily assimilated into television as part of the creative components, it follows that the Media Arts are really a "Poly-Art"—a collection of many to make up one—their only limitations being those self-imposed by the creator or the presently-undeveloped potential within the electronic equipment. In addition, one may safely assume that television is the supreme communicative art. It is also the supreme teacher, as our age is only now beginning to recognize.

Since, however, an ancient concept of the artist is that he is an individual who, by extraordinary talent combined with extraordinary skill, creates a perfect work of enduring quality (said worth being universally recognized by many generations), it would follow that because neither film nor video tape (his basic creative tools) are materials which have the capacity to endure physically, his product, therefore, cannot be art. Those who argue this would also add that since the final product of the artist is essentially a one-man creation, group creativity activity cannot, therefore, result in art.

But those who argue so have forgotten the artists' centuries of dependence upon the technologists who supplied them with the materials from which they made their art. Historians of the arts are well aware of art's dependence upon such technological developments—just as we are equally aware that technological achievements are dependent upon art itself to be able to transmit an idea from the brain to sketch to drawing board to finished product. No plane that flies, no space module that lands on lunar soil arrived at that action point without having once waited upon the creative fertility of a brain to conceive it, an art process to visualize it and a whole series of artistic and technological functions to bring it to fruition. The inventive creator deals in abstractions which need symbolism to become realities. Art supplies the symbolism representing reality—technology makes it real.

We are, in a large sense, living in an "art unconscious" world. This is a plus for media education, for where there was once a sharp distinction between art as art and Art as it was used to create things, that chasm has closed. Since art is so evident in every phase of our civilization (whether we choose to think of it as art or not) and since technology is able to help provide us with more time for leisure (thus causing a greater volume of participation in the arts), our position to advocate the further use of the arts as the ideal vehicle to advance knowledge via the technologically-created Media Arts is unique. Further, since media (in all forms) causes this civilization to exist as mid-wife between the abstract and real, it follows that media is of itself the single greatest asset we have to continue and develop the civilization. And if we allow ourselves to encircle all arts within the all-encompassing sphere of the Media Arts, we can begin to recognize the importance of training future artists to create in media instruction, thus achieving a plateau until now impossible to conceive, much less attain.

We are, peculiarly in education, earth-chained with traditional symbols—largely words—in the transmission of ideas and information. The arts in their very creation have involved emotional expression in addition to "intellectual" processes. It is this factor, "emotion," which is the universal element in the communication and learning process.

Were we to take time to analyze some of these emotional characteristics inherent in the arts, we could easily recall the built-in patterns in music which trigger emotional responses in varying degrees of power and intensity. We could also recall the emotional factors of universally acknowledged symbols for hate, love, sorrow, happiness, friendship, religion, etc. used in Fine Art, as well as the emotional power inherent in gesture and movement represented by dance and mime, the power of

39

light and dark, of color and atmosphere created by symbolism in both words on paper and words spoken from a stage. Rather than spend a long time on this at the moment, however, let us freely acknowledge what is already known to be without further needed proof and add to it a concept of utilizing the standard arts within the framework of the Media Arts. Let us capitalize on our knowledge of these emotional factors to create (constantly) educational units prepared with the intention of intensifying the emotional experience in order to make a positive reaction to the informational content. We are not, as you may have gathered, speaking of the educational theory of "affective domain" and "cognitive domain." Instead, we speak of utilizing the Media Arts to create a single domain in which the creator and the consumer *both* exist on an identical plane interdependently. We shall say more on this presently.

In short, all disciplines (irrespective of subject content) will be successful in their adaptation to media presentation in direct ratio to their involvement of the arts in the packaging of information. If we are to achieve a learning experience through emotional involvement with the subject material, it may be accomplished only through the arts. This may be best achieved through their employment in the Media Arts.

Any long-range, large-scale program to up-date traditional academic procedures, then, should take into account as a prime requisite the study and preparation of media instructional materials, for without this awareness and involvement the program is doomed from the outset. If we are to develop this mind-to-mind transfer electronically, the whole body of knowledge to be used (as well as those who prepare its availability) must become involved in (a) the tools of the Media Arts, (b) the principles involved in the learning process and (c) the use of the arts as the greatest single ally in the process of electronic learning transfer.

If we are to accept these truths of emotional involvement in learning transfer and the arts as a medium of emotional power, doing it best through instructional procedures utilizing the Media Arts, we must re-evaluate our present instructional

40

programs in the light of "Why are we teaching this?" or "Are we using maximum effectiveness in present procedures?" I would not presume to challenge the areas of knowledge distribution as they are normally set up within a curriculum (even though I am reminded of the charming book, *The Saber-Tooth Curriculum*) nearly as much as I would challenge teaching procedures. I feel that the instructional media route is the only solution to the basic problem of human interpersonal relationship, whether on a one-to-one or global scope Until we have developed a universal literacy and have learned to communicate internationally and inter-racially with clarity, precision and intelligence, our complex civilization will destroy itself needlessly. Since we haven't done this through conventional methods, I propose that it is time we tried it through the Media Arts. When we have completed our re-evaluation and begun to investigate the potential of instructional media, we will quickly discover that the arts are uniquely qualified to offer a format or pattern of teaching since they have for centuries practiced a one-to-one teaching philosophy in which the student truly progresses at his own rate.

In addition, there is another demonstrable success formula related to the arts as practiced in dance, music ensembles and drama: group accomplishment of an abstract function done by unification of the whole under the leadership of a single person. This is understood clearly when we visualize a great conductor (great choreographer or dramatic director) utilizing a precise procedural outline supplied by a composer (author) and utilizing the skills of a group to produce his "sound" (which itself is an intangible). This accomplishment, from beginning of training process to final performance, is a result of a highly-charged emotional experience which achieved oneness or near perfection in group participation because one person assumed control over each individual skill within the group.

One may argue, "Yes, but the score itself (the play or the choreographic notations) was the catalyst which enabled them to obtain this result." While it is true that at that moment it was the enabling structure, without the combined skills under single leadership, the format of scores, plays and dance patterns would be nothing more than markings on paper.

Thus, in instructional media we must assume the role of the creative artist in our attitudes. We will coordinate the total elements into a whole, and each segment will depend absolutely upon the other for the fulfillment of its purpose by having one mind direct all responses to the degree that the complete effort demands each participant to achieve learning. Since we do not deal with groups (such as an orchestra, a dramatic cast, or a ballet company) in media, our problem of unification is not necessarily group unification. Rather, it is the evoking of a total response by the individual student. Thus, it becomes even more apparent that we need to create an emotional involvement similar to that which is involved by the arts in learning. The demonstrated proof of learning will be in the performance.

If follows that, if within the art performance this happens, by creating our instructional materials in the form of art and by making the learning process achievable only by emotional involvement of a leader-follower relationship, our needs for the known emotional characteristics of art become so dependent that we can think of no other way to proceed than by the arts as the carrier of thought, the transfer agent and the catalyst in developing emotional interdependence between student and teacher.

Some educators argue that the development of psycho-motor skills, such as those which are required by all performers before they can perform in reflex, is not as necessary in order to achieve a high degree of performance in intellectual achievement. My feelings are that they are exactly the same The process of training for "conceptual" areas (even to the point of abstractions) is the same as that required to develop the psycho-motor skills involved in demonstrating that something has been physically achieved, although the manifestation of such skills is unquestionably different, just as pitching a no-hitter, playing a concerto, or painting a portrait are by-products of psycho-motor skills that can be visualized in contrast to ability to think in the abstractism of mathematical formulae. In every instance there is also a product—after all, it was mathematical concept that brought space exploration from theory into reality.

The arts demand tremendous psycho-motor skill development. The arts also rely on being able to create via abstractionism for their very own existence. Music and dance particularly rely on the symbolism of a flexible language almost altogether, for while they are created in exactness, they continue to allow fluidity of modification within the framework of exactness. As an illustration of this, a composer may write a musical passage in the key of B minor to be played by a clarinet. Simultaneously, he writes supporting harmony for strings and a counter-melody for an English horn. In each instance he supplies a dynamic marking and a tempo marking. The conductor, however, makes the decision about the relative qualities of volume and tempo and adjusts the melody, counter-melody and harmony in a relationship which he finds nearest to what he believes the composer had in mind. It may well be that he interprets precisely what the composer wanted and that the instrumentalists play their parts precisely as the composer intended. But, for all of this exactness, the composer does not supply information about where and when the music should be played, such as whether it should be performed in daylight or under artificial light, whether the people involved should be Caucasian or Oriental or whether they should be dressed casually or formally. In short, he does not, nor can he, supply the extra-curricular specifications for his performance even though each of these contain inherent factors contributing to the emotional values of the music when it is heard.

Nevertheless, the composer, dramatist and choreographer are able to use their specific set of symbols to "see" (or hear) a total product both before it is created and during the process of its creation. Although their language is exact enough to allow them to communicate through it, it is not so rigid that it must be performed identically to the original concept in order to give its values. It is precisely that which enables the

43

emotional factor to prevail. Otherwise we could write music for machines or create ballets for robots to perform.

To a similar degree, the graphic artist and writer do the same thing. Because the language in their case is more directly understood, however, they deal less with the abstract. In neither instance does the interpretation interfere with the inherent values of art work. It is the development of psycho-motor skills in both instances which permit the reflex to perform the tasks, leaving the emotions free to interact with the creative or interpretive process.

All of the psychological implications of the craft, most of which the artist is only intuitively aware, are brought to bear upon his audience, although not deliberately to evoke an exact response or to trigger a Pavlovian reaction. Instead, he subconsciously realizes that the color combination, the word grouping, the harmonic or melodic sequence, or the gesture will form a communicative force which will be understood because of the universality of the basic emotions.

I am sure that this statement may be challenged because of the broadness of the view. Let us add to that challenge by asserting that art itself is mood or organized emotion. Let us further state that no art work of itself is complete merely by having been created—it requires involvement by others who possess a similar set of emotions to those of the creator. It is indeed the emotional factor which drives (compels, forces, inspires, etc.) the creator. All people are capable of creativity—only those who have sharpened perceptions and who have acquired a communicable language create. No matter how sensitive the man, nor how creative he may allow his brain to be, nor how capable he is of daydream, fantasy, or originality, nothing happens at all until he has developed a capacity for expression. The creator himself may be likened to a giant water tower. To get his creation from his brain to the pen in his hand, he must have developed motor skills so that nothing can clog the passage between creative impulse and its translation into whatever language he uses.

So if art, because of its enduring qualities and its emotional response generation after generation, can transmit itself to others by emotional response to itself, think how effectively it can be used as a tool in transmitting all information, especially if we believe, as I do, that all learning begins and becomes part of the permanent human resource only through emotional involvement.

We need to take a hard look at the structure of the arts within our educational institutions. Our service in the arts may well be directed to media instruction, thus giving to all departments of arts activities an added reason for existence. Training programs in all branches of the arts should be developed for participation—and this without detracting from what the arts normally do. Fine performers would still perform, fine painters would still paint, fine actors still act—all in the conventional mode. In addition, we will create new stages and new performance demands through involvement in the Media Arts. Best of all, we will create new needs for the arts themselves.

In our curriculum the Media Arts, those which relate physically to the electronically produced media, should be organized into courses that would train people to create the elements which contribute to the packaging of the whole. A major effort should be made to mobilize the resources of an arts division to participate in the preparation of graphic art needs: drama to fulfill the various needs of the Media Arts in creating informational packages and music to create and perform the vital needs of Media Arts. Courses should also be developed to train students (and faculty) for creative participation in media efforts. Courses should be designed to help the student learn to do so that his doing would produce a usable product, contributing to a unified program—in short, a total effort to involve the creative processes of many, the by-products of which would be used by one to create the final product.

I return to my analogy of the symphony score. The creator of that score, using a set of symbols created by many other individuals, combines his own creative abilities with emotion and psycho-motor skills to enable him to develop a chart or map or formula which represents his creative ideas. In actuality this score is of no value unless others participate in the ultimate function of art by using it for themselves.

The individual performers are contributors of small but highly important segments of the whole. The conductor (who doesn't make any sounds at all, at least none related to the score) having studied the score in detail and having acquired a concept of the composer's ideas (through using the very language the composer used to write it), superimposes his ideas upon the group to achieve the sound the composer was after initially.

So it is in a media instructional unit. There are symbols: some may be expressed verbally, some musically and graphically, some with color and gestures, with light and costume, some with photography and even some with silence. All these components are under a director or producer. His role is to combine according to the intention of the creator who, in the instance we hope to achieve, is the artist-teacher. This producer-director's function is comparable to that of the symphony conductor. His tools are electronic equipment instead of strings and brasses. As in the symphony, the art product requires a unified effort of all components placed precisely in space and time. In this case it is the teaching-art product.

So both the creative and re-creative processes are the same. The only difference is that when the work is done there is a physical product in the hands of the media instructional creator. It is not a paper to read, not lectures to hear in classrooms, but a media package which now begins to do its job as the creative work ends. All values remain the same. As in the symphony, we would no longer need the concert hall, conductor, or musicians had we put the sounds on a tape. We can hear it again and again. We need no audience except ourselves, no facilities except the gear to reproduce it. With the media instructional package, the same thing happens. The lesson, having been created to be delivered through the unification of all necessary components, now becomes permanently available.

Perhaps if I had used the analogy of an opera, a play or ballet (involving as they do so many other elements to re-create their author's original ideas), you would be able to better understand the process of utilizing many art elements to make a single one. It is in the comprehension of this joint responsibility of many involved people that I call upon the arts to develop processes of training which will provide students with a new outlet for their art products. Thus, within the greater area of the Media Arts they will enable education to achieve a goal which no longer is dependent upon campus or classrooms.

In the arts, then, we could create ensembles whose playing personnel would be relating to studio needs, not public audience. Our actors would no longer occupy the conventional stage, nor even the thrust or round. Instead they would be working within a studio. The initial audience would have television cameras for eyes and microphones for ears. All of the traditional skills taught by arts divisions can be given added purposefulness through use of their products to reach new audiences via audio and video production. And since this CAN be, it is foolish for the arts not to recognize the great potential or to fail to take advantage of it. Not only will the individual student be served well by being better prepared to function as an artist in a dollar-sign world, but we will generate a new spirit of creativity. The creative artist needs his work to be used; the performer needs to be heard. The direction I am proposing offers them the opportunity to be extended beyond the traditional arena to infinity. I would urge you to adopt a philosophy for the perfection of the individual component to fit into the larger composite, to acquire the media skills related to the technology, to transform these skills into creative potential and to understand fully that your leadership will not only increase the value of the departments to the institution as art, but will become that all-important unit through which all other academia must express its ideas if it is to use the Media Arts for instructional purposes.

The traditionalist will argue that there is no parallel between creating an opera, a play or a ballet and creating a unit of instructional media in history or mathematics. He is wrong, of course, but why and how is he wrong? The opera or play (he may argue) is designed for divertissement, mere entertainment, and is not, therefore, an educational experience. While it is true that the creative artist in every field has first the desire for self-expression in creation, he accommodates himself to the obligation of arranging the elements of his creativity so that audiences may participate in his products. He knows he must have an audience in order that his products may be consumed so that he may stay alive. I do not mean this in the physical sense of staying alive as a result of money made by selling his products. I mean that psychologically (whether or not he will utter the thought aloud) he depends upon an audience in order to create. He may never know the audience personally, but he knows the proto-type: a mirror of himself. So he creates purposefully. His primary objective is the transmission of his thoughts. His subject content is not limited by art itself. Rather, he uses his art mode to say whatever he desires and wishes to say. He does not set out to educate in the sense of a teacher setting out to educate a class, but in his processes and as a result of his creative efforts an educational experience results. He avoids the direct, relying on the subtlety of his symbols. He succeeds as artist only when his thoughts provide a stimulus to the receiver, who in turn is motivated into a creative response himself.

Few people view a painting with regard only to the technical processes involved in its creation. They view it, either in whole or in part, emotionally. It pleases or displeases. They are moved or unmoved. They respond or reject. In short, the complexities of their own experiences are brought to bear upon the work of another as they themselves, most of the time voluntarily, involve themselves in the art product.

It is an educational experience in the generic meaning of the word "education"—but it is more than that. The painting and the creative experience of the artist now become a part of them. It is to be there always for their use as needed or desired.

There are some obvious conclusions we may draw at this point: (a) the artist knew what he wanted to do, (b) he used the full resources of his craft to do it and (c) he came up with a product that requires its use in order to give it meaning. Although he was not conscious of it, he involuntarily involved the consumer of his art in reacting, to that degree of capability, to his own creative emotional response.

The application toward instructional media is again obvious: the artist knows *why* he is creating (this may be no more than a compulsive urge caused by any number of psychological factors), and he creates to the sum total of his assimilation of technical skills involved. He gives full play to his own need for self-expression by use of symbols or (in the case of the verbal arts) symbolism, which may be responded to emotionally by others, whether or not they have any intellectual comprehension of his use of the crafts involved. In instructional media the teacher is the creative artist. He is no longer in the conventional classroom, however, so his performance skills are required even more than they were before. His basic objective is the transmission of ideas, a leadership, as it were, through the charted path leading from the unknown to the known. His dual objective is to provide the necessary steps for assimilation of needed information in order to bring the student into a state of reflex use of that knowledge, and to motivate the use of that knowledge by the student and get him to do something with it.

Thus, the "why do we learn this?" assumes an importance equal to the acquisition of the knowledge itself. The teacher-artist is in the business of producing a product; one acquires skills of course content and comprehends the reason for acquiring these skills to the point of being able to use them to generate creativity within himself. It is a subtle point, but all learning requires an understanding of *why* it must be learned before it can be learned. Here we come back to the premise that all learning is based on emotional involvement with the thing to be learned—with the added involvement of need to understand why it must be learned *before* a learning state may be reached.

Since we recognize this truth, it follows that the use of the arts through the Media Arts helps us create the emotional environment necessary to the learning process. If we involve ourselves in the recognized success patterns used by the arts and, further, if we create a product which can be used by the student to do something purposefully, we are on our way toward becoming teacher-artists rather than being only dispensers of information. And we can do all of this more efficiently, more enduringly, through media instructional methods than in any other way—at least until we can provide one teacher constantly to be of service to only one student at a time.

There are many ways to give a student the "why" of the learning requirements beyond our standard reward system of grades. We may create media to explore the results of having learned, that is, investigate the career potential which follows a student's study. If a student can be helped to peer into his own possible future by substituting himself for the now-successful accomplisher whose career is being examined, he has a reward factor of infinite value. Media is ideally suited to accomplish this. It will succeed in helping the student understand both the purpose and opportunities inherent in the discipline he is studying.

If we provide a chemistry major with full knowledge of a career potential for himself and are able to help the student realize that the acquisition of skills in the lab and information from his texts are but preparation for his achievement in the great outside world, we will relieve ourselves of much of the *burden* of teaching. We will assume a new position in the eyes of the student, for we will become the one who will reveal to him how to achieve a superior place in society. It is he, then, who motivates *himself*, knowing full well that unless he does he will not participate fully in the areas where diligent preparation could lead him. Certainly this principle has been in the arts teaching methodology for many generations. No performer may achieve the right to replace (or join) the ranks of the immortals unless his motivation is supported by self-disciplined application in study and practice.

This leads us to still another observation: viz., doing can best be motivated when theory is supported by hands-on experience. In the arts, of course, this happens constantly, and achievement can be seen in demonstration by the performer. This is not peculiar to the arts, although understandably it is more apparent, since acquired skills and craftsmanship are demonstrated in performance. It is also apparent in the language arts where its effectiveness can be measured by student demonstration of reading and speaking skills. One should observe, however, that language is one of the communication arts. It is true that in those disciplines where the student is required to do something to demonstrate comprehension and ability, instructional media can be used more efficiently than traditional practices in teaching. But it is also true that there are few disciplines if any where this does not apply.

The complex skills needed to be a pilot of a great jet liner are acknowledged readily. Equally necessary are the skills involved in captaining a super oil tanker or commanding a space module. There are training programs presently in existence where these skills are taught—through media. Their procedures are sophisticated methodology, combining media with hands-on, step-by-step instruction. Finally, when all intermediate steps have been successfully negotiated, the student is placed within a simulator, a highly complex capsulized re-creation of reality, identical with his captain's bridge, his 747's crew area, or an exact duplicate of his space module. Everything about the simulator is precisely like the real of the ship, the aircraft, the space vehicle. Every switch, tab, button and gadget is connected to apparatus which give him a feeling of actually doing what he is being trained to do. Even down to the vibration of the deck, the sound of the engines, the weightlessness of the capsule interior, the trainee is subjected to a highly-charged emotional environment. For all intents and purposes everything he is doing is real and not an exercise. Instructors have told me of seeing flight captains with years of experience emerge from the cabin after such a simulated flight trembling from reaction to having crashed his simulator. It was *actuality* itself. When the ship's captain, the pilot or the astronaut complete their simulated training, they move into the real with assurance, for they have accomplished the right to

51

do by having done. Industry and government have recognized the value of investing millions of dollars to create these simulated experience modules. Education has a lesson to learn from each—both are dealing in human lives. While a freshman English major may not crash at the end of the runway because he didn't learn his grammar, he is a victim of a system which was not real enough to make him want to learn it. And whereas industry and government have acknowledged the values of media instruction as a more efficient and less expensive way to train, education by and large drags its collective feet.

If we were to summarize our thoughts, we would first recall that we believe all arts form an art we now call the Media Arts and that combined with the technology of media, the arts of themselves must now move away from their tradition-bound arenas into the broader area of media—specifically audio and video. In addition, we laid stress on the emotional factor inherent in the arts to communicate through emotional involvement, concluding that these inherent emotional powers can best serve all instruction and that the logical approach to teach through media should be through them.

We discussed the similarity between the one-to-one approach used by arts in their teaching procedures and that of media. We pointed out that creativity in the Media Arts and re-creativity in the arts is a one-man assimilation of many elements to achieve the whole. We stressed the necessity for reorganizing the arts themselves to train for service through the Media Arts to all education, and we recognized the need-to-do and the need-to-know-why factors common in the arts but not yet in general practice elsewhere in academia.

We urged the transition to the Media Arts for education in order to extend the range of both its efficiency and influence. And we suggested that research be done into the proven psychological implications of the arts and that these factors be utilized in creating within the Media Arts.

Most of all, we advocated the creation of the artist-teacher who, now freed from conventional classroom, uses the arts as a way of combining knowledge with technology. He creates in order to cause students to become self-motivated because they will understand that it also takes *them* to accomplish the intent of the teaching creation. It is a large subject—one needing the creative efforts of thousands to develop the perfect product. But it must be done, and it will be done through the Media Arts.

There will be a day when the university will not be a gathering place for people who come to have knowledge served up to them. Instead it will be a gathering place of great creative minds who will organize knowledge into distributable units designed to be used by people who want to learn, whenever and wherever they may be. That day, of course, is still years away— but its eventuality is predictable with certainty. Shakespeare's line "All the world is a stage" may now be modified to "all the world is a classroom." It is a classroom just big enough for one at a time, through the courtesy of the art of media.

CHAPTER III

INSTRUCTIONAL MEDIA AND LEARNING

Educational institutions by-and-large are in a production mode: their product is people of all ages, people trained (in most cases) for someone else's use. Those institutions which are not a part of the structured formality of schools are more direct in their training philosophy. They want to take advantage of their training programs in order to be a benefit to the organization itself. They also have a clearly defined motivational attitude both for themselves and for their students. Many times the motivational incentive is money; sometimes it is prestige, and at times it is life or safety.

These non-school educational programs are frequently involved to a high degree in the use of instructional media. They achieve more expeditious results, produce better trainees and—quite importantly for them—they save money in the process by utilizing media instructional methods. It is easy to understand that a company which can produce more income through the development of people-skills, and can also save money in the process of development, is more eager to grasp the media concept than an institution which has been involved in the traditional approaches to training.

Most major airlines train ground crews, sales and service personnel, stewardesses and pilots with highly sophisticated systems of media plus hands-on techniques. Many major businesses utilize media processes along with on-the-job training in developing executive, management, sales and accounting personnel. Unions, attempting to keep pace with the technology involved in using heavy machinery and in supplying base education for the not-yet-graduated worker, have long utilized media-oriented courses to expedite the training process with better results. Police, fire, marine service and many other career areas in which human safety is of prime importance have used and are using media in some form or other for training. The military, blessed as it is with qualifying budgets, pioneered many of the presently-used media systems, and their use of computer-assisted instruction and simulators in the space program is a marvel of training through media. Almost without exception their training programs (irrespective of the differences in *what* is achieved) are headed by teams of experts in human engineering and experts in the media arts who combine their particular skills to program their students to perfection in task accomplishment.

Unfortunately institutionalized education has no such similar set of objectives. I say "unfortunately" because the motivational problems would not be as great as they are if they did have such objectives. Perhaps this lack of objectives lies in the fact that most educational institutions are confined to places and times. We go to school and we receive an education in a structured time period. Media will change all of that. It will make our present institutional systems much more flexible and increase our potential influences far beyond the campus itself.

As professional educators we are sometimes prone to look down-the-nose at what is known as vocational training. This is largely because of the connotation the word "training" has acquired as it is practiced in secondary and trade schools. Yet, with all of our lofty idealism in our own stated objectives, we practice training for many livelihood areas, including professions as diverse as engineering, medicine, law, business, music, coaching—and teaching. We call them professions although we do not act like professionals do when they re-train our products. Perhaps our own attitude should be to train every student as if we were going to use his services ourselves. If such were the case, I'm positive we would throw away our present structured course concept and re-tool our educational programs at once.

Just as non-institutionalized educators know they must invest in training and plan for its use, so nust we, especially

55

since our prime reason for being is service—service paid for by students wanting a fair market value in return for the money they invest.

Lest you think I am demeaning institutionalized education, let me hastily deny it—for I am not. I do, however, question the continuation of its procedures in the light of present technology, as I also question its objectives in the light of society's demands.

I have included this comparison between the two attitudes in contemporary educational procedures because I believe more positively in the realistic approach than I do in the traditional one. For this reason, the present chapter advocates the re-tooling of our service industry (the schools) to assume the objectives and obligations of the other. This can be done through the media in all of the implications of that term.

In order to do this, we must look at our curricula, our discipline and courses, our learning theories, our options in media systems and our obligated philosophy to the human who comes to us for education, whatever the reason, at whatever age.

I think if I were to set about building a program in media instruction, I wouldn't begin with any specific discipline in mind. Instead, I would begin with people, for it is from individuals that knowledge comes. God Himself used people to transform knowledge of Himself through the man-written, divinely-inspired words of the Bible. And having withstood many a test through various centuries, it remains a model of teaching efficiency (even if you do not accept the divinely-inspired concept). Its subject areas are ideas and deeds related to time and place, and its conveying mechanism is words through people.

So, following the example of a successful teaching method, I would collect the names of a few hundred men and women, all of whom did one or more things vital to the creation of our knowledge-mass. I would then develop a series of media packages (audio tapes, slide tapes and video tapes) about them, making each of their lives into an exciting and dynamic presentational unit. I would portray their deeds, ideas and times in

56

an attempt to rediscover (through them) the truths which they brought to light. I would make use of every production skill I could muster to create these human show cases, and I would use them as the basis of general studies.

Let's take a for instance: Euclid, the great philosopher-geometrician, who contributed vastly to world knowledge by codifying truths from natural law which formed the basis for geometry. To understand what he did and why he did it would be our objective. Since he was a flesh-and-blood human, possessing the same physical-mental-emotional needs that we also have, we need to understand him as a man in his times, learn of him as a person and attempt to enter his mind as he discovers the principles which have been so important to the way we think and live.

To do this we must know the man. We must identify with him to the point of being involved in his environment, his thought patterns, his deeds and with the people who were his contemporaries—in short, to determine the "who, what, when, why and how" of the Euclidian fatherhood of geometric truth. Thus we would be studying geometry, not only through the practice of theoretical knowledge but through re-discovering Euclid's thought processes—processes leading to understanding and, as a result, to use.

This process of person-involvement, or to use my term for it, "transient identification," does not consist of some mysterious, occult, incarnative mystique. It isn't even unusual for those of us who are practicing Christians to involve ourselves very much "in" Jesus, His deeds, His associates, His times and His ideas. We try to be like Him, to emulate Him, and attempt to become the same "Christ-like" figure even though we have no idea of what Jesus really looked like. This fact, however, does not prevent our involvement with Jesus in a very personal relationship. Indeed, we quote His words (although He did not personally write them down) and apply their meaning to our lives in a way that governs our every living moment, whether or not we are consciously aware of it. All of this is to say that, whether or not we are believing or practicing Christians, it is in fact true that a large part of the world exists in what is called

"Christendom." So the believing and acceptance of Christianity has nothing to do with the validity of the truths He taught.

We need not, therefore, use a truth because it exists. The theorem evolved by Euclid, "All radii of the same circle or of equal circles are themselves equal," is a statement he deduced from his observations of natural law. Its truth is unaltered whether or not we use it. But the goal in "transient identification" is to discover the processes by which truth is derived. You may say, "Yes, But Christ was divine. Euclid was only human." Actually that wasn't a fair thing for me to have you say, but because we are taught that Christ assumed human form, we conclude that He arrived at His state of truth through human processes (aided by His Father who also created the natural laws which Euclid observed and charted into codes). So, just as Jesus, living in perfection, obtained truth, Euclid, deducing from perfection, discovered truth.

This parallelism is not intended to be theological. It is only to show you how the study of men, by emulation, identification and involvement in their beings, is a potent force in the learning process, not to "worship," as in the case of Jesus, but rather to attempt to occupy, however transiently, the minds of the discoverers in their time-place zones AS they discover in order for us to have comprehension to understand AND to make use of their discoveries, in order to know what use the world has made of their findings. I used the word "findings" instead of "creations," for the knowledge was already in existence. It simply took an individual to locate it, define it and use it.

To attempt an understanding of the "how, when, where, what and why" of the "who" presupposes that we have access to him in order to begin the identification process. However limited our biographical information about Euclid, for example, we do have access to his writings. His four treatises are entitled "Elements," "Optics," "On Division" and "Phenomenon." If studied, they would reveal a great deal about the man's thought processes. And we have no trouble seeing the results of his having discovered the things set forth in these treatises. By knowing of others in his time zone, we can assume or by using his own process of reasoning deduce much of how he acted within the society. We can discover which of the various religions or philosophies he may have espoused and what kind of clothes he wore. While we do not have an example of the "why" of his discoveries (as we do with Archimedes and the case of the King's golden crown), we would be able to understand his actions in the light of the fact that there was a philosophy of "discovery for discovery's sake" which could have motivated him. We might even deduce that it was an ego factor in victory-desire and competition with others trying to discover the same truths. Perhaps he had an unconscious reaction to the needs of the world and fulfilled them, whether or not he had any personally-related problems to solve.

Let me carry this idea of transient identification a step further because of our need to understand it with respect to a later phase of our "curriculum" assimilation within electronic media. All of us have experienced the feeling of identification with characters in a play, a film or novel. For a brief moment as we leave the theater (or as we read the story) we are in that transient state of being that one with whom we have empathized most completely.

We may even assume the physical stance, adopt the inflections, pacing, style of speech, walk like "our hero" and even momentarily assume his mental and emotional attitudes. The transient state is achieved in direct ratio to the empathy you project toward the actor (on screen, stage) or character in a novel as you involve yourself in a character who (though unreal) is actually real to the direct ratio which the actor (or novelist) has empathized himself into the role.

We may continue this identification over a long period of time, or it may be a fleeting experience. At the moment of the identification, however, it was to all intents and purposes real, although it was not real in actuality. Prolonged identification with the subject may actually cause one to assume permanent characteristics typical of the person with whom we identify. In this way one may become like John Wayne (if he is his hero) or Napoleon (if his tastes are different). On television we frequently see impressionists who seem to become the person they are impersonating because they have so copied the physical of the one they transmute.

We are familiar with the classic story by James Thurber, *The Secret Lives of Walter Mitty*. Thurber's character was able to fantasize himself into actually becoming the men he wished he could be—the ubiquitous hero—and while it is only fiction, Thurber himself had to go through transient identification with the characters he created in order to be able to create them. Most of us will readily admit to fantasizing and day-dreaming. It is the acceptance of this inherent capability to so identify which is the basis for our recognition of the necessity of the "men of knowledge" approach, relying upon media to strengthen the environmental circumstances so that this can take place more easily.

The late Arturo Toscanini, eminently distinguished as a "Maestro," often said, "It is necessary for the conductor to go through the pages of the music to find the man." He meant this in two ways: beyond the need to absorb the music is the need to know it so that it becomes (reflexively) a part of himself, and hence, he needs to go beyond the pages of the music to know the man who created it; in addition, he meant that at the point of actually recreating the music, the conductor actually becomes the composer. He, Toscanini, would become Beethoven. At a rehearsal of Beethoven's music, one could almost see the transformation from the real Toscanini to the transiently identified Beethoven. I must conclude that the realization of the Beethoven pre-supposes Toscanini's achievement of the same mastery of music which Beethoven achieved. By using that mastery he himself relived the emotional and intellectual creative processes while conducting Beethoven's music—this in addition to all that was also Toscanini's own personality.

An actor portraying the role of Iago must—in order to perform it as Shakespeare visualized it in *Othello* (for Shakespeare's creation of Iago was as real in every respect as were the sounds in Beethoven's head when he was writing a symphony)—become the Iago of the mind of Shakespeare and not himself playing a role. To that extent he is able to assume that identity, he may involve the listener-viewer in empathizing. By this means Shakespeare's Iago is transferred through himself to the audience.

Christ simplified the explanation by saying, "As a man thinketh, so is he." One may extend this idea to mean "as a man thought, so was he," and "as a man will think, so he shall become." While Christ did not say "as a man thinketh *he is*, so is he," He did encourage us to follow Him, to be like the Father. He spoke in parables to encourage the involvement of self in situational conditions which teach truths. We may use this "as a man thinketh, so is he" to mean that we, as a result of all our thinking, will become the composite of all we think rather than to sense in its implication that we may become that which we think about. As we learn to think as Christ, Euclid, Beethoven or Shakespeare thought, we may become Christ-like (but NOT Christ), Euclid-like (but NOT Euclid), Beethoven-like (but NOT Beethoven) or Shakespeare-like (but NOT Shakespeare). Although we do not "become" them, we may, through application of their truths, so identify with them that their truths are revealed in us.

Whether you realize it or not, I have been trying to get you to think as I think so that you may discover the truth and the application of it in your involvement with media. My media here has been the entirely visual use of individual letter-pictures arranged into a commonly-understood vocabulary placed sequentially into recognizable thought-patterns which you, by your reflexive understanding of the symbolism involved, are able to admit into your own mind. Along the way you have entered into my mind involuntarily and simultaneously have brought all of your own being into acceptance, rejection, comprehension and understanding. You may already have decided whether or not you care to use the idea in either the teaching or learning processes in which you are engaged.

I am using a medium consisting of letters, combinations of letters (words) and sequences of words (sentences). You brought to this medium your personalized reaction (pro or con) and your utilization of identical picture symbols to take the words from the printed page and transfer them to your own mind. At the moment you do this, you identify completely with me through word symbols. How much this identification means to you depends on your understanding of *why* I am thinking as I do (although I have already told you that). I have told you that I want to utilize all communication media, concentrating on the electronic because it can do in an instant, non-verbally, what it has taken pages for us to do in print media. Because of its nature it also makes the identification process easier since in our age we are as accustomed to identification with (even transiently) media as we are with real itself.

One thing about media expression is that it not only remains expressed, but it remains expressed in the way it was expressed. You'll notice that you didn't use up a single word on this page by just reading. Instead, you became the person who wrote it. But you also remained you, just as I remained me. Whether or not you choose to use any ideas that have been expressed in my media does not alter the fact that you were involved in a process of thinking identical thoughts to mine on one plane while continuing to think your own thoughts on a parallel plane. Another thing that has happened is that the time-space elements here have become entirely fluid. The time and place of writing and reading has no absolute meaning because of the media. Euclid's writings, done somewhere around 300 B.C., are of the moment you read them when you read them rather than of the B.C. time zone. You may read them in Dubuque, Iowa; he wrote them in Greece. None of that affects the values inherent in what was in his mind, and we may as easily enter into his mind from our point in time (*c.* A.D. 2000) just as he himself allowed his mind to enter ours from his time (*c.* 300 B.C.).

The words of this chapter also transcend the time-space elements. I am in a specific place at a specific time. Where (in space) and when (in time) you make the contact doesn't matter. Neither of us could have been in contact (as we now are) until I had written (with all of the background preparation that implies) and until you read. Having fulfilled my obligation to write when and where I did (for whatever reasons), this medium eliminated the time-space barrier existing between the mind-to-mind contact necessary for people to have such a relationship. In that relationship, I would say it—you would hear it; I would leave and only my thoughts would remain. In this media relationship, I wrote it when I wanted to, you read it when you wanted to, and there is plenty left over for millions to partake of the same if they wish.

This is media's prime function—and this is also the prime function of truth. Both must be valid without respect to time or place.

Our process for transferring truth through media communication strengthens the transient identification factor which I have described. As for its application to media other than written language, I will chart a conceptual course which you will follow—hoping that you will bring within the vast potential that exists in media your own creative skills. Many of these skills will be detailed in later chapters as we address the "how to" of writing, directing, photographing, etc. But the learning to do will not be nearly so important as showing you how to convert those potentials into a discovery mode through transient identification with the world's great minds, living and dead. I have been successful in creating a concept of it using only a single medium to this point, but we may also be able to develop a concept of its application in ways far more energizing than print media because of the involvement of non-verbal communication made possible (in this release from time-space isolation) through electronic media.

Earlier we mentioned that another phase of our curriculum in media would have to do with transient identification in a different way, while simultaneously producing emotional involvement which results in an understanding of why we must learn. This involvement of discovery is not joy in the Greek-Euclidian philosophy of discovery for discovery's sake, but in the practicality of existing within a continuously-moving time-space realism called "now."

This has to do with the preparation of a video series which I shall call (for lack of a better title) Career Investigation. It is a series which would use as its basic presentational format one of the several "interview" styles. My task would be to find the "success symbols," to present them in a showcase of "achievements" relating both to an individual course and an entire discipline, representing "rewards" and giving "answers" to the "why" of course and discipline study. These answers would go beyond the basic motivations involved in acquisition of knowledge for its own sake—or grades. What may happen to a student in the "job" market when he stands at the exit gate of his Alma Mater, his newly-gained diploma clutched in his hand? Why should he have studied as. he did to be where he is? How may he utilize his knowledge to be in the world that is definitely "off-campus"? Such questions as these demand answers. Our obligation is to show students the variety of careers available to them, to indicate background knowledge necessary to achieve success and to provide information from people who are in each career. Successful people would provide substantiating reasons for the "why" of the curriculum which students are required to study.

I am aware that what I am projecting is not particularly innovative and that it has been used by counseling services in vocational guidance. But the way I suggest that we use it is vastly different from that currently available. It is different in its presentational approach and in its application in relation to each course and discipline as well.

As I write the following paragraphs, I have beside me a curriculum outline for a degree program in music. I have selected music for the obvious reason that I can speak more authoritatively to the subject. I have been an active career participant in music specifically, as well as in the Media Arts, and in both instances as a professional as opposed to being a campus-bound theoretician.

My catalogue information for the music department indicates that a student may elect to major in applied music (performance), church music, music education and music theory-composition. As I look at the course requirements for each degree, I am able to see a pattern that shows (on an undergraduate level) a broad base of music courses common to all of the degree programs. In addition I see that all music students, irrespective of their field of interest, are required to study a large number of courses in the general studies area in which they participate with others (irrespective of THEIR field of interest). This is to provide them with a common core of knowledge representing a substantial percentage of their campus study time. In short, they all take English, History, Mathematics, Science, Language, etc. The courses included as the liberal arts side of their total education are not necessarily correlated with their major.

I also see that music majors (except music education majors) are required to study twenty-two hours of music theory, that all are required to pass a proficiency test in piano and that all must participate in a minimum of eight hours of an accreditated ensemble. All majors, with the exception of theory-composition students, are also required to take from fourteen to twenty-two hours of study in applied music, depending upon their major. All take conducting; all take music literature and history of music.

By examining in detail the total music curriculum, I can see that there is very little concentration in specialties leading to career qualification in any single field, with the possible exception of music education. This leads me to conclude that the curriculum has been designed to prepare *all* music students to have the benefit of a common-core designed to help them first to be musicians and then to be specialists. So we may reduce the major's program into:

a) performance skills (solo and ensemble work),

b) concepts of how music is made (music theory),

c) study of literature of music (the various kinds of "already successful" music),

d) study of people who have made music and its theories (music history),

e) philosophy and methods (music education, church music),

f) creativity (composition),

To do an analysis of the career opportunities available to the music major, we must see how many possible job potentials exist for those who are musically educated either solely or in combination with other disciplinary skills (music education, music therapy, church music). The following is a compilation of immediately recognizable livelihood categories available:

1. Professional symphony/opera player
2. Professional band/dance-band/studio orchestra (recording, TV,-films)
3. Solo performer (entertainment circuit, clubs, restaurants, etc.)
4. Solo performer (vocalist)
5. Specialty group performer (chamber ensemble, country-western, rock, Dixieland, etc.)
6. Music educator (classroom, ensemble, administration, supervision)
7. Military music
8. Music therapist
9. Music librarian
10. Music editorship (publisher oriented—words and/or music)
11. Musical stage (opera, musical comedy)
12. Chorale singer
13. Music specialist: media (films, broadcast, educational, recording)
14. Recording engineer, studio technician, recording and/or broadcast supervision
15. Arranger (from jingles to symphonic material)
16. Music copyist
17. Composer (from jingles to symphonic material)
18. Music critic
19. Music research and authorship, commentator, script writer
20. Symphony/opera/band/ensemble conductor in multiple fields
21. Concert artist (soloist, instrumental or vocal)
22. Vocal coach (opera, pops)
23. Accompanist
24. Church organist
25. Private teacher
26. Church music ministry
27. Music management
28. Music consultancies (publication, industrial, medical-psychological oriented)
29. Music publishing (any related phase)
30. Music merchandising (store, traveling salesman, exhibitor)
31. Musical products field (equipment for music use)
32. Music instrument manufacture, design, demonstration, management, repair
33. Musicologist, historian
34. Music rights societies.

Most of the preceding could be sub-categorized, but this is enough to show the varied potential in store for those who designate music as a choice of livelihood. Many of the categories are highly competitive, some requiring extraordinary degrees of skill and talent, but all are achievable. Music schools, under the misguided assumption that if you are a musician you can do anything, generally devote their teaching energies to areas sharply divided between cultural and practical, with little or no attention being given to the meat and potatoes programming. We seldom educate the whole musician. Instead, we leave a substantial part of his education to be developed by hands-on experience in the great outside world.

In order to carry our "emulative" concept further into the field of music, one would secure the success symbol personalities representing these endeavor areas for interviews to define the nature of their work, the study background required to do what they do, the related studies (apart from music) important to their success, the life values they see in their careers, their own progressive experiences helping to achieve present status, the prestige (power) values and their advice to those contemplating careers in the field. It may be that you would want to extend the scope into school work by talking with people from all areas of educational activities. Instead of one concert artist, you may make representations from several varieties of performers. The number of individual units you have is not restricted. Each will add new dimensions both to the emulation of and to the discovery in the lives and careers you examine.

How does one become the conductor of the Philadelphia Orchestra, the music critic of the *Saturday Review*, the Dean of Music at Peabody Institute, the commander-in-chief of military music, the supervisor of music in the Minneapolis public schools, the editor-in-chief of Boosey-Hawkes, Inc. or the president of National Music Camp? What are the musical requirements for each? What do you have to know of business, language, public relations, marketing, education and human relations? How does what you have to know for a career relate to the curriculum at your disposal?

Since this approach could be unilateral, designed to serve all the course-disciplines specifically and most of them generally, our directive toward accomplishment would call for much effort in planning and production. Our result, however, would be a body of video tapes uniquely designed to serve the student in his quest for "what-to-do" and "how-to-be-able" information. It would provide the viewer with a success symbol to emulate in behavior so that he, by using the values of the training program, may advance nearer the time when he may be able to replace the imaged success symbol by being one himself.

Phase three of my suggested stage for media use would be to redefine and restate the whole objective of our educational philosophy. Perhaps you may feel that this should have been first on our list, and you may well be right. However, had I begun the chapter with what I am about to write, I might have lost you altogether.

What I am about to do is reduce our objective to what you may consider simplicity to the point of absurdity. In the light of what I have said previously, however, I think you may agree that although you have known this to be true all along, you just had never thought of it (specifically in its media affiliation) in just this way. I would claim that our job as educators (from the very outset of education) may be stated as follows: the objective of the educator is to teach his students

a) how to speak	d) how to figure
b) how to write	e) how to think
c) how to read	f) how to behave

While at first glance (as I predicted) you may believe this pattern has reduced the whole educative objective to being absurd in its simplicity, it is neither simple nor absurd. Let us take a moment to see why.

All six elements are interrelated and their sum total spells "communication." To exist in our generation (or any future one), one must know how to use his native language orally. After all, he transmits (and receives) the bulk of his information in oral language. He even thinks in a combination of oral patterns. His delivery and receptivity of speech depend upon the reflexive assimilation of word meaning. Knowing how to

68

speak requires vocabulary, grammar, delivery styles and adaptability to environment (where is the speech taking place?). In short, he must learn to speak because he cannot exist in contemporary society without knowing how to speak.

One should certainly know how to write. His writing must be capable of transmitting ideas in multi-word energy, be expressed coherently within the regulations of the native language (or others) and reflect the author as a person. Thus the writer must know form and style. He must also know that there is a reader for his writing, just as he knew there was a listener to his oral projections. He should also know how to read. It seems such an absolutely obvious statement, but he MUST know how to READ, that is, if he is to be a part of all that surrounds him. Our times demand at least a basic working knowledge of mathematics, of budgets and taxes, of money, of economy. It is absurdly simplistic that we do not recognize the need. It is even more absurd that we rarely attempt to meet it. In order to help one think, there are models of thinking procedures available for him to study. They are neatly labeled by such terms as "inductive," "deductive," "conceptual," etc. Their patterns are set for us by many philosophers, scientists, poets, mathematicians, historians and other scholars. Our task as teachers is to show the way to use created knowledge creatively. Before one thinks, one must have a language for thinking, whether it be real or abstract, factual or symbolic. We must develop the processes of using patterns of knowledge-use so that new knowledge may be discovered and used.

All five of these elements relate to our sixth: "how to behave." Think what the obligations are! How should a person behave with respect to himself, his home, his community, his world? How should he involve religion, law, history, art—what of race, recreation, morality? What more can we give our students than this knowledge of how to behave? Yet, we give them nothing at all if we do not give them all.

Thus far our media instructional program has involved itself with the people, the creators of knowledge, plus the how to media that covers the basic ingredients of human need. Not until we have developed the instructional units to accomplish the broad goal of meeting these needs would I suggest building specific units in the individual disciplines. We might find much of it already highly involved in the disciplines themselves—to speak well, one must study the style, form and vocabulary of speech. To use it well, one must know the techniques and styles of writing as well as the content of literature. This, in turn, imposes the techniques and skills of reading for comprehension and retention. To use figures, all of the preceding elements are needed in addition to the basics of mathematics, business, economics, reasoning procedures and their creative application. To the principle of action (as Jesus said, "As a man thinks, so is he") we might well add, "As he reads, writes and speaks, so he acts." The whole is the sum total of all the parts. "He" who "is" through study "may become."

How does one, with all of preceding criteria, convert the "learn to earn" disciplines into media instructional units? I have no final answers to the swiftly-developing circumstances of media. Some positive suggestions, however, allow me the luxury (as I said earlier in "beginning from scratch") of making a broad, general outline of worthwhile procedures.

Our first step would be to analyze the courses within a given discipline and to divide them into these categories:

a) The "to do" courses—those which require a manifestation of performance skills to demonstrate achievement.

b) The "to use" courses—those which require the assimilation of learning in order to make application.

Category (a) is psychomotor training plus category (b). Category (b) is assimilation, concept and application plus varying degrees of category (a). While it might appear that both are the same, there is a difference which we will try to indicate by this example: A freshman biology course is divided into the elements "to do" and "to use" in its normal classroom-laboratory structure. The lab section is hands-on experience, both learning the tools and then utilizing them in the accomplishment of the learning goal. It transforms theory into reality by the application of performance skills to concept. One must know what the concept is before proving its validity; one must be able to use the tools to demonstrate understanding of concept.

70

In order to speak, write or read a language (physical manifestation of knowledge by demonstration), there are certain psychomotor skills involved in doing—that is, new physical positions required to say *lingua* or *idioma* or *langue* instead of "language." These skills come only with practice and must be learned to the same degree that a reflex enables us (as we speak, write or read English) to use the word without analyzing its components or thinking where to put our tongue or move our lips. Reaction to the language, whether oral, aural or visual, is instantaneous. The theory of the language is arrived at conceptually; acquired psychomotor skills allow its application in use.

When we have looked at our course content and have analyzed it in terms of the two basic categories into which the material falls, we then need to place the individual course in perspective with the total required courses which make up a major within that discipline. Obviously we have already sequenced these courses into what we have previously determined to be the most direct route to the achievement of the completion of the study. We would then look at the common elements contained within each course and the common courses contained within the separate majors.

Science in its undergraduate curriculum, for example, offers a large number of courses which are common to several majors: pre-med, chemistry, physics, biology, medical technology, mathematics, etc. Making a determination of the common elements within each of these courses would enable us to prepare instructional units on each of their common elements. I shall give a brief illustration of this in a moment in my authoritative field (music). For now, let it suffice to say that one will soon discover that this approach will develop units which can be used within all of the courses and disciplines, not to teach specific subjects, but to use the materials within the subjects to teach science AS it applies to the specific subject.

In music, specifically, there are five courses which provide information (for one use or another) about the oboe. Music history is one (as we examine the "when" of it, its principle users among composers, its use in orchestration [the art of combining instruments together to produce orchestras, bands

71

and various ensembles]). Students need to know how to write for the oboe; a conductor needs to know about it because he needs to know all he can about each instrument he directs. It is taught in music education courses where music literature, elementary and secondary methods and instrumental technique are studied. Knowing the value of a media unit on the oboe, we would create one geared to the specifics required in each of the several courses, thus making it practical for all to use—not merely, as we said, to learn to be a conductor, a music educator or an orchestrator, but to be a musician who must have knowledge of this instrument in order to function as a musician.

With this specific unit, we could amass an additional body of already-available material on the oboe ranging from performance recordings, tapes, film or film strips to available video tapes on specific artists doing music involving either solo or important ensemble work with the oboe. Utilizing this same material gathered together for the oboe, we could then use it as correlative material for form, style, harmony, etc. See how it works? All of the elements within a discipline are individual energizing forces which, when combined, enable the student to apply the parts in order to gain understanding of the whole.

Once this detailed analysis and dissecting of courses has been accomplished, we may begin to address issues involving the type of media to be utilized most expeditiously in accomplishing our teaching-learning goals. Some of the following questions are pertinent:

1. Is the unit to support classroom instructional methodology within the classroom itself?

    Is it to be used in the classroom before a "live" audience by means of an audio tape, slides or perhaps a combination of all elements of media—or if facilities are available, by film loop, super-8 projection, film strip, overhead projector?

2. Is the unit to be self-contained, needing no teacher-textbook support to achieve learning?

    If so, it may be done as a purely audio or slide tape, or produced as video tape or video tape transformed to 16mm. or super-8 film.

3. Is the unit to be used together with hands-on equipment demonstration of learning achievement?

This type of presentation is especially valuable to the audio-visual-tutorial lab where the student has access to equipment and materials under the supervision of an instructor. It is truly individualized instructional media, since its success is dependent upon the student's control of the playback equipment and the adjacent availability of the hands-on materials.

4. Is the unit to supply information that must be learned through rote memorization?

Technical terms, vocabulary, language pronunciation, identification of varied items (lab tools, anatomical areas, definitions, punctuation, etc.) can be produced on audio slide-tape and in some instances used by students independently of a teacher. Best results may be achieved with an audio tape and an illustrated handbook rather than slides. Ample proof of student participation may be determined (a) by immediate response or (b) by testing over each unit. These tests could be incorporated into media. Programmed instruction techniques can be used in preparing the scripts so that each bit of information could be tested before the student proceeds to the next step.

Thus far we have talked about the body of materials in lives of the people who discovered a segment or segments of the knowledge-mass. We have talked about the importance of career investigation to relate the "why" of learning to its livelihood use. We have discussed (and distilled) the educational objectives we should maintain. We have advocated the re-thinking, the re-examination of course–discipline–degree requirements in terms of the common, unifying components identifiable with the whole. We shall conclude this chapter by discussing some of the media transfer units and systems, examining our options as to available equipment and delivery modes and attempting to determine which techniques (or combinations) may be used to the best advantage. The following list will provide us with the components for our discussion:

1. Audio (or audiovisual) tutorial labs
2. Audio-video retrieval systems
3. Audiovisual classrooms

4. Closed-circuit television (microwave, cable and within-house transmission and reception)
5. Audio, slide-tape and video packets
6. Computer-assisted instruction
7. Public broadcasting and/or educational radio-TV

While there are variations of these components, those listed represent the basic availabilities currently in use. Each of them offers advantages; each has limitations. Let's think about each of them briefly:

1. The audio (or audiovisual) tutorial lab (used widely in science, language, music studies) is a very successful teaching system.

   This implies having media systems plus the immediate availability of hands-on equipment (or some variation of the "demonstrate to show learning" method). One moves from the media instructional information directly to the application of theory in practiced reality. It is both group and individualized instruction. It has the benefit of being non-structured in a "time" concept, although it does retain the feature of the student having to be in a specified place to learn. It permits service to large numbers of students on a more personalized basis than could be accomplished in a lecture hall. Its best use is in the area of instruction which, as a result of theoretical input, requires the student to demonstrate his understanding by doing.

2. Audio-video retrieval systems utilize a delivery source of media transmission by means of audio and video playback equipment which supplies many reception areas on a closed circuit.

   This is usually, but not necessarily, confined to a central listening-viewing area. Several systems are currently in use, such as (a) a dial-access or touchtone signal utilized by the student to obtain delivery of service to his carrel or study area, (b) a direct telephone request to a delivery center for transmission to a specified area, (c) an automated delivery on a scheduled basis, either manually or time-clock controlled, or (d) combinations of these. The retrieval system is a complicated, somewhat inflexible, extremely expensive system to buy and maintain. It is capable of delivery of many audio-video units simultaneously, and its delivery capability is limited only by the number of playback units available. It also has the capacity to serve many students at the same time by varying the number of receiving sets available.

Reception centers may be placed in single, large areas (such as Learning Centers) or they may be interconnected to the campus facilities, such as classrooms, labs and dormitories.

Since this system is designed for large-number use rather than individual control of the playback equipment, it delivers the "whole" of something. Much like commercial radio or TV, each unit is presented in its entirety. The student's dial-up may either activate the remote mechanism to playback or, if the unit is already in progress, it tunes in at whatever point the unit is then playing.

The positive features include capability to deliver materials to large numbers simultaneously with undistorted audio-video reliability, and capability to service distant, off-campus points through microwave or cable. The negative factors include the extremely expensive equipment required and maintenance costs.

3. An audiovisual classroom is a classroom modified to deliver the output of various media equipment which is generally permanently installed to assist the teacher in the presentation of audiovisual materials.

Some classrooms are automated to the degree of easy remote activation of the equipment from a lectern panel. Others may be totally programmed to be operated by "pre-sync" audio tape. Many are equipment-supplied to be operated either by the teacher or an assistant. The classroom may be theater in design (and ideally should be so). If possible it should include an instant response system for testing of the students. Equipment needs include opaque and standard overhead projectors, super-8 and 16mm. projectors, audio control and lighting system, film-loop, filmstrip, carousel slide projectors, audio-tape playbacks, videotape playback (ideally projection video), rear and front screen projection capability, and, if possible, both mobile and fixed-position TV cameras, turntables, display areas for large graphics, maps, charts, etc. Some audiovisual classrooms may require science lab fixtures and others may need playing areas for multi-voiced productions.

The audiovisual classroom is, as you will begin to understand, a veritable production center in which the elements normally used

75

in producing TV materials are assigned in order to permit a display live and in larger scale than on the ordinary TV screen.

Of all the systems yet developed, the audiovisual classroom (equipped as we have described) is the most dynamic setting for group presentation of media instruction. It does become theater capable of utilizing live and prepared elements. It has many effective qualities which we do not obtain in other forms of presentation, and they are related primarily to the flexibility available to the user.

Fully equipped, it is expensive. Its maintenance problems are fewer, however, than retrieval systems. Since it requires performance to make a presentation, much time is involved in programming. This procedure usually requires the services of a technician-plus-teacher. The system is flexible because the classroom may be used for standard lectures or lectures involving only part of the equipment. The time of preparation involved is actually a good thing, for no media production should ever be used until sufficient time in planning and preparation has been given. The teacher himself is the fundamental creator in this media type, as well as in all others. One other positive asset this media type possesses over any of the other forms is its ability to use copyrighted materials without the usual restrictions. It also has an infinitely larger capability of using resources already in existence.

Were I compelled to select a single system of media use (apart from the use of standard audio and video cassettes, etc.), I would suggest this approach, with a minimum of two fully-equipped rooms.

4. Closed-circuit television via microwave, cable, pickup of standard band TV, or a central dissemination system normally services (but is not restricted to) classroom monitors or similar reception areas elsewhere.

Many school systems, both local and statewide, use this method to mass-deliver instructional units for class viewing. Normally transmission is made from the central delivery system via wave-lengths unobtainable on home sets. The usual procedure on such systems is to schedule on a time basis the transmissions available during that time slot. Such systems have many advantages in the capability of setting up two-way transmission between distant points, permitting interaction from students gathered in one location with a teacher broadcasting from distant points. While this type of capability is presently limited, it is easy to believe that there will be a day when satellites will be used to service great geographical areas via microwave.

The cost of procuring equipment, its maintenance and personnel will depend entirely upon its size, the amount of service expected from it and the number of locations it is required to maintain. Like the retrieval systems, it has the tremendous advantage of being able to transmit to many students simultaneously. It has the disadvantage of being inflexible (if anything but live programming is done) in its service to the individual student.

5. Audio, slide-tape and videotape packets utilize audio cassette (or reel-to-reel) tape playback equipment, carousel slide projectors, and videotaped materials capable of being used on individual video-playback units of either cartridge, cassette, or reel-to-reel players.

Slide-tape units may be transferred to videotape and thence to film, used in classroom presentation, placed in viewing areas for use by individual students (who operate the equipment) or obtained from library check-out areas. Thus their use is quite advantageous because of their flexibility. Videotaped units may also be transformed to film for class viewing or used in fixed areas where playback units are available. All three of these presentational types have the distinct ability to be used without respect to time or place, may be operated by the student to repeat or re-study in whole or in part and they may be combined with various types of print media to allow the student the option of individualized pacing. Since he is not restricted to a scheduled transmission and since he may elect to use the materials either alone or with a group at a place and time limited only to the availability of the playback unit, he has a distinct advantage over any of the other locked-in time-place conditions.

The audio-cassette is, of course, the least expensive and currently the most widely used media equipment. Video units are still (and will be) comparatively expensive. It is assumed that this will change when mass-production is achieved. Any video unit or film (with proper copyright clearance) may be transferred to cartridge, cassette, or small-tape video units. Slide-tape packets have one other advantage: they may be combined with other equipment (film-loops, filmstrips, etc.) for additional flexibility in live presentations. Equipment purchased for slide showing (even if it includes such items as the programmer—for automation—and the slide dissolve unit) is not overly expensive. The champion, of course, in the low-cost field is the cassette tape recorder. It is also the most efficient piece of audio equipment available at present.

6. Computer-assisted instruction is obviously an enormously expensive but valuable instructional tool.

Programming the materials for the computer is a highly specialized skill, but it has tremendous flexibility of interplay between student and computer-teacher, allowing for assimilation of other media and immediate student response. It is of itself the nearest one may get to the one-to-one teacher-student relationship via media apart from a human teacher. The values it loses in personality-to-personality are counterbalanced by the quality the programmer can design into the instruction of the computer-teacher unit itself. Fortunate indeed is that institution which has computer-assisted capability. While it is not the all-in-all, it does have fantastic possibilities.

. Public broadcasting and/or educational radio-TV is one of the most underrated sources of media potential easily available to those who teach in an area large enough to have both commercial and educational TV.

This is also valuable to those who have only commercial broadcasts available. While it may be that TV is indeed the "vast wasteland," as it has been described (and I argue even with that), there is a great quantity of scheduled material (usually in public service areas) which is good. Any consistent analysis of a month's programming, for example, would turn up a number of things which could be included in an overall instructional program. It is relatively simple to get advance information so assignments may be made to view within the "on air" schedule.

The values of TV are in direct ratio to the number of channels available and/or the number of educational broadcast services in a given area. Many such public broadcasts originate as a joint effort between schools and the stations. Some stations permit in-house viewing of their units and sometimes permit taping privileges for delayed viewing. One could, if he were creatively inclined, combine all the available radio-TV broadcasts with local movies and recordings to develop a quite healthy media instructional program.

78

The disuse of public broadcast availabilities for instructional use is often caused by the schedule conflicts that frequently occur between broadcast time and school time. Many times teachers are reluctant to assign viewing or listening without having had the privilege of seeing or hearing the material in advance. Because we are so accustomed to the time and place concept of teaching, we tend to unconsciously resist the exterior forces which are ours to use. One may sum up pointedly that the educator who fails to take advantage of his opportunities to incorporate these factors into his program is failing his students miserably.

Since I have been in a position to suggest *what* you should do and now *that* you should do it (and *how* you can do it), and since we have been assuming from the beginning of this chapter that we are beginning a media instructional program, I feel free—no, obligated—to set forth my recommendations about your equipment usage. This is especially so in view of the time I have spent advocating the adoption of new learning theories as we move from standard classrooms into the dissemination of knowledge via media.

I would gear my production toward (a) audiovisual theaters, (b) individualized packets through cassette-tape, slide-tape and videotape cassettes, as well as (c) utilizing public media wherever available. I would be less inclined to utilize any sort of retrieval system, would engage in microwave/cable reception if available and probably would not advocate use of ultra-expensive closed-circuit or computer-assisted instruction at all—unless there is absolutely no problem finding money to use. Here is the order I would follow:

a) Audio-video, slide-tape checkout packets
b) Audiovisual theaters
c) Audiovisual tutorial labs
d) Public audio-video transmission

Before purchasing even one piece of equipment, I would research the market for availability of resources already in existence as instructional units.

This chapter ends with no set of high-sounding inspirational words. It has no promises of an easy life ahead if you go the media route. Rather, it assures you that there are hours and hours of hard labor ahead—that is, if you are to utilize media fully as an energizing force of incalculable values to the student whose life's programming you, the teacher, are directing. In the chapters ahead we shall consider how to write, how to make graphics, how to use music, how to take care of your media library, how to use photography, how to direct and how to find some of your available resources. I hope you combine theory with hands-on equipment so that your skills may become reflexive to the pinnacle of learning's achievement— to be able to create, with media as your art form.

CHAPTER IV

SYMBOLISM:
THE LANGUAGE OF THE MEDIA ARTS

If I were to capsulize this chapter into its briefest meaning, it would be that "Symbolism is the totality of communication." Since the thought processes involved in the creation and performance of the arts are communicated by the use of an organized body of symbols classified into notational systems, we may conclude that the use of such an organized body of symbols is a positive force in the stimulation of thought-generative patterns. When these symbols are learned well they enable the user to create and perform with a remarkably high degree of efficiency and effectiveness.

Of all the arts, music has the most positively-defined system. Yet dance, mime, drama, the graphic arts and the "word-arts" (poetry and prose) all have systems of determinative meaning, although most of them overlap. Mime, which is an embracive art form included within dance, drama and to some extent music, uses a symbolic language based on movement of shapes and forms. Its symbolism is "imitation of being." As an art form it is practiced by more individuals than all of the other arts combined, although subjectively in most instances. Symbolism even reflects itself in written language as simile, metaphor and euphemism and in oral communication by gestures, inflection and volume. In the graphic arts represented by painting, drawing, design, sculpture and ceramics, form, shape, dimension, color and perspective, plus a multiplicity of effort symbols (brush strokes, textures, material types) represent the basic symbolic language. The word-arts are also symbol-filled, since they themselves are symbols in reality.

In all instances, works of art are generated from an emotional-spiritual experience expressed through the symbolic language of the individual art. In addition, these symbols (either in creation, performance, or both) are artists in direct relation to their ability to understand and use the symbols individually. That is, in applying their own individual personality-plus-potential to the employment of symbols to express self, artists express their creativity. One who enables the symbol-thought to become evidenced reality in product or performance with the greatest degree of skill is called a "master," and his work is called a "masterpiece." It should be noted that the notational systems of creation are brought into being one item at a time (such as musical notes, brush strokes, handwritten or typed words, gestures and inflections). Within the creative process *and* the performance process of thinking via symbols, however, thought patterns move with amazing swiftness within the mind and into the mind. This latter observation will be of value as we contemplate the potential in a philosophy of symbol utilization as an educative process to function similarly in all knowledge creation and performance. The educative process inevitably leads to greater efficiency and effectiveness for teacher and learner alike.

Symbols are "representations" of reality rather than the reality itself. Take, for example, the word "now." "Now" is "now" only when it is the *now* that is being experienced. The now which just occurred becomes "then," and the next now awaits its "nowness" in the instant of becoming "now" on its way to becoming "then." The arts have learned to capture *now* symbolically so that as it *was* at its meaning of "nowness," so shall it ever be. While written language may have begun with meaningful marks on their way to becoming words, it is more likely that those marks (symbols) represented meaning (without oral expression). It was that artist in primitive society who first painted on walls who accomplished the time-stopping event of using symbols to represent the real.

In all the Media Arts (electronic and otherwise) that "now" is static in its time-space relationship. This is made possible through the use of symbols drawn one-by-one from the mind to form the whole in evidence of creation. Within the mind of the creator, these symbols moved with incredible swiftness to allow him to see or hear the whole before it became manifest by his one-by-one representation of it. One hears or sees or feels ˙ the results of that creation, and it relates its meaning to those who hear, see or feel—not as symbology itself, but as an in-presence representation of individual thought. It is experience expressed in that which we call "art." It was a "discovery" of new knowledge based on individual manipulation of an organized system of symbolism within the framework of mutually dependent creative-performance potential.

While the arts themselves are so organized as to be able to give the nowness in a permanent quality, it is not theirs alone to do so. Electronic media, in fact all media which represent more than the transient use of symbology to capture time, have this capability. The thought processes represented by art's acknowledged achievements and used as concept in creation and performance with media's assistance open new realms of possibility in education as we consciously use simulation of real to represent real. Not only can they be utilized as such in the creation and presentation of ideas symbolically, but also through the multi-gadgeted resources called "media" which have the capability to retain ideas in some retrievable manner. For all media (written, electronic, photographic) art is merely simulation of real.

A picture of your mother is not your mother, no matter how many tender and wonderful (or terrible and awful) memories of her may be evoked by your viewing it. Neverthe-less, it is representative of your mother's physical likeness to the extent that one mechanical eye can reproduce it in facsimile color and two dimensional plane. The picture's symbolism represents a totality of factors represented by your experience as a child of that motherhood. Your memories of her are now simulated, since all memories are themselves only simulations of the real, and are activated by a photograph which represents a multi-stimulus capable of activating (as does the word "mother" itself) hundreds of responses. Even the memory of

83

the photograph becomes simulation. Not only is the intellect activated by the symbolistic picture, but recall will provide emotional response. All of this is done swiftly within the mind of the viewer through energy released by the explosive-implosive crystalization within the symbol represented by the picture and the symbolic word "mother."

Media then (itself a simulation of experience) enables the mind to ingest the informational input as a pre-determined experience (one guided by the maker of media), investing the participant with the dual role of being an experiencer (real) of the media output (simulated) as well as being in a state of involvement with the simulated experience represented by media. As a result, the viewer participates in vicarious experience and actual experience simultaneously. To that degree that media can be created to simulate experience which is transferred into reality, media itself (of itself) becomes real instead of simulated. In a symbolic sense, this is like eating predigested foods, such as honey. The body assimilates the food into the blood stream without utilizing its full digestive processes. Not that this insures total benefit, for if the honey-makers did a bad job of selectivity in the honey-making process, or even if the consumer had no need or willingness to consume honey, the product itself would have little value. The intent of creativity for use plus the need for and willingness to accept the product also becomes a major factor in determining values. No matter how great the honey, it amounts to nothing if it remains as honey. It must be consumed to make its contribution.

Our plans for the use of the concept projected in symbolism plus media must also include ways of designing the product so that its internal potential may not only *be* palatable and nourishing, but also desired, enjoyed and needed. It is not enough to motivate (in the old sense), but we must show the student *how* to learn. To revert to our homespun analogy, we must show him not only that the honey is beneficial to him, but also that all that is left on his plate and chin will never do his body any good at all. Our task in this chapter, then is to suggest a state of awareness of the potential in the use of symbols AS

THE ARTS USE THEM — as factors in creativity and performance to provide a simulation of the real through a simulative ingestion of learning materials in ALL THE DISCIPLINES. In short, because of the kinetic potential of all symbols and because symbols represent totality of communication, we should utilize them for their capabilities to "explode" an idea into consciousness.

In the pages that follow we will discuss symbols because we want to re-awaken your sensitivity to and your awareness of them. We will also suggest the power of the mind (or minds) and try to define the potential of media to extend sensory capabilities. We will think together about thinking processes. We will postualte hypotheses and suggest theorems, suggesting to you that as the mind itself is capable of being able to leave the body to range far and free in imagination, so the Media Arts may be used to transport the mind in ways the mind of itself could not otherwise go. We shall talk of media itself as being symbolic of reality and propose that "experience real" and "experience media" both become "experience simulated" once the experience has been consumated. We will also assert that media is "predetermined experience potential" capable of multiple repetition whereas experience real (once experienced) must rely on what we will call an additional sense: the memory sense — itself simulation. We will argue that media has capabilities of extending the senses far beyond the customary power of the individual (particularly in auditory and visual), and that it has the capability of doing all this with no particular reference to the media-experiencer being in any given time or place.

We shall point out that media itself has developed (and is constantly developing) a highly sensitive body of symbols which enable the practiced user to create and perform with extraordinary skill. We shall talk of the unconscious mind and the explosive and generative force of symbols as informational inputs. We shall define symbol as "representation of multi-meaning expressed in single unit form." In all this we shall remember that each member of the human species is an individual, conceding in advance that there are no hard and fast laws which can pertain even to one individual, much less to large numbers. As we strive to arrive at some basic conclusions about the concepts put forth here, we will operate on the philosophy of these three short sentences, themselves symbolic of totality:

I am.
You are.
We are.

Our key word is "awareness." Our motivational verb is "suggest."

To begin, I'd like you to take a look at this group of symbols and see how many meanings of each you know.

1. O, 2. =, 3. +, 4. →, 5. <, 6. X,

7. T, 8. ☞, 9. ℞, 10. √‾, 11. ■, 12. 卐,

13. L, 14. ⇌, 15. ♆, 16. †, 17. ( ), 18. ◠,

19. ©, 20. A, 21. ⚕, 22. $, 23. %, 24. #,

25. ÷, 26. λ, 27. ♭, 28. ☆, 29. △, 30. ? .

Actually there are more symbols there than you thought at first, for the commas, the period and the numerals are also symbols. Beginning with the number one, we see a circle. What does it mean to you? A circle? Perfection? The symbol for oxygen in chemistry? Zero or nothing? It represents a circumference to the mathematician, or perhaps a pint as an apothecary measure. It could be an annual plant to a biologist or botanist, or represent a full moon in meterology. A circle with a dot in the center might represent the sun in astronomy or the earth if it has a horizontal and vertical diameter included in it. In other ways it means "degrees" (in both temperature and measurement) and the letter "O" of the alphabet. And what of the "plus" sign (+) in number three? It can mean "in addition to" or a unit charge of positive electricity. It can also be an "x" which is sometimes used to sign one's name, or represent the sign of the cross.

We recognize some of these symbols for single usage instantly, and we can find the meaning of them all in a good standard dictionary. Perhaps it is what we do with them that causes us to use symbols as natural expressions of thoughts—or perhaps it is where we are. Symbols like the "dollar" sign ($) may represent a currency amount although it may not always mean "dollar." In Mexico, for instance, they do not read it for dollar but for peso. The triangle might mean several things. It could refer to the eternal triangle, for example, or to finite difference (math), or even to the notes for a musical instrument named the "triangle."

This sampling of symbols could be extended indefinitely. Many of them would have a single meaning; most of them have more than one. In the case of the two raised fingers, the meaning might depend on who was making the sign, as well as why and where they were making it. It also might depend upon to whom the sign was being made. A crowd of dissenters wanting physical action would not be well dissuaded by a "peace" sign, nor would one be likely to interpret the sign as "peace" if numbers were involved. Even if there may seem to be a single meaning in a symbol, many factors govern its interpretation, including the individuality of the interpreter and the circumstance surrounding its use.

The largest part of our symbolism then may be considered capable of transmitting meaning over and beyond mere sensory interpretation. We and "it" arrive at "its" meaning for us. Thus, it is possible to see a circle and have the whole meaning of circle symbolism already understood in whatever relationship we want to make it meaningful for us. It is like mentioning the name of a familiar tune. We don't have to hum or sing it all the way through to know that we know it. Not only will a fragment excite the intellectual recall, but it may also trigger the explosion of emotions. It is already there, and the mere mention of it instantly brings its totality to mind for demonstration or use.

Many symbols may be interpreted in a broad general sense to add richness to a variety of thought patterns. Rain, for example, may be a soft and gentle springtime thing, a raging jungle storm, a summer shower, a picnic-spoiling rain, a crop-saving rain, a cold and stinging winter's feel or a source of drinking water. Fundamentally it is rain. What it does to us personally or how we want to think of it determines its meaning for us and our meaning for it. It is instant representation whether we feel, see, taste, hear, smell or remember it. Our language, oral and written, is rich in such variables. Fortunately, language rigidity sets in only when we attempt to or actually circumscribe a symbol with one meaning only.

There are symbols which tell us what to do: stop, go, turn, exit, speed, act! We also react to symbols environmentally. We smell a skunk and generally try to avoid the immediate proximity, or we hear a rattlesnake and flee the scene. We see a flashing red light while hearing a siren and translate the sight and sound into an ambulance, police car or fire truck. We are affected emotionally (and therefore physically), and we are affected physically (and therefore emotionally) by shapes, sizes, temperatures, situations, sights, tastes, smells and sounds—whether real or simulated, actual or memory. In short, in our body displacement of space-time we are directly and indirectly affected by all forces around us—just as in some small measure we also affect all other life around us.

We used numerals as numbers in the illustration and words symbolizing numbers in the explanation. Our alphabet is an example of the use of such symbols to communicate. To one customarily using these symbols, the meanings and sounds are less important to comprehension than the symbol itself. Each letter of the alphabet, for example, is a picture-symbol. These picture-symbols are used one at a time and combined into word-symbols. In speaking, we also use them one at a time (at times), but we are more accustomed to using their combination as "meanings" rather than thinking of their individual force. Some of them are even word substitutes or actually words themselves. For example, the letters "I," "O" and "X" are used of themselves as words. The sound of the letters "B," "R," "C," "Y" and others may also be used as words. We could use a phonetic process in writing: I M I, U R U. Y? O, I C. Remember that bit of doggerel about "ABCD goldfish?" We might experiment for a moment to substantiate the truth of this symbolism.

In written language, capital letters assume an implied importance (such as capital "H" when used with reference to God). There are strict rules governing our use of capitals, and we adhere to them in order to be clearly understood. Mechanically reproduced letters (such as print or typescript) limit, to some extent, the meaningfulness of letter-making since it is depersonalized when compared to the manuscript or handwritten copy. When typing we may shout by SHOUTING with capitals, subject to the limitations of a machine. We can shout with the letters themselves only to the extent of the mechanical latitude. In handwriting we can shout all over the paper if we like, although most of us conform to a relationship of mechanically produced lettering. The size, color, style and position of the letters do have meaning, as do giant letters on billboards and buildings, smoke letters in the sky, letters formed by marching bands. In animated cartoons letters themselves take on semblance of human form as they become "alive" as well as stationary symbols.

Since we're dealing with letters only, let's proceed to abbreviations and their incursion into the language as words. The following sample of abbreviated words should prove instructive: AAA, WAVES, NATO, CARE, ENCO, POW, TV, PS, AMA, PDQ, DOA, COD, FBI, RIP, VIP, MPH, EKG, NFL, NG, RSVP, TLC, AA, BTU, AC, DC, AM, PM, KC, RBI, BVD, CIO, ETA, PTA, NAZI, FM, EEG, VA, GP, MO, FCC, IRS, etc.

Some of these abbreviations actually spell out word sounds. All of them are used as symbols representing word groups, the pronunciation of which is the sound of the letters. We call AAA "Triple-A," making a new word out of old words which represent the American Automobile Association. "Double-A" may represent Alcoholics Anonymous or Athletic Association. The "KC" can mean anything from kennel club, Kansas City or kilocycle to Knights of Columbus. The endless list of such symbols leads one to suspect that we are unconsciously trying to develop a language which can be spoken at a greater-than-usual speed, just as we have developed a whole set of symbols in speed-writing and shorthand. While we have increased speed of symbol reproduction (as in computer language) to undreamed of velocities, spoken language has not yet adapted itself to such increases. However, we can hear at enormous speeds as we do when we listen to the multi-sounds coming from a band or orchestra at tremendous velocities.

But because we are not mechanical or electronic ourselves, we tend to develop word forms and new words which combine a number of ideas into "meaning groups." We use them so that we may speed up the process of oral comprehension just as we have done visually and aurally. Just as we may now transmit (electronically) great volumes of information in single "blip" sounds which are to be reheard later in proper word speed as words, we will someday be able to have access to micro-words in sound storage as we now have them in microfilm. Not only that, but we will be able to listen comprehensibly to hundreds of words per minute. In the meanwhile, we must be content with symbolism speed-up—a symbolism which is growing more and more apparent as we replace names with numbers on credit, bank and social security accounts.

While I have been typing out this collection of symbols one by one, I have used another form of symbolic language called "punctuation." Punctuation, like the alphabet, has assumed some sort of universality of meaning irrespective of the language used—at least among most of those who use written language in Western fashion.

All of our punctuation marks have names: periods, commas, semi-colons, colons, question marks, exclamation points, parentheses, brackets, dashes, slashes, hyphens, apostrophes and elipses. These all have meaning not only as written language, but through inflection and phrasing they have meaning aurally (if done correctly orally). Their function governs the interpretation of thought groupings, and they are used according to a fairly rigid set of rules.

Since our punctuation marks indicate meanings both read and said, we could speak the words in a manner (using the wrong inflection) which would entirely negate the purposefulness of the original intent of the words—no matter how well they had been punctuated. Let's take this example, "Mary, I love you." In this instance the quotation marks indicate that someone else says to Mary that he (or she) loves her. If this statement were written as it appears in some scripts, it might appear differently as: Mary: I love you.

In such a case it would be Mary speaking to someone else (or to herself if she were Narcissitic). Inflective words might be added which would convey the delivery or reading attitude:

Mary: (pleadingly)	I love you.
Mary: (angrily)	I love you.
Mary: (hastily)	I love you.
Mary: (happily)	I love you.
Mary: (anxiously)	I love you.

Both the inflective and attitudinal styles can be altered to a degree by punctuation marks. Try this yourself by repeating the line in the form of a question and then as an exclamation. Then give stress to all three words in turn: *I* love you? *I* love you! I *love* you? I *love* you! I love *you*? I love *you*! Thus the three symbols ("I" and "love" and "you") assume a dimensional potential through inflection, emphasis, attitude and situation which they could not achieve in their ordinary written form. In short, WE have brought to THEM these dimensions of meaningfulness. In so doing, THEY now HAVE them. Later we will examine the worth of these multi-meaning symbols in terms of learning procedures applied to media.

Parts of speech, particularly adjectives and adverbs, are also symbolic. While verbs indicate that action is taking place, adverbs tell how it takes place. In the following illustrations pronouns will indicate who is taking the action: "He ran pantingly, she spoke haltingly, he wrote furiously, they danced energetically." With pronouns we may also define or delineate the sex of all words. By adding adjectives the action may also be directed: "His face, sweat-beaded and grim, peered sightlessly into the black silence of the midnight hour." Prepositions (of, with, for, if, as, at, between, among, in, into) are determinate words which help locate time, space and condition— in short, they move us from a pre-position to another position. They are also conjunctive, but not so much as conjunctions. Conjunctions (and, but, or, nor, for, so, yet) unite thought patterns and we add prepositions and conjunctions conjunctively to provide energy impulses which move a narrative along.

We also have people symbols and representations of people (animals and things) which are symbolic. Among people symbols we could list: Lincoln, Churchill, Hitler, Stalin, Washington, Jefferson, Franklin, Napoleon, Caesar and Christ-- all figures of great intensity. Our representational symbols could include Santa Claus, Uncle Sam, Smokey the Bear, Robin Hood, Winnie the Pooh, Mr. Clean, the Jolly Green Giant, St. George, King Arthur, Scarlet O'Hara, Peanuts, Superman, Dick Tracy, Kilroy and Mickey Mouse. With birds and animals we can be as silly as a goose, graceful as a swan, strong (brave) as a lion, happy as a bluebird, saucy as a jay, sly as a fox, or as white as a lamb. We are much aware of hawks, doves, eels and snakes during political campaigns. We can be as hard as a rock, soft as down, high as the sky, low as the bottom of the sea, warm as toast, tight as a drum, tough as leather, sharp as a razor or as nutty as a fruitcake. There is, you see, no end to these symbolic combinations— they are as endless as grains of sand on the desert.

And colors? What of them? How important are they and what advantages can we take of known physiological-psychological influences of color intensities and their symbolic meaning for media instruction? "Red" can mean shame, anger, revolution, danger, monetary loss, valor or sin-stained. We call Indians redskins (although they aren't), we get red-hot (enraged or super-charged with luck), we may get caught red-handed, or encounter red tape (officialdom), a red light (traffic signal or symbol for prostitution), become red-eyed (tears) or even red tag something important in our files.

"Green" can refer to newness on the job, jealousy, growth (nature), illness, envy, immaturity, spring-like, fear, foodstuff (turnip "greens"), recreation areas (putting green), or safety (green light). Green is an energizing word used to symbolize action, movement, potential, as well as disposition. It is a "life" color.

"Blue" also has a widespread usage, for it can mean best, as in blue-chip, blue-ribbon, blue-blood and blue-book, or it can mean evil: "the air turned blue with his curses." We turn blue with cold, or enact blue laws to limit business on a given day. A woman may be a blue-stocking if she is learned. One may see nothing but blue skies and bluebirds of happiness or have the blues of depression and loneliness.

"Yellow" connotes cowardice, jaundice, sensation, illness, strength, caution and springtime. It is also the color of the sun as we see it and therefore powerful, of gold, of yellow-lighted caution on traffic signals, and of the many yellows of springtime flowers. Yellow, for all its sensationalism, cowardice and strength, is also an at-ease, safe color. And if you want to know more about yellow, look up a good bookstore in the yellow pages—hmm! Yellow also must be revealing!

"White" has all the colors of the spectrum and shouldn't rightfully be called a color at all. White symbolizes purity and innocence, freedom from blemish, honesty, square-dealing and cleanliness. It shows intensity (white heat), hypocrisy (whited sepulcher), surrender (white flag), age (white haired), miscarriage of justice (whitewashed), untruth (white lie) and heroism (a man on a white horse). White is a symbol of sinlessness in Christian religion—white is germ-free, sanitary, purity. It is also the color of legrosy, and when one's strength fails he turns white. It is the opposite of black and is used as such in contrasts. When we want to know the certainty of something, we ask to see it in black and white. As "black is beautiful" is a popular slogan, so also is "white ugly" as the "whities" of the world are learning of the reverse symbolism of black and white. And that combination, expressed in any way, is "pretty ugly" (how symbolic can you get?). White is black when the light is off, but black is still black with or without light. White is a pretty mixed-up word, I'd say, representing life to some cultures, death to others, beauty to some, ugliness to others—one thing is certain: white is a potent word which energizes the mind into all sorts of reactions when we see, feel or hear it.

"Black" represents the absence of light (darkness), the dismal (the future looks black), evil (the man in the black hat, black marks, black book or a pirate's flag), as well as the loss of consciousness (blackout). It can also mean prosperity if your accounts are in the black or disgrace if you are the black sheep of the family. The magic of witchcraft is called black magic. Blackmail is a form of extortion, blacklisting deems one uninclusive, blackhearted is the absence of integrity and the fascist were blackshirted. It is odd that the Bible, a symbol of life, is bound—more often than not—in black.

"Gray" identifies uncertainty (not clearly defined), wisdom (gray matter), age (gray-headed), lack of cheer (absence of color), fog (density factor of light and moisture) and mystery (shadows). As a non-color mixture of black and white, gray represents the legal-but-immoral (as in gray-market) as well as the beginning of light or darkness at dawn or dusk. There are gray-ladies who cheer up hospitals, the graybeard is venerable, the gray matter of braininess is magnificent. It has no motion. As a color it seems to try to avoid making a decision.

We can think about hue combinations: rainbow, red-white-blue, black and blue, red-cross, blue-cross, white-cross, candy-striped, polka-dotted, etc. All these are representative symbolisms which have rushed song writers and poets into mass production.

What we do know for sure is that colors are mood reflecting and mood reflectors which act differently on all people because we are all individually different. There is enough basic data available to enable us to use color, especially the intensified color that media is able to produce, to create atmospheres more stimulative and conducive to learning experience than can be obtained in gray shades of inaction. Color is a multiple-symbol energy force. The timeworn phrase: "all cats look gray in the dark" may well reflect education's previous lack of employment of light factors in determining the value of color in setting the stage of the mind for dramatic action within it. There once was a command, "Let there be light; and there was light." It's time we let the light let the color perform its symbolic miracles.

CHAPTER V

SYMBOLISM AND MEDIA INSTRUCTION

We've talked of words and letters and colors and shapes and forms as symbols—now let's talk of sounds, not inflective and modulative sound meanings or music, but rather sound that has come to us in these past fifty years or so from sources other than natural—that which comes from speaker systems. We have been conditioned through these years to hearing sounds in various volumes and intensities from such communication systems as telephone, radio, television, recorder and public address devices—all of which transfer sound with much more intensity and almost as much realism as the real sounds. We have also developed a dependency on these devices. Psychologically, the telephone is the most demanding of any single stimulus in communication, for involuntarily we are responsive to it as we are to no other insistencies upon us. The ubiquitous radio may be found in cars, homes, classrooms and offices, on picnic outings or as a travel companion along the way. I'm sure most of you have seen folks at football or baseball games listening to a radio while they are themselves in the midst of watching and hearing the same game.

As individuals we not only have a sense of urgency to respond to the potential available from media, but we have accepted its output as having been given from an authoritative plane. We are prone to believe, to accept, to credit those things which occur on media: "He is recorded by RCA Victor; therefore, he must be good." "I heard it on the radio, so it must be true." "But it said in the newspaper. . . ." We accept the fact that when people achieve the performance-acceptance necessary to be on TV, on records or in books, they must be a star of superior status to those who have not so arrived. Therefore, if something comes from these sources, it contains truth, is status-delivered and is automatically acceptable (on the whole) from media *because* of the media.

This does not mean that we may not disagree or disbelieve in specific instances. It only means that fifty or so years of activation in the sound-spectrum delivered by mass media have fixed us—as a group—into a pre-conditioned reflex to media that is, in some instances, more responsive than the same experience under natural circumstances. We believe the guy on the radio more than we believe our neighbor.

We hear the media voice and see the media picture (in the electronic media) with willing belief simply because it is they who are inputting into our consciousness. We are so accustomed to the instant transfer across continents or to the moon to hear voices from miles away on telephone and radio and to see via satellite that we simply do not distinguish (although we are perfectly able to do so) that one experience is simulated while our "in life actuality" is real.

We hear the voices of people long dead and see them on motion picture screen or television tube. They are dead, but there they are! We accept the miracle of it all with jaded reflexes because it has happened to us so often. Even our emotional responses (sometimes even our physical responses) to the simulated are more energized than similar or identical experience would be if it were real. Without editorializing on this peculiarity of the era, I am merely being aware of the phenomenon that exists.

Having accepted, through long periods of conditioning, that which is in books as more important than that which is not, and having adopted a stance of believing more readily that which comes to us out of loudspeakers than what we may believe in actual experience, we have become media-susceptible as individuals and as a society. We are already pre-conditioned to participate, already pre-conditioned to accept and believe and already pre-conditioned (through previous participation) to receive simulated experience from media with at least the same intensity as that with which we accept the real. Since our

96

memories are filled with sights and sounds of infinite variety, since we think in speeds greater than we are able to speak or read or write and since we do this in thought patterns made up of symbols, it follows that if we input with greater intensity (into minds pre-conditioned to accept in value-perspective) using symbolism constantly, we enhance the capacity both to perceive and to conceptionalize.

We readily accept the simulated experience from media because we are accustomed to simulating experience through imagination, daydreams, real dreams and forms of controlled fantasizing—as well as permissively allowed or deliberately provoked uncontrolled fantasy. From childhood we have played the game of pretend. As a matter of fact, most of us never outgrow it—a most fortunate thing for humanity. When we were young we translated fantasy into reality (or reality into fantasy) by pretending that mother's dress was a gown for a princess or that a stick was a great white horse on which we galloped off into some marvelous adventures as the hero. We still play such games when we envision inordinate fame, wealth, happiness or discovery for which the rest of the world pays us obeisance in some super-superlative way. We hold imaginary conversations with the boss in which we always win arguments, receive approval, or perhaps we get fired, demoted or otherwise suffer humiliation.

In more grown-up situations, too, a controlled fantasy may result in a new symphony or opera. The composer (fantasizing, or utilizing symbols to change non-reality into imagined reality and thence into reality), utilizing a conglomerate of previously perceived and conceptionalized sounds and sound symbols, puts them on paper. Another may see a picture in his mind which causes him to reach for brush and canvas. Still another may see a statute lying inertly within a chunk of marble and go after it with chisel and mallet as he releases it from its prison. Another person, hearing voices and seeing things "no mortal man ere saw before," translates his in-mind symbols into identifiable outer-mind symbols, which results in a play, a novel or a poem.

97

We wrongly attribute to such people ultra-special talents endowed with special gifts. While the endowment may well be God-given (and I'll not deny that), the process involved in creating is man-made and achieves a state of perfection which is invention, architecture, music, or any other creative function to the extent that there is coordination and utilization of symbolic units with psycho-motor skills. He sees, feels or hears and then does. Such achievement capabilities are within human endowment, given to individuals along with their status as members of the human family. It follows that if there are some who create to perfection, some who create to mediocrity and some who create transiently without visible proof of the creation (within and only within the mind), all have creative capability. It also follows that if it is as a result of symbolism that we think and create, if what we do create is the input, then the greater the variety of symbolistic input we provide, the greater will be the product of the mind to be used by others in comprehension and creative application.

Let's get back to the controlled fantasy idea and see how we as educators can utilize this energy as well, for instance, as do the advertisers. We are bombarded from birth by stimulae urging us "to do." The advertising industry has paid far more attention to motivational symbolism than have educators. They have capitalized on the truth that all of us are susceptible to suggestion, both subtle and direct. We receive their suggestions to do via print media (in all of its forms), from radio and from television. Words, pictures, music and sound-effects are combined (with people) in television to suggest that if we are thirsty, we should either drink a type or brand-of-a-type liquid now or, if we do not have it on hand, we should buy it as soon as possible to alleviate our thirst. They go beyond the mere alleviation of a thirst factor by suggestion that we may also enjoy its *taste*. Even more, they suggest that by the mere drinking of the product, we will be transported into a self-situation resembling that in which we see others (in their high state of euphoria) drinking their drinks—all of this merely a result of our having seen them in the process of drinking the product. The implantation of the fantasized suggestion will more often than not trigger both fantasized and real response. Their idea of a real response is to have us buy their product. Our idea of a real response is the fantasy of enjoyment of their product to the extent that we are supposed to enjoy it because they showed us we would. That there is validity in their methodology is reflected realistically by their upward-spiraling sales charts.

It is really wild, isn't it, that teams of experts spend countless hours and expend energy beyond measure to create a response to the "coffier coffee," the "gusto" life (in which you only go around once) or the "tiger in your tank." They suggest, with maximum intensity of motivational input, for whatever reason YOU may think you are buying their product, that you DO buy it. Take time to look at commercials with this objectivity. You will learn much more, much indeed, about the power-packed suggestions they input with super-intensity so that you WILL do what they want you to do. Friends, if it works in advertising, it will work in education, although we may have to create a more "educatively education" to achieve the same ratio of motivated doers. At least they offer a product which in the light of much educational philosophy in action is hard to find either by us or the student.

We may also have uncontrolled fantasies such as those which occur in dreams. Even without knowing the symbolism of dream fantasies we are aware that much attention has been paid to dreams throughout history. The Bible gives us many accounts of dreams and their meanings, and if you don't want to rely upon the Bible's veracity, there are innumerable accounts published where ideas occurred, problems were solved, futures were foretold and mysteries were solved during dream states. Uncontrolled fantasies caused by mental and emotional illnesses sometimes cause people to believe that they are, in fact, Napoleon, Lincoln, Christ, etc. Society by and large, especially in formal, structured, institutionalized education, frowns upon fantasy—controlled or uncontrolled. We are too prone to disallow the values of such endeavors mainly because we fantasize on a different consciousness plane and, therefore, do not appear to be doing anything at all. It is a truism, however, that it was the "staring out into space" which finally accomplished the reality of being there. I mention these things merely to suggest that you have an awareness of these unutilized powers, to have you acknowledge the truth of it and to regret together that we do not take advantage of it very much in educational procedures.

We acknowledge great power in mind control exercised by individuals upon themselves in varying degrees of concentration. We admire those who have will power, who can withdraw from the real world in order to live fully within the mind for a time in what we call "concentration." Most of us have been exposed to the fact that there are many levels beyond the so-called conscious mind, but for the most part we are afraid to explore them lest something "dangerous" happen. We want to control our own minds with little regard for the truth that we are constantly exposed to control forces from without. Most of these control forces come from media of one sort or another. My own pre-occupation with media as an educational force is motivated by my own questions to myself. I have inquired about what media has done to me during the years I have been exposed to its intensified inputs. What have I received involuntarily from these inputs which I would not have put into my mind voluntarily? I have no answer, but I do choose to advocate that media become the prime tool of the educator for the same reason it is the prime tool of the advertiser, the opinion maker, the evil world forces and, to a lesser extent, the good. Media IS education uncontrolled as dreams are fantasy uncontrolled. Uncontrolled forces can be destructive. Controlled forces which generate creativity are constructive.

Let me explore for a moment a function known as hypnosis. I mention this, not because it is a control exercise in which one mind controls another, but because it is a control exercised by one mind upon itself—aided and abetted from suggestions made to the mind by a secondary force. The free will of acceptance or rejection of suggestion is ever present. Used in this manner, it is media. I am not advocating that hypnosis nor any form of it

100

be used as a part of the educational process. I am merely alerting you to the power of suggestion given during the "I want to" stage. On a number of occasions I have used this power of suggestion to effectuate amazing results in rehearsals of choral groups, bands and orchestras. It is actually a simple preparation of those minds who have come willingly and needfully for help in achieving a common goal of musicality to accept a mental state in which they themselves will draw upon their fullest potential in combined and individual effort to perform as perfectly as their abilities will permit. I have also noted that they memorized at speeds much greater than conscious effort would allow as they self-directed themselves to perform to fullest capacity.

Through media, our capacity to receive stimulae is extended infinitely. Media instruction, packaged in the utilization of the arts, within the framework of instructional philosophy which works so effectively within the arts, will provide us with the *modus operandi* through which we can initiate the energy forces physically, emotionally and spiritually to cause the mind to direct itself to the learning state. The Media Arts, expressing as they do the symbolization of sensory capabilities of the species and utilizing technological as well as live communicative forces, are themselves symbolic to the extent of providing experience in simulation of real experience otherwise unobtainable. They also deliver that simulation to the sensory receptors with energy forces more intense than the real itself. If we postulate the theorem that the real experience having been once experienced itself becomes simulated in the memory sense, and if we further state that a simulated experience also becomes simulated in memory sense, then we may argue that media is to simulation in memory as memory is to real experience depending upon the ratio of energy input intensity during the moment of either experience upon the conscious mind.

Let me tell you a story of simulated experience in order that we may be on the same plane of understanding as we discuss "simulation-equals-real" in memory sense. Norman Leyden, composer-conductor-performer-educator, wrote his doctoral

101

thesis on the conducting techniques of Arturo Toscanini. The largest part of this research was done from films (kinescopes of telecasts) provided to him by the Toscanini Archives. During his study, made after the Maestro's death, he was able to analyze body movement as it pertained to the conducting art and to draw some definite conclusions on the relationship between Toscanini's motions and orchestral response in performance. Dr. Leyden was also the conductor of an exceptionally gifted group of teen-aged musicians, the Westchester Youth Symphony. It occurred to him to wonder, since the Maestro's impact on the film was so overwhelming, what would happen if the Maestro (on film) were projected to a screen in front of the young musicians who would play while watching the screen instead of a live conductor. I attended the rehearsal where the film "Death and Funeral March," from *Die Gotterdammerung* by Richard Wagner, was performed. It was selected because the Maestro's face and body gestures were present throughout the entire performance with the exception of one brief, ten-second cutaway.

The young musicians had been well rehearsed by Dr. Leyden. Prior to their performance via media direction, he played the kinescope (film made from TV performance) for them, asking them to listen, watching their parts and the screen simultaneously as if they were mentally playing their instruments. He explained to them what he wanted them to do next: watch the screen and let the Maestro conduct *them* as they actually did play their instruments—letting the figure on the screen become their conductor as he had (in the moment of the film's making) been the conductor of the NBC Symphony. He reminded them once again of the basic tempo of the piece, turned the sound off and started the projector.

The result was almost magical. The young musicians were transfixed as they responded to the Maestro's direction, inspired to perform at the high standards required by Maestro of all of his players. Many of them were so intensely involved in this new experience of ecstasy brought about by playing under his baton that their faces seemed to glow, and tears streamed down face after face. When they had finished, they sat silently for a moment, too moved to act—until suddenly a great spontaneous shout went up, and there was that mass happiness that comes when something very, very special has happened. I talked with many of them later, and they told me that they did not see a film conducting, but they saw the man on the podium and he was conducting—not another orchestra—but them. And in fact he was—or rather, he was conducting the music of Wagner. The totality of the physical and spiritual language transcribed in a life situation was transmitted, via film, to the spirit and senses of the young people involved.

The experience for them was part real, part simulation. Certainly they lent their imaginations wholeheartedly to the experience. They willingly provided reaction in response to super stimulation. It was a symbol—not only Toscanini with all of the symbolism of perfection that he, himself, represented, but the moment itself was symbolic as are those moments when intensity overrides human normality and creates joy in perfection of achievement. Yes, it was a simulated conductor, power-packed with traditional symbolisms of conductorial language plus the known values of the representational figure, but the human involvement in it transformed it from simulation into very real reality.

I have talked with many senior airline pilots who, as part of their training, used a device called the "simulator." This highly complex training equipment is a facsimilie in every detail of the flight deck of various models of aircraft. It has the capacity to simulate in-flight conditions with a computerized system of control-response that does (simulatively) precisely what the pilot tells it to do by using the hands-on equipment in the area. Thus, he feels the vibration of the craft, hears the sound of the engines, feels the tilt of the wings, feels the simulated air pockets—in short, the experience provided for him is one which is comparable in every detail to that which he will encounter in actual flight. The computer is programmed so that weather conditions of all sorts may be simulated. Emergencies are created which must be met by the trainee. He feels and to a large extent actually sees the results of his experience.

Pilots tell me that the transition from the simulator to an actual plane is almost like moving from one real aircraft to another. They have experienced the aircraft in more ways than they will ever experience it in actual flight. They are now able to cope with emergencies and to use their simulated experience as real. As professional pilots, they brought hours of actual experience to the training simulation and were able to use the media-plus-hands-on experiences to make the transition from simulation to actual as easily as we may transfer any learning situation in which going from the known into the related unknown is the process used.

But, as if in contradiction to the philosophy of these conducting and flight stories, let me tell you of the Italian composer Ghedini who, when asked if he had gone to Siberia to get the environmental background to enable him to write his opera about that country, replied, "Did Dante go to the Inferno?" While these two dissimilarities may seem contradictory, they are in fact one and the same—the composer utilized his symbolic bank to generate his product via a creative process which is identical to that which the pilots use in creating the illusion of reality at the moment of actuality-simulated. Perhaps our concept of media instruction needs this happy combination of simulation, which includes the excitation of creativity, to arrive at that state where simulation and actual both become real at the moment of their happening. None of this may be accomplished fruitfully, however, unless the learner evidences a need for and a willingness to accept instruction, as well as the "why" factor as it relates to his own personal accomplishment and the learning goal which he and the educator suggest as being ideal. Thus, we need to be able to create an awareness within the student of need plus want, with understanding of why, and serve as his tour guide from his known into our related unknown. We need to pre-program him to the capacity of his self-power in order to utilize the energy forces of experience which (through symbolism) literally explode into his consciousness as well as the various planes of his unconscious mind.

Perhaps we may create a formula to use in this process: Experience is the energy force required by the intelligence to enable the intellect to function. We may further state that experience-real and experiece-simulated both become experience simulated once that experience has occurred, and it is *all* experience-simulated in the memory sense. In addition, as the sensory receptors are to perception, so is the memory sense to conception. Our nervous systems makes no distinction in its reflexive action between experience-real and experience-simulated. We may conclude that experience (energy explosion) plus intelligence (both species pre-patterned and awareness) equals intellect (function) or, to put it another way, energy exploded plus intelligence imploded becomes intellect functioning: $E + I = F$.

Let us examine the validity of these statements by using a rather symbolic analogy of what takes place when we drop an Alka Seltzer tablet in a glass of water. When the tablet and the water make contact, an explosive force is generated as a result of their chemical action upon each other—one repels, the other accepts. We actually see the action at work as the pellet is consumed—the greater implosive capacity of the water surmounts the explosive force of the compacted granules of chemicals within the pellet. We see and hear effervescent action and watch the totality of the pellet burst into tiny bubbles which then burst upon the surface of the water. All of this is not a single action, but many, many tiny actions. It is a process which shows the entire tablet being exploded and absorbed a fraction at a time. If we wait long enough we will see nothing of the tablet except some spattered residue on the glass rim and sides. The rest of it, having been absorbed into the water by the water, becomes a part of the water—which is, chemically, no longer the basic component of H_2O but is now H_2O *plus* the new ingredients.

Two forces are in evidence in this illustration: the capacity to explode and the capability to implode. Their meeting causes energy to be dispersed and absorbed. The finality of the meeting results in one becoming the other *plus*. Put the tablet beside

105

the glass of water and nothing happens to either it or the water. Place them together and the action causes a reaction which, in this case, is absorption. Put a drop of water into a glass filled with Alka Seltzer granules and an explosion would result—but this time the absorption factor of the granules would be greater than the explosive power of the water droplet. Let the symbol (Alka Seltzer) represent the crystalization factor and let it contact a force capable of absorbing its explosive capability. The symbol is the kinetic explosion absorbed by the imploding force of the receptors.

Intelligence is also an imploding-power factor; the symbol is the energy-explosive power. The absorption by the greater power-factor is fuel for the functioning power of intellect. Just as the pellet enters the glass of water, oneness is achieved irrespective of further use of the combined substances. Ingested, it may have beneficial results—or, under ideal laboratory conditions, it may be resynthesized into the original chemical components of H_2O *plus*, since each is capable of being separated into its individual components.

Were we to share the experience just described in actuality, our relationship to it would be in proportion to the intensity of the experience as we reconstructed the scene in our minds. Had that same experience been video taped (without either of us knowing it), we might look at it later together or separately and in an objective way (with memory sense) not only see the event taking place again, but be more aware of the events within the event. While our conscious concentration was focused on the glass and energy of water and pellet, our unconscious selves would have been accepting stimulae from any and all exterior forces independently. While the conscious mind would have been provided with intensity ratios which would affect our use by the memory sense, our unconscious selves would have accepted stimulae with no particular regard to their inherent conscious explosive potential. There they were, so they were accepted.

Those who have experienced or read of hypnotic experiments are aware of the capacity of the mind to recall, under suggestion that it can so do, even the most minute bits of information related to the environment in which an experience took place. Under hypnosis, even years after an experience, one may re-live the event, not merely re-living it, but re-living it with an awareness which did not penetrate the conscious mind at the moment of experience. Capturing the experience of two of us watching an explosion of granules take place within a glass of water might be compared to this recall through hypnotic suggestion: we now look at the event as recorded in taped memory and have shifted our perceptory emphasis from concentration of a part of the whole to a representation of the whole itself. Although we still participate in the event (as observers watching ourselves participating in the event), our awareness of total detail is more defined than it was in the first state of mind. Media then might be said to be able to bring us a greater comprehensiveness of the whole through objective participation. If we believe that the unconscious mind absorbs all stimulae (willingly or not), presents itself with a totality of information which is not biased by stimulus choice or its evaluation, and that our conscious mind responds to stimulus based on intensity ratio, and if we further allow ourselves (as in the analogy of the Alka Seltzer and the water) to be responsive to each explosion-implosion to be reassembled as one after the event, I think we can begin to grasp the vitality of media systems of *themselves* as communicative agents with enormous power potential.

Let us further examine the power factor of both explosiveness and implosiveness for a moment. If we were to drop the Alka Seltzer table in the middle of the Atlantic Ocean, there would be only a momentary reaction. Its effect on the total ocean would be small indeed. Nevertheless, however small, it still has an effect. On the other hand, should we dip out a glass of water from the ocean and pour into it a dozen or so Alka Seltzer tablets at the same time, the fomenting and fizzing would overpower the water altogether and most of it would be blown out of the glass. The glass itself, however would scarcely be affected by either of these forces because of its superior power factor.

107

Thus if we equate intelligence with "container," that is to say the capacity to accept explosions implosively with that precise balance where explosive capacity may be absorbed constructively to cause unification of the combined ingredients, then we may say good has resulted. To put it another way, explosive energy results for good only when the absorption of energy equals the exploding force. It is within symbols that we find these explosive idea-forces, these capsulized knowledge packets, where one input may interact with many responses. If we want this generative factor in both creation and performance of learning, the only possible route is the codification and use of symbols related to all disciplines and used as the arts use them.

Our somewhat lengthy discussion of symbol-power has been included to indicate that symbolism is already available to us in general terms as we begin thinking of it in media use with reference to the various branches of instructional discipline. Within the disciplines themselves, each educator already has a wealth of symbolic materials available which need only to be used as symbolic power-factors in order to do our task magnificently. In the Humanities, for example, there are people and product symbols in abundance which may be associated with that study grouping—History, Languages, English, Philosophy and Religion are also mother-lodes of symbolism. Sociology and Business both are potent areas for analyzation and use of symbolism. Science, with its already formulated grouping of use symbols, has but to apply them in the concepts already used by the Arts to function as the Arts now do. Perhaps a Creative Science (and the continuation of Science depends upon creativity) may evolve with this methodology.

The symbols are, we believe, already in existence. As we mentioned in an earlier chapter, there is such an abundance of symbology within the natural law that, by the use of what we have together with the continued observance of those laws, we may one day reach a universality of communication use of the symbolism that is even now universal. Science has enabled us to observe that there are organized symbols within sound and

108

light. It had discovered to pictorialize these symbols not only within recorded sound and photography, but through the oscilloscope, and magnified observation of the symbols has shown us a picture of the picture we see on television. It has developed ways to show us the actual structural symbolism of the wave forms that represent the picture. One day we may find a way to utilize the symbols as writing materials and by-pass the necessity of the go-between in such a way as to communicate directly through symbols on master tapes and films. These would be created entirely through symbolism. It really isn't such a wild idea at all. We already have learned to do it in servo-systems to obtain directed responses. The next step may be the use of the symbols themselves in direct communication—with people to people.

Scientists have established a mode of symbolic thinking already. They have concerned themselves with the whole being as the combination of particle-mass and with the concept of "particles plus particles equal X" have created things. They have accomplished in a sense (by their discovery of a provable theory) a symbolic proof that God can be everywhere simultaneously in any time period because, as universal power source, He is the universal intelligence represented symbolistically by the particalization of energy. With this theory it is possible that energy forces are available for us if *only* we can discover how they are already organized into symbols ready for use. Man of himself creates nothing. He only rearranges the already-existent into patterns of function based on the potential of a predetermined energy force. While the mind may boggle at trying to grasp the significance of the universe being a balanced plus-minus force factor which keeps planets in their orbit and arranges determinates which we define as natural laws, it seems to be true that all of all is all. If this be true, then all of all is codified (somewhere) awaiting our discovery of its components to be used in communication from somewhere to something and somebody. It may come through an extrasensory route, through telepathy, through tapping the universal God-force, through the creation of a universal intellectual-emotional language little dependent on words or, in more likelihood, it could be through the discovery of a communication factor already existing as symbols—simulated representations of the X-factor of truth-energy force.

While discovery *is* being made because the intelligence of the species is set upon discovery, we may at least observe the universality that exists in similarities (since there are no identicalities in human species except the lack of identicality) and, forgetting the differences caused by cultures (characteristics acquired environmentally), see what does exist in the human family that is *known* to exist simply because it does exist universally. We may include the instinct factor, the acknowledgement of basic (if not equal) intelligence factors, the similarities of bodily-function factors, the thought capability universally existing in reason, the creative factor with which all members of the species are endowed, the consistency of curiosity commanality, the spirit and soul factors, the preprogrammed physical-neural response factor, as well as the desire and need factors.

There are existence needs for food, water, sleep, air and for bodily functions. In short, there are universalities of similarity in response to heat and cold, self-preservation, companionship, worship, etc. Our five senses are used fundamentally in similar ways. Many of these similarities from worship to sexuality have become symbolized in a general pattern as art forms of dance and mime. Although they differ from culture to culture, they all contain the same basics.

I am not suggesting that dance or any other of the arts will ultimately achieve this universal communicative factor. I am only pointing out the probability of some sort of symbolism which will accomplish it. Within music we have already developed symbolism which has far-reaching, if not universal, power as represented by both intellectual and emotional factors of organized sound. A string quartet, made up of a Chinese cellist, a Nigerian violist, a Russian second violinist and a Hindustani first violinist can play the work of an Austrian composer to an audience of Greeks, Turks, Latvians, Americans and Japanese to the degree that intellectual comprehension of the musical symbolism in intelligent non-verbal communication will result. But neither dance nor music can directly communicate between people a translatable common understanding.

Such experiences as those provided by international involvement with scientific symbols, various international codes and species similarities represented in the symbolism used to express dance, mime and music can be shared or communional moments at present. At those times, they must be entirely within the language of the participant instead of being transliterated, without benefit of word meaning, into species intelligence. What we may do with the extra advantage of media is intensify those experiences which do have this species similarity. Since the creative artist has a need to know for whom he is creating, our media efforts could take the cultural differences into account when using such elements as hunger, sorrow, sleep, sexuality, nature, danger, work, etc.—all these experiences may be magnified via film and video tape to represent the simulation of reality.

What is all of this doing in a chapter about instructional media? Only this—we have already discovered ways of representationalism in the arts which communicate most of the human similarities in terms of physical, emotional and spiritual universality. It may well be that the answer to all communication may be found by using this as a basis for going from the known into the related unknown. "Particles plus particles equal X" could well be the theorem we need to complete our search. It's worth thinking about.

All of that almost brings us to a proper summing up of some of the statements which, at least intuitively, I know are true. First, symbolism is the totality of communication. In addition, media, itself a composite symbolism, is the educator's strength because it may intensify sensory perceptions to extend human capability far beyond itself as it removes the time-place restriction and because it enables us to function creatively both in developing and using materials in a mind-to-mind relationship. We stated that symbolism is the means which enables the involvement of multi-levels of the intelligence to provide the intellect with the capability of doing. We equated experience as energy, saying that experience equalled

111

energy-force and that experience implemented with known powers represented by symbols would provide greater input of energy into all levels of consciousness, but primarily into the conscious mind.

We said that symbols represent a capability of ingestion of energy-force, by-passing the normally required digestion of informational input. This results in the facilitation of the conceptual. We further said that all experience, once experienced, is simulated within the composite of all senses, the memory sense, and therefore the simulated function of media may provide the memory sense of the conscious mind with energy. This would be so not only when the real experience is unavailable, but even when it is becoming even more potent because of the capability of the mind to participate in the experience from (at least) two mind levels simultaneously. Throughout our discussion we advocated the codification of symbols available to all disciplines *by* those disciplines for use as the Arts use them— in the creative and performance capabilities available to all educative areas. The result would achieve efficiency and effectiveness in the arts on an enduring basis, both philosophically and technologically. We also equated "need" and "willingness" plus "why" as those ingredients which allow the mind of one to be entered by the mind of another.

We concluded our first chapter with the statement: "Nothing of itself happens by itself except nothing." We now suggest that your awareness of the truth that the granule of explosive energy-force representing knowledge lying beside the container of explosive force representing potential, needs the verb "to do" in order to arrive at the verb "to be." In the chapters ahead we will acquaint you with the tools and their functions and discuss the means whereby they can help you understand the theory and potential of their creative use. Using these tools well will enable you to give your students microscopic and telescopic eyes as well as super-sensitive and supersonic ears. You will help them exercise their minds so that they can travel in and out of the world with you as their tour guide. What this whole media process really does is transform you from the standard, five-foot-something, easy-to-lose-in-a-crowd species sample

112

teacher into a giant-sized knowledge symbol, owning more wish-fulfillments than an Aladdin with acres of magic lamps. I suspect, however, that when Aladdin went into the magic business, even he had to make a few practice passes at his lamp before he got the hang of it and could do it every time.

CHAPTER VI

PACKAGING THE PRODUCT

Creating an instructional unit for TV or audio presents a number of problems which can better be solved when the creator has an understanding of the media and the potential it offers him in creative presentation of factual materials. This chapter discusses both the media itself and the resources available in creating learning units. First and foremost, a determination must be made regarding content. What should the unit achieve and how can it function more usefully than the standard classroom approach? Should the unit be a part of a whole series or should it be an individual component, self-contained and complete within itself? These two questions must be answered in advance. Preparing and planning a unit series is not unlike that process involved in making up a syllabus for a course. First know WHAT should be taught within the course and then determine HOW MANY units it will take to convey the required information to fulfill the learner's need. When the "what to teach" has been determined, the "how to teach it" may then be discussed.

Media instructional units, beyond their capacities to be repeated via TV or tape recorder, should not be considered at all unless they produce results that cannot otherwise be obtained in the classroom through the use of standard audio-visual equipment. After all, we do have slides and slide projectors, 16mm. and super-8 film and film projectors, film-strips, cassette film loops, tape recorders, overhead projectors, charts, maps, diagrams, chalkboards, display tables, exhibits and probably other things available to us in the classroom. Most teachers have used one or more of these devices throughout their careers as illustrative aids to help them present materials more efficiently. Failure to use them in the classroom is due more often to the extra trouble it takes to assemble the materials than it is to the lack of available resources. It *is* also more difficult for the teacher (working as a one-man equipment operator and lecturer) to handle more than one audio-visual technical piece at a time. Utilizing them simultaneously or in sequence calls for rehearsal and preparation time almost equal to that required in preparing the lecture which they illustrate. Therefore, it is fundamental to the successful presentation of a unit that media segments be carefully planned and rehearsed. This is especially so in the classroom where electronic means, such as a closed-circuit TV system or audio listening lab, are used. Presentation of a unit via any system other than the classroom simply means that all of it can be prepared in advance (under professional guidance) to be sure the unit develops smoothly and without hitches caused by poorly operating equipment or other such technical flaws. Once it is prepared, it may be repeated as often as necessary to convey the content to the student under environmental situations not confined to the classroom. It, like his textbooks and reading lists, becomes a learning device used as a study aid NOT requiring the teacher's immediate presence to do the task.

When it has been determined that the way to present the materials most effectively is by use of audio or visual media, the question should be asked: "Can the student grasp the information presented here simply by viewing or listening to the unit or is he still dependent upon other factors (textbook, reading lists, etc.)?" If he can achieve what is necessary from the unit alone, it is a successful product. If he cannot, the unit needs re-evaluating and re-doing until it can achieve this objective.

Media themselves are not the only answer to learning. It must be admitted that they are part of a trio of available tools, the composite of which will produce the fulfillment of the teaching purpose. Nevertheless, we must go about teaching by media as if they WERE the only contacts the student has with the materials he needs to learn. We know from experience that there have been many successful self-teaching texts.

recordings, training films, etc. We also know that many individuals are self-taught through disciplined attention to the resources available to them. However, in preparing media instructional packages we must determine whether or not the student could still accomplish the goal of the course if we as teachers are NOT physically present in the learning process. Thus, the primary goal is to create media units capable of education totally apart from a classroom experience, even though we are fully aware that the student will have the distinct advantage of textual aid plus the personal element of the teacher contact in a classroom setting.

When we have therefore determined our purpose in offering instruction via electronic systems and have divided the course into its fundamental components, we may move on to examine the available methods of presentation: i.e., the unit format. There are several such formats available to us, and we need a detailed explanation of each.

1. *The lecture.* In the lecture, a teacher is processed electronically (video, audio, recordings plus film strips, etc.) in order to make him available to teach without the necessity of his physical presence. There are as many variables in this mode of presentation as there are styles of delivery within the classroom. The principle difference is time itself, for while a classroom lecture may be confined to the schedule of the class meeting times, it is necessary to be much more aware of time in the unit presentation through media. There are two reasons: the expense in preparation (involving as it does both materials and personnel) and the awareness of the rate of interest decay involved in prolonged periods of required attention. Network programming, for example, is carefully planned not only to sustain listener or viewer interest but to keep it as a high level of receptivity. In commercial broadcasting the reward is keeping the listener or viewer tuned in while the penalty is losing him to another station. In our situation we may keep him bodily present but lose him mentally if the material is not equally well-planned and placed in a time segment that is compatible with the average listening or viewing interest rate. Media units

must be shorter than classroom lectures, regardless of which format is used.

There is a certain rare breed of individuals who are equally at home in front of a microphone, video or motion picture camera. Their personalities or *charismata* are evidenced at the outset and people respond to them with unlimited attention. In such instances time is no criteria. But these are indeed rare people, and for our purpose we must consider the ordinary mortal whose experience and background have not prepared him for the electronic environment and whose charisma is not up to power-house supply.

Generally, then, we must prepare lecture materials in a concise and lucid presentation in which the teacher first tells WHAT is to be learned, proceeds to teach the WHAT and sums up by restating the areas fundamental to the material offered.

In educational circles, such programs are often called "the talking face." While their value cannot be discounted, there are generally more acceptable ways of presenting material. At best the availability of such units are for the benefit of students who may have missed that particular lecture in the classroom or who need to hear it more than once to grasp the essentials.

In this type of presentation, the teacher is processed while delivering the lecture. He may (a) read the lecture, (b) extemporize from an outline and notes or (c) utilize (if on video) the available charts, maps or any other resource materials at hand. If he does, it is no longer a straight lecture and therefore falls into other categories of presentation.

In video media the lecture format is normally successful in direct proportion to the communicative ability of the lecturer plus the believability of the media made possible by the production crew. In audio tapes the problem is more acute, particularly when the student is listening on systems instead of hand-operating his own equipment. Please understand that there are always exceptions to the rule, but by and large the read lecture (in the delivery of an untrained reader) quickly becomes dull and lifeless, while the extemporized lecture (even from outline and notes) tends to be wordy and rambling.

117

It would be our suggestion that IF there is any other possibility available, another way should be found. Certainly except for the convenience of the student in making up a lecture, for the convenience of a participating star teacher or aging authority in the subject, or for the professor having multiple class sections, there is little reason for utilizing this talking face format.

Before we continue with our discussion of video formats, let us pause for a moment to discuss the processes of putting units on audio tape, particularly since an understanding of this process is fundamental in creating media instruction. The various procedural options available in production of audio tape will be stated as follows:

a) The reading of material (or extemporizing from notes) in the audio studio requires the "reader" and an audio engineer.

b) The tape is then edited to make it free from error. The teacher himself should be present at such an editing session to make sure that all mistakes have been eliminated and that no portion of the materials has been omitted.

c) If the taping is unsatisfactory to the teacher it may be completely redone or portions re-recorded for insertion into the tape. The editing composite should have teacher approval before anything else is done.

d) If nothing but the words of the teacher or his designated voice substitute are wanted and there are no errors, the tape may then be readied for playing.

e) If the teacher-producer agree that music, sound or special effects, other voices (in the case of quotable materials or dramatic reading) are desired, these may be added to the original tape by "mixing" the other elements. When the final mixing has been done, the teacher should approve or reject the result. Production specialties can make the tape more listenable and create an environment of learning which will transmit the information more palatably with better results. But in all instances, the teacher himself must either participate in the various stages of the tape's preparation or designate the authority to the producer assigned.

In this age of super-systems and advanced television technology, the lowly audio area is often sorely neglected. It has, however, an infinite capacity to deliver information and is a much more cost-effective teaching-learning tool. Remembering the former power of radio to involve people by invoking an imaginative response from the listener, we must not discount audio in favor of the glamour of TV. Instead, it should be utilized extensively as a prime force in creating instructional media packages. Certainly in list of the low-cost availability of cassette recorders and the almost over-whelming amount of commercially produced educational audio cassettes, it would be foolish for instructional planners to exclude it just because sound has taken a back seat to sight in the vastness of electronic mass media.

I interject another stance at this point by saying that there is no difference at all in the production techniques involved in either audio or video packages except for the purpose for which they are designed. One is primarily entertainment, the other educational or instructive. By using show business techniques, we enter (in a real sense) into show business ourselves—not in content, of course, but in use of similar methods to produce instructional materials (in whatever discipline).

We should not forget that the generation we are teaching has been nurtured on sights and sounds obtained by their contact with radio, recordings, television and the movies. They will have a tendency to judge our product, perhaps unknowingly, by comparing it to those to which they have been accustomed in commercial media. Our standards of production should be no less. If anything, we need to try harder as we produce to educate than others who use it only for entertainment.

2. *The slide-tape unit.* In this format, we must again begin with the script itself. While in the case of audio units we have kept in mind the resource options common to taping, in preparing the slide-tape the creator of the content materials must keep the visual aspects of his materials clearly in mind. If he doesn't a series of non-essential, more-distractive-than-effective pictures will result. BEFORE the script is ever written, much less recorded, visual materials should be determined. Once such visuals have been agreed upon by the creator and the producer, the script (or content material) may then be put on audio tape and mixed to its final form.

119

In the slide-tape format the visual materials consist of 35mm. slides. There are two types of slide materials: a photograph obtained either from life or from another photograph, and information slides which have been prepared and then photographed. No matter how we prepare them, for our purposes they should be 35mm. slides. NOTE: not all 35mm. slides are adaptable for video, and if the program creator plans to do his own photography, he should note the limitations imposed on him by the media. This will be discussed in the chapter on "Television Photography."

When the visuals have been prepared or selected from existing slide libraries, and when the sound track has been approved, the final technical operation is completed as the visuals are placed on video tape simultaneously with the audio track. If the slide-tape unit is prepared for classroom use or is to be used in prescribed listening-viewing areas by students, the slides may be arranged in proper sequence in carousels which may then be operated in an automated mode by programming the audio playback unit. In Chapter X this process is also explained in detail. The options in picture choice are infinite and you are limited only by your own ability to imagine the final result in fulfillment of your instructional needs.

There are a few "do" and "don't" suggestions to remember. No picture should be included which detracts from what you are saying. No picture is better than a bad picture. Unless the picture totally represents your need for it to visualize your oral material, it should not be included. In short, while slide-tape units should strive to pictorialize or provide visual stimulus to the learning process, pictures for the sake of having pictures are meaningless.

Let me give one brief example. Suppose we were writing about or discussing some phase of Lincoln's life and referred to the Lincoln Memorial in Washington, D.C. A photograph of that Memorial would be more revealing than any number of words you might conjure to create a word image of it. If, on the other hand, you went on to discuss its size, its cost, the number of tourists visiting it annually, the same photograph held endlessly on the screen would soon become a meaningless symbol.

120

You would more effectively use the media by providing simultaneous projections of photographed graphics containing your information. Another foolish method would use a series of photographs of the interior, exterior, building plans, etc. unless they were DIRECTLY related with what you wanted the students to learn from your words. I repeat that in the preparation of this type unit, the visual potential should be investigated to its fullest BEFORE final content material is organized and written. Just as you would not be likely to use Sousa's "Stars and Stripes Forever" as background music to an audio-tape reading of the "Sermon on the Mount," you should not use visual portrayals which have little or nothing to do with the subject you are presenting.

Effective slide-tape units are DIFFICULT to achieve, but they are very effective teaching units when properly done. They are included in this discussion for two reasons: they are the simplest unit to put on video-tape because of cost in that they involve fewer production personnel in the final operation, and they can also be utilized as a package in themselves. They can be taken into the classroom, checked out to students for library use or packaged on video tape.

3. *Slide-tape-plus unit (for video only).* This unit type has all the ingredients mentioned in the slide-tape format. The "plus" refers to the addition of one or more of the following resources:

   a) film loop
   b) film strips
   c) charts, graphs, pictures, maps, posters, etc.
   d) display tables or objects
   e) chalkboard
   f) overhead projection
   g) additional slide projection not involving film chain
   h) film segments
   i) special effects

In this format the variety of illustrative materials is increased and the visual presentation has a flexibility not obtainable in the non-video slide-tape unit. The preparation of the content material should take into account the visual options available and all such options should be pre-determined before the audio portion of the unit has been finally completed. In addition to determining the availability of sources one must also determine, with the producer of the unit, the technical capability of the video equipment which will permit a multiple selection of resources.

In any production facility equipped with a film-chain, it is possible to put a slide on the screen and at the same time superimpose another picture or vice versa. We may, for instance, display the skeleton of a bird on a stand and the same moment superimpose an information slide relating specific data to the student as a visual illustration of the material contained on the audio tape. If we wish to use a film segment showing the bird in flight and show a 35mm. photograph of the bird plus the information slide at the same time, this more complicated procedure would require additional preparation and planning on the part of the script or unit creator as well as the production supervisor. Film segments can be introduced into the show; their inclusion is limited only to the technical facility of the studio itself. Unless such inclusions contribute to the final learning results, however, we do not really accomplish anything by including them except proving our production prowess.

Let us again return to the Lincoln Memorial illustration. A slide could show the Memorial but it might be more exciting to move to a film clip of it, adding movement to the picture. Nevertheless, even this would not be a contribution unless the picture and information were correlated. Great care must be taken in planning the visual area in ANY of the new options offered in resource availability. No amount of production "know-how" can save a unit from being visually inadequate if the unity between the oral and visual is not sufficiently planned. It is indeed a time for the teacher to be willing to put himself into the hands of trained production people and to arrive at a style of presentation which can produce a learning experience fundamental to the student's progress in whatever discipline is being taught.

4. *The slide-tape-plus unit and you.* The "you" in this format is either the teacher or his designated representative in the studio. In this instance we immediately lose the opportunity of the smoothly-prepared sound track with respect to the

teacher's voice. We may, however, integrate taped segments of sounds, other voices or music into the sound track. This should not be ignored altogether simply because the teacher is in the studio, for it remains one of the most vital elements available to him for use in his teaching process. The teacher himself now becomes an integral part of the show, whether he is reading a lecture or working extemporaneously. Admittedly, reading a lecture poses fewer problems for the production crew, but the aliveness of extemporized materials can bring an element to the unit which continuous reading loses. Ideally a, mixture of the two should be used.

In addition to delivering the subject matter, the teacher may now become active in displaying books, magazines, hand-held objects, maps or charts, working at the chalkboard, etc. He may interview an individual or make use of a number of individuals simulating a classroom situation. He may, in short, serve as the visual catalyst for all of the other visuals which go to make up the unit. He humanizes the show, as it were, and his very presence lends a credulity to the unit which it may otherwise lack. He represents authority in the studio and the visual options he selects become audio-visual aids in the classroom. The principle difference is that he can NOW do things that he cannot do in the classroom and he uses this fact to think through and organize his materials so that he MAY use the options to his student's best advantage. But here, as in all video preparation, concentrated planning and preparation are required to bring about a smoothly flowing, technically flawless production. Nothing less should even be considered.

5. *The interview unit.* This unit is produced with an interviewer (the teacher) talking (in most cases informally) with an expert. In short, it is a process of presenting information via the question-answer method. The success of such units generally depends altogether upon the ability of both parties to extemporize lucidly, to stick to the subject projected in the opening moments of the unit and to provide a summary which will be important to the viewer or listener. As in the case of the other video formats, one may introduce exhibits, slides or other such devices which will further strengthen the presentation.

Variations of this unit would be multiple participants where more than one person would be interviewed or selected students would be asked to join in the questioning of the guest.

6. *The dialogue unit.* Here the teacher may select a student or students to ask prepared questions designed to bring information to the viewer or listener. Although prepared answers could be read in response to the questions, extemporaneous answers add a humanizing element. Indeed, extemporization produces a more exciting and believable unit. As in previous units, additional pictoral information can be introduced here as desired and needed. Variations in the teacher-student dialogue can be made by the inclusion of additional students.

7. *The factual unit.* This unit is relatively easy to produce It generally contains information to be used in drilling students in such areas as vocabularly, spelling or materials requiring repetitive experience to achieve. One example of it could present a series of words which give the proper pronunciation of tools used in a lab with accompanying pictures to help the student identify them and to learn something of their use. Another example could be drills in language vocabulary, with the combination of sight and sound helping the student to *see* what he hears and *hear* what he sees. Normally the narrator would pronounce the terms correctly and define them on the audio track while the video portion would simultaneously give proper spelling, phonetic help and in some instances pictoralize them. Customarily this is best achieved in slide-tape format, but there are many ways to present such materials within the body of any unit. When the student sees and hears the word, he is invited to participate in the learning process by repeating the information aloud in order to obtain facility with pronunciation while acquiring meaning. Such "how-to-do" units may find real use in many areas of instruction.

8. *The film unit.* There are several possible uses of film. Most obvious thus far has been the inclusion of film segments within the body of the unit for special instructional purposes. Films or film segments may also be created directly for use within a given unit and are often made in order to facilitate production within the TV studio. Moving into a laboratory or

into a field-trip situation with super-8 or 16mm. camera is often more feasible than trying to recreate that environment within the video studio. These filmed segments are apt to be more expensive than other forms of prepared video illustrations. If the budget is available, however, they can perform great service for the student.

Although there are many forms of film available, let us discuss the use of the commercial film which has been produced for classroom use. There is an infinite variety of these, as perusal of any major film rental service will reveal, and since many of them have been produced by unusually expert educators and film producers, their classroom use has been widespread and valuable. Many films are also available for TV screening, provided the proper clearance is made, and transferred to video tape, their use on a system serves a good purpose. It is our belief that such video units would be better served by film if the teacher requesting their use would appear before camera prior to the videotaping of the film to delineate the purpose for the students watching it and again after the film to sum up, re-enforce or add additional materials not covered by the film itself. By his appearance the teacher can add much to the viewing and understanding of the film. Should he desire, he may also stop the film at any given point to discuss the materials by stressing the salient points live, by utilizing a brief slide-tape unit or by using some other varieties of media presentations. The examples we have given will go a long way to help the teacher in his contemplation of the problems of unit-making if they are utilized properly. Let me remind you to be sure to obtain rights in advance for use of film or video tape (even for closed circuit systems). Penalties can be severe in case of violation.

A long discussion could and probably should ensue concerning testing the effectiveness of the completed unit. I believe the main criteria applied would be simple: "Does the student learn what I am teaching him via this method?" If objectives are clearly stated at the outset, if the objectives are fulfilled in the teaching process and if the summing up re-enforces the stated objectives, then most units can be tested with the same methods used in testing a classroom lecture or a reading assignment. Testing should be done as soon as possible after the unit is heard or seen. While course syllabus outlines should be a part of the whole procedure, with individual unit outlines to be read prior to the media use, I strongly object to use of fill-in-the-blank questions to be done during the viewing itself. Note-taking should be permitted if the student desires, but distractive activity should not be encouraged. To do so penalizes your well-intentioned use of the media itself.

If units are properly made they will be able to convey information to the student easily and creatively. Media instruction units are not, however, miraculous short-cuts or instant knowledge devices. They are what they are, another vital tool for the teacher to use. Viewing should be required not once but several times. Teachers do not expect students to scan a book chapter and absorb its factual content at one sitting or one reading; neither should they expect it from media presentations. Unit viewing should be both introduced and following by seminars whenever possible. If this is not feasible, the unit creator may at least take pride in the fact that he has prepared his information capsule so expertly that it can fill the knowledge gap necessary for the student's growth in and of itself.

The student owns his text and may study it at his convenience, but he only hears the classroom lecture once. With media instructional units he may have a built-in teacher whom he may summon at will. Our job as teachers is to make sure that when he summons, we will have prepared what he needs.

In summary, let me say that: (1) audio and video instructional units should be prepared by the same professional standard which are common to commercial broadcasting; (2) all units should be capable of conveying information in and of themselves, with no additional need for information sources; (3) an understanding of the media and its potential is fundamental to the unit creator's success in planning and producing a unit; (4) close cooperation between the creator and the production personnel AS the unit is being developed is a prime requirement to its success; (5) time is the great factor

126

in planning; nothing should be done unless time is available for careful planning and execution.

Media are most effective when they have been prepared to be self-instructive and when they can be used along with textual materials to achieve learning requirements. In media the classroom teacher is not supplanted by any means; rather he now becomes the master planner whose ideas can extend his influence far beyond his immediate presence through electronics. Those ideas can enter in the minds of countless numbers who cannot possibly be served otherwise. Media are not miracles; neither are they mysteries. They are exciting ways to provide students with "round-the-clock" access to their teacher in performance modes which no teacher can himself supply within the time-space, structured limitations of the classroom. If the product is packaged artistically and creatively, the contents will be consumed avidly and digested effectively. Even better, they will also create an appetite for more.

CHAPTER VII

WRITING FOR MEDIA

Writing words to be *read* by others is one thing—and writing words to be *heard* by others is still another. Our objective in this chapter is to write words to be read by you which will describe the processes by which you may best write words to be heard when read aloud.

It is not a simple process; yet we may approach the problem with some assurance since we communicate most of our thoughts orally, speaking much more often than we write. Whether we are lecturing, making a formal address, conducting a seminar, or merely having a casual conversation, our method is the spoken word. It is, for the most part, a natural and spontaneous use of the language to convey an idea. And, since most of us are adept at this, we should use our "talking to be heard" style in writing, relating it as closely as possible to our normal speech habits.

Most of us, when we have a writing task, tend to change personality completely. We have a writing vocabularly, and we frequently employ words not found in our normal speech. And, while we usually speak in short, concise sentence structure, we tend to create complicated sentences when we write to be read.

Perhaps most of us would do well to use the letters we write to friends and relatives as a basic model. In them we tell the family news, discuss our work, ask questions, and generally reveal our own minds to others in a pleasant and informal manner in order to get them to reply. Many of our business letters have a similar purpose—we want to convey information and to get an answer.

128

The main thing to realize is that there is someone *to whom* we are writing—someone important enough for us to take the time and effort to write. The style we use in such letters could well be the real us. As a result, we can examine our letters as a possible style to use in instructional media.

Perhaps you may already be disagreeing with me, thinking that writing letters to friends has nothing to do with writing a script designed to teach students. However, your letters might easily be considered teaching your friends about yourself. So, before you discount the idea, try it. Take your own discipline and write a make-believe letter telling what you do, what you teach (and why) and how your students respond. Add a P.S., explaining how you know when your students have actually learned as a result of your teaching. Do this in the same informal style you normally use in writing to friends, and you will be surprised to see how well you can adapt your style to the presentation and exposition of content material.

If you have a tape-recorder handy you can do the same thing. Tell somebody about yourself, what you are teaching, what you want them to learn and why they should learn it. After all, if you as a professional teacher are industrious enough to have accomplished an advanced degree in a study, you should be able to tell someone about it. When you have made the tape, listen to it. Compare it with the letter you have written on the same subject. Somewhere within your letter-writing style and talking tape style lies the best media writing style for you.

You will find, I am sure, that your "spoken" letter is more spontaneous, more natural, more the real you. This is mostly because your think-write habits are not as practiced as your think-talk habits. One means of correcting this is to practice writing, for writing does take practice and the more you write, the better you become at it.

As teachers, we have the long-formed habit of preparing an outline for our lectures. We do this partly as a memory aid and partly to make sure that what we are going to say will justify the goal of the lecture. We have already done our research, we have the subject matter well learned and we understand it thoroughly. So, our outline serves as a mental road-map to guide us in the proper distribution of our knowledge with the ultimate objective being that an entire class will learn and comprehend our material.

Take an outline of one of your class lectures and give it the letter writing treatment. Tape a sample classroom lecture in your study and listen to it. Do this several times and your own response to yourself will teach you more than volumes on "how to write."

What will you learn? First of all, after you overcome your own self-consciousness at hearing your own voice, you'll find your command of language is more natural when you extemporize; it is easier to understand and freer from complications than even your informal letter writing style. By the way, listening to your own voice will upset you at first because you are accustomed to hearing yourself from behind your voice. In recorded material, the sound comes toward your ears. In video you see yourself from the front, as in a mirror, and you won't care for it too much because it simply doesn't fit your private concept of how you look to others or sound to yourself.

Be that as it may, your experience in listening to yourself and making the comparison with your written style will be a rewarding session, for you will decide that your real forte is extemporization and realize that your real task is to write in a manner which will create the illusion that what you are reading aloud was just that very second created.

If you are still disagreeing, I would invite you to take one more step. Transcribe your taped words and, combining the best section, create a script. When you have done this, record it all again. Chances are, unless you are an expert reader, the result will be less than hoped for, but at least it will be you—"you" in the sense of your having arranged words in the way you normally use them when you speak. You have found your "style," for better or worse, and it is the style you should use in your preparation of instructional material for media.

There is a journalistic style of writing. Some newspapers and magazines have individual styles to which all writers adapt themselves, most notable in this regard are *Time* magazine and the *New York Times*. Some publications reserve the basic journalistic style for hard news, but allow variation of styles in columns, feature stories, society news, sports writing, etc. Traditionally the journalist begins his article with a sentence in which he tries to include the "what, when, where, who, why and how" involved. It begins with a lead sentence from which the reader obtains a synopsis of the facts to be presented in the entire article in more detailed form.

An example from the *Dallas Morning News* of Friday, June 11, 1971, will illustrate this point. "Salem, Ill. (AP)—the City of New Orleans passenger train derailed at more than 90 miles an hour in a hail of twisted metal and flame Thursday, killing 10 persons and injuring 94." The statement is a capsulized version of the entire story, telling what heppened, when, where, to whom, why and how it happened:

the what:	death and injury of rail passengers
the when:	Thursday
the where:	Salem, Ill.
the who:	City of New Orleans train and passengers
the why:	derailment
the how:	train wreck

The first sentence of this news story was a terse statement defining the subject to be discussed and furnishing factual materials of the time-space situation in which the facts originated.

This style of beginning a news story is an accepted journalistic practice and might well be emulated in preparing the opening statement for an instructional unit. But there are as many styles of writing as there are individuals who write. For example, we can read passages from the Bible and recognize them as being biblical. Similarly, there are Shakespearian, Emersonian, Dickens, Thurber, Joyce, Guest, Hemmingway, and Poe styles. There are also styles related to various fields of publishing: pulp magazines, slick magazines, religious publications, scholarly and scientific journals, etc.

Writers often adapt their natural styles to the requirements for acceptance of materials to be published by such magazines or journals. Your own analysis of several of these would be helpful, for you would find factual, narrative, poetic, scientific

131

and other styles in use in the various magazines you choose to examine. You might also examine a number of textbooks and find a definite textbook style of writing. A quick peek into any sports section would reveal a distinctive approach to writing not found elsewhere. Looking at a copy of the "show-biz" publication, *Variety*, would also reveal an individualistic approach in all articles contained within the magazine.

It would be well worth your time to do this, if only to satisfy your curiosity about different stylistic approaches. A writer who is doing a story for *True Romance* takes a different stance from one who is writing in a scientific journal on the space program. An author engaged in writing a story for a "shoot-em-up" western publication writes quite differently than one preparing a study on Paul's letter to the Corinthians, first *or* second!

Select paragraphs from some of these publications and try to write something of a similar nature yourself, using the style of the author you are studying. Make a comparison of the same news story as it might be written in *Time, Newsweek, U. S. News and World Report,* the *Wall Street Journal,* the *Christian Science Monitor* or your campus newspaper. After you have made the comparison, write the article yourself in your preferred style, using the facts you have obtained from those articles. If you do not have immediate access to a large number of publications, examine a *Reader's Digest,* which offers a variety of styles in their various condensations of articles and stories.

The *Yellow Pages*, a much read book, is another one to examine. In it you'll find a composite of information and description with its behavioral objectives contrived to make a customer out of you for service or products. The main *Telephone Directory*, however, is largely a statement of fact and information. Both books illustrate the definition of purpose made prior to writing and publication. The conclusion we may draw from this analogy is that we must have that same sharply defined purpose for the use of our product before we write or publish it in media format.

At this point we need to discuss something which, while not directly pertinent to our task of actually writing words, still must be a part of our thinking as we plan units. This has to do with the relationship between the "cognitive" and "affective." The first word means "facts"; the latter (scarcely defineable at all) connotes emotional and spiritual factors which enter into the learning process. The cognitive area may be tested with predictable results but the affective may not be tested with any determinable accuracy. This is largely true because the response to cognitive data is immediate while the affective becomes a part of a body of emotional futures. To see a picture of Vermeer's "Maid Servant Pouring Milk" and to be told that it is indeed that picture, is cognitive, but the observance of the picture in terms of emotional and spiritual reaction to it is not only unpredictable, but it is also immeasureable. I wish there were hard and fast rules which could be provided for achieving the cognitive independently of the affective, but unfortunately humans are not constructed so that such a separation can be made. The same problem may be illustrated by analyzing the difference between knowing that rain is wet and the feeling we get while walking through a rain or the reaction we get when seeing a painting of a rain-swept scene.

Understanding, and therefore the capacity to do, is best achieved when cognitives are assimilated and become part of an affective presentational environment. Since, as we believe, all learning is fundamentally emotional, intellectual achievement (cognitive) can be acquired more readily from within the kinetic potential of a designed emotional climate (affective) than ever anticipated if the two are kept separate. "Just give the facts" may be sufficient for a TV detective, but the facts alone without emotional involvement are not sufficient to achieve understanding which will cause change of the highest order in the student.

While you're trying to work all this out, I will return to our discussion on style. The ultimate choice of styles is up to you. You may adapt yourself to that of another, you may find your own distinctively personal style or you may combine the best features of others. Any style is a good one if it satisfies your sense of the appropriate way to express your ideas so they may be completely understood by the listener. It does not necessarily follow that the natural style of "you" will be dynamic, earth-shaking, sure-fire method of informational dissemination. We only suggest that whatever it is, it be yours, and that it be as closely related to your talking style as possible.

Having said these things about style, I would draw your attention toward the application of style in developing content. You may be a bit startled at first by my choice of illustrative material for this discussion, but I think that you will agree shortly that the analogy I have selected will be helpful to your understanding of the processes of putting your materials into words. The analogy is the "recipe" or "how-to-do" method.

Read a few cookbook recipes and you'll notice that all the necessary ingredients are listed. The suggestions for assembling the ingredients in order to make the pie or bake the cake are filled with "do" directions. You are told to mix, blend, sift, add this or that, stir, fold, whip—in short, in exact measurable proportions the ingredients are put together in an orderly, precise way, one step at a time. When the preparation is complete, it is finalized in a process of cooking or baking at prescribed temperatures and times. The success of the end product is dependent on the quality of the ingredients, the skill of combining them, and the exactness of the cooking process. The behavioral objective was bread, cake, pie or whatever else you might have selected. This objective was achieved by carefully following the directions. When the product is consumed, the consumer reacts in various degrees of enthusiasm or rejection. The point is that a plan was set forth and, given the proper ingredients and conditions, a certain defineable result was predictable. Its acceptability, however, is dependent solely upon the attitude of the consumer.

I am not suggesting that your writing style be as unimaginative as a recipe or as pedantic as a set of directions for assembling a bicycle. Instead, I am only suggesting that if you want your product to be as concisely rendered as that which follows the correct use of a recipe or a set of directions, you

134

must first state your final goal, plan your ingredients, set forth directions to be followed in their development and then provide the proper condition for their production. If it adds up to a cake when you meant to make a batch of hushpuppies, something went wrong somewhere.

You may argue that the results of one process are visible (and consumable) while teaching has no such touchable or edible product. True, and yet the comparison is obvious enough to test its merits as you assemble ingredients (facts), follow directions (outline), mix and blend (illustration, demonstration) to create an environment for its finalization (classroom media). Your product is a learning experience for the consumer. How well he thrives depends on your ability to create and satisfy his appetite.

One does not create a masterpiece each time he sits in front of a typewriter or takes a pen in hand. In writing media instruction we are not engaged in the creation of poetry, drama, novels or any other art form. Instead, we are utility workers in this business of writing. Our job is to select the facts, present them coherently and summarize them accurately. If we, by our lifelong association with artistic writing, apply similar principles to our endeavor with skilled craftsmanship, so much the better. But it is not a "wait for the Muse" process. It is a "tell them how to get from here to there without getting lost" attitude. When we give a set of directions clearly, our task will be easier and the process of writing more exciting. We will produce better results if we adopt this attitude. Our stance will be "I know it and he wants to know it so why don't I tell him?" Try it. You'll find it works wonders.

So far this is pretty heady stuff but, apart from suggesting ways for you to find your own style, no really significant contribution has been made to your comprehension of the writing skills needed to create instructional media units. We'll add to your ability to communicate via the "written-aural" method by suggesting a few of the "do" and "don't" areas which will prove helpful. There are no definitive rules covering these procedures, but the suggestions which follow will make your writing task easier and more acceptable to your students.

1. Write in short sentences wherever possible. Avoid complicated sentence structure. A sentence written to be read from textbook or novel may be as complicated and involved as you care to make it, for in the printed page the reader has the advantage of re-reading if he has not understood at first sight. This instant replay possibility is not always available to him in media.

Should we construct a complicated sentence like the present one, where we utilize a variety of phrases or clauses dependent upon one another for clarification of meaning (and insert additional explanatory or qualifying conditions by using parentheses), and further complicate it by trying to explain what we are doing to make it complicated, we succeed only in confusing the issue, creating chaos where there should be coherence and probably making a resolution never again to write such a long sentence, no matter how much we may feel the need to do so, unless, of course, our intention is to demonstrate (as here) the uselessness of such sentences for inclusion in media instructional materials.

In such a long and complicated sentence as the one you just waded through, we would have lost our listener at about half-past parenthesis. In writing for media then, we can achieve results better by using terse, concise, simply constructed sentences. Otherwise we lose our listener in the aural labyrinth resulting from over-complication.

Now by "terse" we don't mean the "Run, Jane, Run!" type of brevity. Instead we suggest using your common sense in evaluating each of the sentences you write, reading each aloud to yourself to check its validity as an idea carrier and, if possible, double-checking it with someone else to see if he understands exactly what you mean. This business of reading material aloud while you are in the process of writing it is a very good thing to do while you are still in a position to make the necessary corrections to make it understandable.

2. Avoid repetition of the same word within a sentence whenever possible. Our language has vast resources in possible word substitutions and we should use (employ, utilize, write,

select) them in order to get (obtain, achieve, accomplish) variety. Also try not to use "sound alike" words.

Here is an example, although it is an improbable one, which will illustrate the inherent dangers in using such homonyms. "In the scene you have just seen, the king's daughter, having tangled her foot in the fisherman's seine while swimming, was almost insane with fear as she struggled to free herself in the turbulent ocean. The young Prince, hearing her cries, knowing that he could never reign in peace until he had rescued her from the sea, swam desperately through the rain and fog. The Prince's deed in trying to save her would win her heart and hand from the King, .and so he swam through the mist and fog toward the direction of her cries. He almost missed her entirely because he couldn't see because of the sea's turbulence. But he made it and the one he won through his bravery and so on and so forth."

Sometimes a combination of two words will result in aural confusion. "A rest" sounds like "arrest," "a parent" may be heard "apparent," etc. Possessives also play havoc with meaning on occasion: "clock's tick," "house's location," Possessives often sound like plurals and the "s" sound may seem to be at the beginning of the following word rather than at the end of the one you meant it for. Words ending in "ish" should not be used before the pronoun "it" unless you know that its reading can be accomplished without embarrassment.

3. Foreign language words should be translated aurally (or on screen) immediately unless they are proper names or the titles of established, familiar works. In any event, you would do well to furnish the correct phonetic guide if you yourself are not doing the proper pronunciation. You will have to decide for yourself whether you want to "anglicize" foreign words or have them pronounced in the tradition of their language.

4 Try to avoid "tongue twisters," that is, words which have similar sound elements: Sally Simpson sold seashells at the seaside. Things like "Shelly shall," "Xerxe's zeal," the "Thessalonian thesis," "Montezuma's monarch," etc., may seem exaggerated, but unless you are constantly on guard, similar

tongue twisters will have a tendency to creep into your word patterns. The use of alliteration is also dangerous because, while similar sounds seem a suitable style for saying something, it soon sidetracks the student from your main thought as he is caught up in seeing how long you can continue to alliterate.

5. Don't coin words if you can help it. There are already enough words in the language that can do the job for you. Slang and current expressions should also be used with care. Language changes constantly and what may be an "in" word one season, such as "cool," "neat" or "tell it like it is," may rapidly become as dated as last year's political promise and a new crop of students may find your "in" words "out." Know that your "cool" is now archaically tepid, your "neat" now cluttered, and your "telling it like it is" now a "was" and "has been." Unless you intend to update your materials constantly, it would be best to stay away from this slang usage. Communication between teacher and student does not require your learning (and using) his contemporary idiomatics. Rather, the idea is that he is here to learn yours.

6. Abbreviations, except very familiar ones, are not as easy to grasp as the words their abbreviations signify. Such frequently used terms as NBC, AMA, USA, COD and TV are acceptable because of their familiarity, but the huge volume of abbreviations used as governmental short-cuts (changing almost daily as one agency is formed and another dissolves) demands explanatory words except for the very familiar ones. In the following list of abbreviations, see how many you recognize immediately upon reading them: DOA, REA, SEC, NSF, RFD. Customarily the complete word grouping is identified at least once before any abbreviated use is made. We frequently find simulated words evolving from initials describing agencies, and we may be even more familiar with the representative word, NATO, CARE, UNESCO, VISTA, than we are with its exact meaning. Other such simulated words such as COSIP, TAEGER, METROTEK, may be less common and their usage need explanation. We might even make one up for our own use called

138

WRITE, which we could translate "written right to insure top education," but we won't (make it up, that is).

All words which are not a part of the common vocabulary deserve an explanation when they are used. This applies especially to those terms involved in a discipline which are directly related to the understanding of that discipline itself. It is not a waste of time to define terms. The student will respect your willingness to offer him a mutual area of communication. Incidentally, I'll suggest here that a dictionary is the writer's best friend and should be as much a part of his writing tools as are his paper, pencil or typewriter.

Our objective is always clarity. We want them to understand us. So, unless abbreviations, foreign terms, terms germaine to particular disciplines, slang terms or coined phrases are immediately identifiable by the hearer, we have failed to achieve the goal of clarity. There is no real rule about all of this except one we can make up right now—"when in doubt, spell it out."

7. Quotations can also confuse, for the student can't see or hear quotation marks when you are speaking. Therefore, you must indicate that you are quoting by calling his attention to it specifically through such patterned phrases as "and I quote," "Abraham Lincoln spoke the words you are about to hear," "in the gospel of John, Jesus said these words," etc. If you intend making a long quotation it needs to be interrupted a time or so with such phrases as "Emerson continues," and you continue quoting, or "Jefferson concludes his statement by saying," etc. All quotations should be acknowledged, of course, even paraphrases of the original. Quotations may be given special emphasis by voice changes; that is, you may change your own delivery style or request another voice to do the "quote" lines.

8. The use of the parentheses can also lead to confused listening. As in the case of quotation marks, the student cannot see or hear the parenthetical markings. Even expert readers (announcers, commentators) find the parenthetical phrase hard to handle. Using the suggested short sentence style will relieve you of this problem for the most part.

In visual media we have the advantage of using the screen effectively to emphasize such things as quotations, abbreviations, foreign terms, simulated words made from abbreviations, parentheses, etc. In audio transmission we have less possibility for emphasis than in video, but we do have it.

Let us examine one problem as it might be handled by both media forms: "Man in space." In video we have available film clips of launchings, moon landings and a multi-variation of other seeable materials. In our brief episode here we are going to involve President Kennedy and his speech in which he dedicates the nation to a moon landing. We may simultaneously show a newsreel clip in which we see and hear JFK as he makes this speech, or we may choose to use his actual words taken from the original sound track while at the same time showing a launching in progress. Also simultaneously we may show the text of his words as he is saying them.

In audio we would have no picture advantage, but we could say, "President John F. Kennedy spoke the words you are about to hear on such-and-such a date." As the recorded words of JFK are heard, one might also provide simulated space sound-effects through music or actual recorded sounds. The possibilities in either form of media are endless. All this sort of thing, however, demands a response on your part to the variables and options available in media usage. At the risk of being considered repetitious, let me say that along with your dictionary, your writing tools and your own knowledge of the subject, your knowledge of media potential is fundamental to your success in script writing for instructional purposes.

We may sometimes cause confusion by using words which have multiple meanings. Such words may mean different things to different people and thus the most universally accepted meaning should be used as it relates to your purpose in transferring your ideas to the student's mind.

The word "thrust," for example, is such a multi-meaning word. An engine may have a thrust of x-power, an idea may be thrust upon you, a hand may be thrust in your face and the new thrust in education is instructional media. Since there are many words, your task is to use them in the exact context of your meaning or employ a less confusing word instead. Other such meaning-traps are word combinations such as "blow out," "side-kick," "take-off," etc. In the latter case you may be referring to a plane's departure, a skit, a burlesque act or an imitation of some real thing. Your use of such word combinations depends solely upon whether or not they represent your real meaning. Our rule of thumb is, "when in doubt, leave it out."

So far we've been suggesting "don't" to you. Let's suggest a "do" called "re-write." Rewriting will be difficult for you if you're the type who thinks each word you write is an immortal saying, a gem, a shiny nugget of purest gold. Fortunately for us none of you are like this. You wouldn't have read this far had you already believed yourself to be such a writer. It is important to rewrite because of the necessity to achieve clarity. Because there are so many ways to say the same thing, we need to make sure that *what we want to say* is really *what we are saying.*

You should reach each sentence aloud at first, perhaps even making changes as you go along. Or you may want to finish the unit completely before examining it in detail for misleading words, word combinations, phrases or sentences. You also need to make this examination aloud, ever conscious of the sound of words. If you have erred, correct immediately. If you're not sure whether you've erred, try it out on someone else. If you do this often enough, you'll do it automatically, thus avoiding word traps and complicated structural formations.

Practice this sort of thing: take a familiar quotation and see how many ways you can rewrite it and still retain the same meaning. After you have practiced with sentences, rewrite an entire paragraph. The process of analysis in determining what someone else has written will help you in maintaining clarity and accuracy in your own meanings.

Since writing words to be spoken imposes the listening factor upon the writer, and since our thoughts are transmitted by voice sound rather than sight, it is the listener's receivability factor which must be given prime consideration in everything we write.

It is the difference an author must take into account as he decides whether to create a novel, in which we read not only what his characters say and do, but what they think and feel, or a play, in which the characters speak their lines aloud, communicate with gestures, create individual characterizations, utilize costumes, set and lighting in order to provide all the information the audience receives—via them—from the playwright. It is also the difference between a stage play and a TV or motion picture scenario. In the first instance the author is restricted to the mobility of action that can be performed within standard "box," "thurst" or "round" stages. In TV and motion pictures he may move easily in time and space, changing scene, costume and situation almost instantly.

In a novel the author must use words to set a scene and describe his characters' actions both physically and mentally. Flip Wilson's funny remark, "What you sees is what you gets," is most appropriate to our discussion here, for unless the author actually sets the words down, you can't read them. If he wants you to know his people, be able to imagine their actions, understand his locale and grasp the reasons for the total activity in his story, he must provide you—word by word—all of this detailed information.

Let us try to illustrate the conceptual differences between novel, drama and scenario by providing a vignette treated in the styles of each. First, the novel: "Bob stood before the open fireplace in the richly furnished room, drenched from his long walk through the driving autumn rain, still quivering from the shock he had felt as he remembered what he had seen at the seedy bar and grill in Chums Corners. He paced restlessly, wondering whether to tell his wife the truth or deny the entire thing." Here we told you *where* Bob was (in a richly furnished room with an open fireplace), *where* he had been (at a bar in Chums Corners and in a rainstorm), *how* he was (wet, cold, nervous, fearful, tormented), *what* he was thinking (whether to tell his wife), *who* he was (a husband with something to deny or admit), and *when* the scene occurred (just after he had walked home through the rainstorm).

In a play, we would need to see Bob come into the "richly furnished room with its open fireplace" and he would have to be wet-looking. His physical and facial actions would reveal that he had a problem. If this cannot be accomplished in a monologue, the playwright has the option of having one of his other characters enter to assist Bob in telling his story. Bob, then, bursts into the room and literally shakes the rain from himself, moving quickly to the fireplace for warmth, demonstrating his cold by visibly shivering, indicating his nervousness by pacing, clenching his fists and running his hand through his hair. His sister Clara enters:

"Bob, you're back. I've been so worried. How did it go?" Bob turns to face her.

"It was awful. If I live to be a thousand I'll never forget what I saw tonight." On and on it could go with each line designed to let you in on the fact that something pretty bad had happened at Chums Corners.

In the movies or on TV, we could see Bob return home as he runs through a driving autumn rain. We could see the lightning, hear the thunder, watch him as he passed parked cars, hear him barked at by a dog, watch him being splashed by a passing taxi. We could even see the action that provided the sense of urgency that was causing him to be in motion. We could watch him enter the room and see Clara join him. She doesn't need words to express her worry about him. The camera can follow her to an adjoining room, watch her snatch towels from a linen closet, and see her help him to dry his face and hair. Her words might be:

"You saw her?" Bob turns slowly, his face revealing his fear and shock.

"I saw her all right." The words were spoken tensely. He turns back toward the fire and continues:

"She was in Chums Corners like she said she would be."

At this point the camera moves backward in time to show us the seedy bar and grill in Chums Corners as Bob enters, obviously looking for someone. The entire event can now be replayed in reality as we hear the conversation between Bob and the "someone" he met there. We even have the option of an

143

additional voice track representing Bob's real thoughts during the conversation.

Even though it was over-simplified in its use, this brief example delineates the problem nicely. In the novel we are dependent entirely upon words; in the play we let action, costume, lighting and set relieve us of much word necessity, whereas in the movies or TV our need for words (of themselves) becomes even more pointedly unnecessary. The novelist knows he must provide all, the playwright realizes he needs to take up where the visual aids leave off and the scenarist recognizes that his scenic potentials are as much a part of his "writing" as are his actual words.

Apply this to our problem and we might well compare the textbook to the novel. In it we depend largely on words to convey information. The classroom situation might well represent the elements of the drama (our set is the classroom, our words are monologues). The audio script might also be compared to the play in that while we need words to convey our thoughts, we do have access to other possibilities such as music, sound effects and recorded voice quotes. We need always to remember that whatever we tell the listener must be either *described* or *shown* in both classroom and media.

Video tape, in our instance, offers the third comparison—TV and motion pictures. In video tape we are not bound to time or place, but may utilize all of the available options to express our thoughts. While we may demonstrate an object or chart in class, in video we have the advantage of having each student see it close up, and while he may not be able to touch or smell it on video as he can in class, our words conceptually designed to give him a sense of smell or touch can help him.

An anthropologist talks of an exploration of ancient Incan culture and brings a small idol to the classroom. He may pick it up, show it from all sides, discuss its probable age, its color, its similarity to other idols known to have been used by the Indians, describe the texture of its material and even point out that it has a slight aromatic quality. He may utilize large charts, show slides or motion pictures and make use of the overhead projector in providing large-scale reproduction of maps and graphs. In short, he may combine within the classroom many of the same elements which he will need vitally when he uses video media.

In case he uses audio, he may give his materials added dimension by providing music similar to that known to have been used by the Incas, but he must rely upon his words to make the student "see" the object he is describing as he attempts to visualize it in shape, color, size, texture, etc.

In video media he may use the same object, the same charts, the same slides and maps, but by using different camera angles be able to achieve the same sort of intimacy that a touching, smelling, feeling opportunity provides. He may show it from every angle both in close up and in comparison with other objects with the set. If video is not in color, he may need to describe it, but its shape and detailed characterization are plainly seen. He has easy access to picture comparison and has provided his students everything except touch and smell. And, he does it once, thus providing opportunity for his students to review his materials by reviewing the unit, a feat patently improbable if not impossible within the classroom situation.

In all of these foregoing illustrations and comparisons, I am well aware of the fact that I have been relying solely on words to create an understanding and solution to your problems with media. Perhaps I could have used media items themselves to provide the demonstratable proofs of my thesis, but since we are involved with the problem of learning to write for media, it seemed more realistic to use writing rather than visual or aural tools to do the job. In this case your involvement is voluntary and you may drop out in the middle of a sentence unless you are motivated by words alone to continue your reading.

Students do not have this option unless they elect to take your course, so while you have a built-in audience based on degree requirements, you also have an additional obligation to keep them in a state of wanting to learn. Thus, words and their placement within your informational packet are prime tools in informational transfer and emotional stimulus. They are, of course, just as much media as the more complex visual aids. If

145

you can agree to this concept, your acceptance of media will be more palatable. Even you, the teachers, are media. Your physical appearance, your personality, your command of language, your charm are vital to the creation of the learning environment. Your classroom situation is itself media and is identifiable as a place to learn, or at least a place in which to be taught. Your desk and lectern are media tools as are your display stands, hand-held objects, chalkboard and chalk.

The principle difference between MEDIA and media is your dependence on exterior forces to perform the function which in other situations you perform singlehandedly. Another difference is your use of words themselves. Where once you depended solely upon words to convey thoughts as I am doing, in most instances media requires that the art of extemporization in speaking be changed to an extemporized writing style. In addition, because of the imposition of the expense factor involved, it also imposes a time factor on the teacher. Where once the teacher had a full hour to present information, to enjoy the time-luxury of repetition, illustrative re-enforcement, demonstration and review, he now is limited to those time areas known to be acceptable lengths of receptivity. In audio and video media, the interest decay ratio is much more rapid than in either the classroom or in studying. All of this must be as carefully taken into account in instructional media as it is in the planning or writing of an entertainment piece. If we elect to use video or audio media as teaching tools, they must be used as if they were your only possible contacts with the student's mind. The repetition factor, the review and demonstration capacity that you have in the classroom, can also be included easily in the video-audio unit. The only difference is that now it is the student rather than the teacher who does these things again, although they are based on your audio or video presentations.

Perhaps this would be a good time to elect a review or reiteration of areas closely allied to our media writing problems.

We have discussed elsewhere the importance of knowing your media possibilities prior to writing the script itself. This applies to both audio and video, although admittedly it is more critical in video. It is common sense to admit the necessity of examining all of our potentials in slides, graphics, movie films, music, sound, etc. In short, pre-writing in the sense of exploration of visual or aural potential is equal in importance to the act of writing itself. When we have ascertained these options, stated our objectives (at least to ourselves), outlined our materials and determined our style of writing, we are ready to begin.

We begin by telling the students what they will learn. This may be preluded by a sentence of greeting and an announcement of the general topic. Actually this topic announcement can better be done for you by the screen than you can do it with words. You simply and directly state what you want them to learn from viewing or hearing your unit, and then—just as you would do in a classroom situation—you proceed to present your factual materials in a logically organized way. You sum up your lecture with a restatement of your objectives and, if you like, by making suggestions for auxiliary reading or additional parallel viewing.

Since you have planned your visuals and sonic effects, use them for reference as you speak. Indicate their values and pertinancy with such phrases as, "the map you see on the screen," "this statue of Simon Bolivar," "the graph we are now showing," etc. There are endless varieties to choose from as you write to visualize, and there are endless visuals to be chosen or created in order to emphasize or illustrate your text.

For example, you might wish to refer to American political conditions in 19th century New York City, with special emphasis on Boss Tweed (picture) and his downfall caused by the *New York Times* through its political cartoons (slide of cartoons) by Thomas Nast (picture of Nast). At the same time, music of the "Bowery" style of the period could provide additional values. Or perhaps you might do a biology unit showing the structure of the human skeleton with special emphasis on naming each bone. Visually you could work with the skeleton itself while talking. At the same time you could project on a screen closeup and wide angle portrayals of your objects, having the names of the bones themselves spelled out on the

147

screen. What the music would be in this case would be hard to determine.

We could go on and on with such illustrations, showing the capability of media to emphasize, reiterate, underline, define, portray or illustrate your spoken word. The important point we would make is that you must keep in mind (both when you are writing and speaking) that there is someone on the other end of that earphone or picture tube whose opportunity to learn depends on you. *You* may be on tape, but *he* is very much alive and your job is to make him feel that you are writing (and talking) just for him. You won't see him physically as you prepare your unit, but you must know he is there and communicate as skillfully as you do in the classroom with words combined with sight and sound to form the whole of his learning experience. You're the tower and he's the pilot—you give the instructions and he receives and acts accordingly.

The "you" of you, plus the media opportunities skillfully combined with your words, presented coherently and with purposefulness will result in a successful product which is infinitely more rewarding than that feeling of satisfaction you sometimes get at the final class bell. There it is over with—in media it goes on and on.

A summary of this chapter is appropriate at this point. First we discussed differences between the word to be read and the word to be heard. We then advocated that you find your own style by writing about your subject (as you would a letter) and recording an extemporized version of it. We suggested that you transcribe the recorded materials and locate yourself somewhere between your letter-writing style and your extemporized style. We suggested that this style would be nearest to your normal classroom presentational style and that your ultimate goal would be to create the illusion that what the student hears is being extemporized. We then look at style in various forms, suggesting that you analyze publications as well as the styles of various authors to see how you might adapt these styles to your own. We gave a number of illustrations of the use of media in reference to their effect on your creativity, insisting that you maintain constant awareness of their potential by investigating media resources.

We gave you a few "do" and "don't" examples involving similar-sounding words, tongue twisters, word traps, abbreviations, quotations, parentheses, foreign words, slang and simulated words. Comparisons were made among the drama, the novel and the scenario, which indicated that an approach should be more closely related to the scenario than to other writing forms. We classified ourselves as utilitarians rather than attenders of the Muse. We then concluded our excursion, but we will not know whether the trip was worthwhile until we begin to see evidences of some of the suggestions being used in your own work. The salient points to remember are simply: you have something to say that your students need to hear; make sure you write so they can listen with complete understanding.

CHAPTER VIII

MUSIC AND MEDIA

Of all of the arts, music possesses the unique power of mind-to-mind communication on a plane more essentially spiritual and emotional than intellectual. Because it is non-articulate, its use in cognitive areas is limited except in association with words. But because its construction, transmission and reception are symbolism in its purest form, its affective powers to generate understanding of content are infinite. Music has power not only to reflect the emotional attitude of the creator, but to create similar emotions in the listener. It cannot project an informational segment on its own, of course, but it can be used as an adjunct in creating situational conditions where such information might be learned more quickly. In instances where words are combined with music in a song, music can also serve to convey information directly. In such an instance it is much a part of the informational segment as the words with which it has been combined.

It is to music as an adjunct to other visual and aural materials that we will confine our study, for music properly used in media instruction is a vital, unifying factor in production. One can realize its effectiveness as a teaching tool by examining the whole body of Christian liturgical music, which is used largely by the church as a means of teaching doctrine, creating moods of reverence and worship or serving as a background against which the rest of the religious service becomes more meaningful. We might also examine the countless numbers of teaching tunes employed in primary education. These range from alphabet songs to more complicated history, mathematics, scientific and language materials. That it is an aid to the

150

presentation of information is clearly demonstrated by the number of singing commercials that are a part of the radio and TV industry. Its present use in children's educational programs such as "Mr. Rogers," "Sesame Street" and "Captain Kangaroo" gives us an opportunity to observe its methods and to evaluate its effectiveness.

Historically, the use of music in theatrical productions is well established, and we are equally familiar with its involvement in the media represented by motion pictures, radio and television entertainment and documentaries, as well as its use as "theme" or "signature" materials at the opening and closing of productions.

On stage the opera and ballet represent the ultimate in the use of music in conjunction with other factors to convey meaning. The stage presentation of drama often uses music, called "incidental music," in a variety of ways to add values otherwise impossible to achieve. Many notable composers (e.g. Grieg, Beethoven, Mendelssohn, Sibelius, *et al.* have written such music, either in direct collaboration with the author and producer of the drama or added later to make the production more vital. In fact there are few major composers who do not consider this form of writing a vitally important work area. From their scores we have obtained many suites, such as "Peer Gynt" by Grieg, "Egmont" by Beethoven, "Midsummer Night's Dream" by Mendelssohn and "King Christian" by Sibelius.

Since it has been such a useful and valid tool in the entertainment media, we must draw the obvious conclusion that it may also serve us well in education. This is particularly so if we also realize that the only differences between instructional media and entertainment media are content and purpose.

For just a moment let us consider the definition of the word "entertain." In common usage it means "to divert, to engage the mind in activities of an enjoyable nature." The word actually stems from the Latin word *tenir* (to hold) and its ancient usage included such concepts as "hospitality" and "maintain." Its use as applied to "entertainers" is still that of one capable of holding the interest of an audience, and it still implies communication regardless of its content or form of

151

presentation. Thus when educators say, "We are not here to entertain, but to instruct," they fail to take into account the fact that (no matter what the situation) they are participating in some form of "show business" and that if they fail to "hold" their audience or "maintain" an interest in their ideas, they also fail to accomplish their intent—to instruct. This is written not to belabor a philosophical point, but to intensify my consideration of music as an adjunct force to be utilized by educators who plan and produce instructional media units.

There are two general classifications of music available to us: (a) music which is already written and (b) music which is composed especially for use in a specific production. The latter has the advantage of being more flexible and more directly related to the content, but it has the disadvantage of being more expensive. The availability of recordings, tapes, music sound track library services or "live" music played from existing publications more often than not actually makes the decision between the two methods, and this primarily because of the cost factor. Given a free choice, the author or producer would select the "tailor-made" score over the one obtained through pre-recorded sources. On campus the cost factor is not as restrictive as it would be commercially, for there are a number of young composers and a large number of instrumental combinations which could be utilized in obtaining the created score. But failing to take advantage of this opportunity, pre-recorded musical sound in the hands of a good music director and editor can provide values almost (but not quite) equal to the music created specifically for the production.

The principle areas or types of music useful to the production of media instructional units are classified as follows in our discussion:
a. Background music,
b. Mood music,
c. Transitional bridges, titles and themes,
d. Underscoring,
e. Special effects,

We shall also discuss available sources, copyright, preparation of the music track (score) and some terms used in abbreviation for inclusion in scripts.

a. *Background music.* Background music is, as its name implies, a type of music which is audibly present for the purpose of providing a "sonic scenery" against which the other audio and video materials are presented. It is desirable only when it does not intrude on or distract from the main purpose of the presentation. It can afford a pleasant environmental atmosphere, which adds another dimension to the product, but care should be taken that this music does not "fight" the content either by its familiarity, activity or tempo. It should suggest its presence without demanding anything in the way of attention. A good rule of thumb might be that something would be felt to be lacking if it were not there, but if it were present it would blend into the total effect, much as wallpaper and furnishings might help to suggest a type of room. A narrative dealing with information that requires concentrated attention to comprehend could be totally wrecked if the personality of the music itself intruded in any way. Selection of appropriate background music follows no set rule except for the avoidance of negative results. What is considered a correct choice of music is more often than not based on what the user himself likes, and the available resources are enormous.

Beyond its use to create this "sonic scenery" in providing environmental warmth and intimacy, background music should be considered by educators because we are dealing with a generation whose habits have utilized music from radio, turntable, or tape recorder to "study by." It is a sound which is more often than not "tuned out" by the conscious mind. Perhaps psychologists could explain how serious learning effort can be obtained in the midst of high-volume sounds and hard-pulsed rhythms. I can't. But I admit that the consistency of this study pattern by a nation of students does not seem to keep them from accomplishing their goals. We won't debate the desirability of this use of music in study-patterns, but we must acknowledge that it is true and that consideration of background music to

153

accompany media learning processes should be included. Perhaps the determining factor for its use depends altogether on whether we can find music that can adapt itself favorably to the role of being "sonic scenery."

b. *Mood music.* Music can create a mood which enhances other production elements. Of itself it can evoke emotional responses from an individual or a group. Ministers are aware of this as they select the appropriate hymn to be used during the "invitation" at the end of a sermon; an acrobat or a juggler may insist on brightly-moving, rhythmic music to lend an atmosphere of excitement to his act; supermarkets and industries use music in shops and plants to motivate a sense of "hurry" to shop or work. A familiar melody can trigger an emotional response ranging the gamut from deep sorrow to supreme happiness. Patriotic music more often than not is used to provoke the desired reaction to its needs, whether it be for awe and reverence during a national anthem or a quickening of the adrenalin glands as marches, bugle calls and drum beats are heard. The music played at funerals is solemn; at coronations or high state occasions it is pompous and dignified; at weddings we hear familiar music by Mendelssohn, Wagner, Cadman or Carrie Jacobs Bond. In short, there is much about music itself which automatically causes a pre-determined emotional response, which induces the hearer to participate more actively in the situational environment. Combining this force with word and picture may, therefore, add dimensions otherwise unattainable by triggering responses whose stimuli cause active participation.

Let me illustrate with an obvious example. Suppose we are doing a unit on Abraham Lincoln and decide to use music which is related directly to the period in which he lived and worked. A prime choice of mood music might be "The Battle Hymn of the Republic," and by using it we have obtained the use of emotional response to the music itself, the intellectual response to its words, the subtle emotional response to the type of melody and harmony it contains and the subconscious stimulus to recall whatever we might know of the Civil War and Lincoln personally. We could also easily include "Dixie," which of itself is a force capable of generating a number of emotional responses, or we could use any of the other familiar war tunes (northern and southern) or Civil War pop tunes. We could, if we wished, use the same hymns that were used at Lincoln's funeral or even include a tune which he himself wrote. This same technique could be applied toward almost any historical figure to obtain similar results. We shall see, as we discuss special effects" and "underscoring," how moods can be developed more deliberately.

Let's illustrate general mood music with still another example. If we were portraying Germany during World War II, music relating to the Nazi regime, its anthem or music of a militaristic nature, depicting Hitler and his colleagues, would be selected. This same music, however, used in a sequence depicting mid-century America would be ridiculed and the mood of the whole destroyed. The mood of the material being presented should be carefully analyzed, and then music which intensifies the mood should be found and used.

Music of this variety can cause an immediate emotional response, for by its nature it can be happy, sad, gay, eerie, violent, romantic, mysterious, soothing, apprehensive, etc. Some music is used so traditionally for specified purposes that its inclusion in any other sequence would immediately draw a negative reaction, because it specifically relates to people, places and events. Chopin's "Funeral March," for example, is appropriate for death in general, as well as at funerals and sad, solemn corteges. On the other hand, Elgar's "Pomp and Circumstance" would be more fitting for processions of royalty and (through years of use) graduation processionals. "Taps" would be used at military funerals or a soldier's bedtime, while calliopes and organ grinders might be more representative of circuses and carnivals. Organs would indicate religious events while a fast "Galop" by a band could depict racing or similar sporting events. Hymn tunes generally represent Protestantism while Gregorian chants depict Catholicism.

Music can be used to suggest actual places or locales. "The Volga Boat Song" would relate to Russia, "Swannee River" to the southern part of the United States. Ireland could be

155

depicted by jigs and Hawaii by music played on steel guitars. The "Marseille" would reflect France and music with an "oriental flavor" would serve to depict Japan or China. Much could be said about "national" music because there are certain identifying rhythms, instruments, melodies and characteristics which put the viewer-listener at the scene by the musical suggestion that he *is* there. Spanish, American Indian, Gypsy, Slavic, Israeli, Scottish folk tunes and rhythms are particularly identifiable. In the United States we could use the "Virginia Reel," spiritual, cowboy tunes or any of the many forms of jazz, while music played by bagpipes could easily suggest Scotland. In short, the variety is infinite in assisting us to select music which has a "built-in" characteristic lending meaning to the mood we are trying to create, the character we are seeking to establish, or the locale we are trying to portray.

Additionally there are music titles and melodies so familiar that we must either use them to represent what *they* represent or not use them at all. A scene involving the Mississippi River would lack believability if "The Blue Danube" or "The Missouri Waltz" were used, just as a scene representing Russian serfdom would fail if the mood music were a Negro spiritual or a cowboy's lament. We could easily establish a western scene with "Home on the Range" or a goldrush mining camp with "Camptown Races," but we would fail to achieve the desired result if we used Luther's "Reformation Hymn" to depict St. Peter's Cathedral or a bright Spanish dance to establish Bombay or Cairo as the city involved in our study. There are many "title" tunes which also represent actual places or times. "Paris in the Springtime" is one which combines both. We can select from such titles as "The Isle of Capri," "Tales from the Vienna Woods," "Chicago," "San Francisco," or "London Bridge," to name but a few of the thousands available for our use.

Our task is to find the mood music which will trigger the proper emotional response in a positive and undeniable way. Just as we would not select a photograph at random to depict a familiar figure or show an office building in an attempt to make our students believe that it is the Taj Mahal, we should not present music which would destroy the credulity of the whole presentation by its misuse.

In ancient times one of the main functions of music was to evoke positive emotional responses from the listener. In India, for example, music was constructed on "modes" which could be categorized into thousands of separate meanings. One melody might transform its hearer into a brave warrior while the next one might cause him to be blinded. Another melody might cause you to burn to death according to legend, and still another might restore your sanity.

This sense of "mood power" attributed to melodies was believed by the Greeks to directly affect human will. Aristotle wrote: "Music directly imitates (represents) the passions or states of the soul—gentleness, anger, courage, temperance, and their opposites and other qualities." He believed that "if one listens to the right kind of music, he will tend to become the right kind of person." However we wish to debate the validity of that concept, if indeed we do, we must acknowledge its historical accuracy. While we regret that the subtlety of the "mood" is generally now lost on the Western mind, we have inherited some of their prescribed stimuli through tranditional usage and have created many others which help us obtain and maintain a mood.

There are a number of these traditional mood-setting musical types which are commonly used in movies, television and other forms of media. They will be listed here. The brief commentary on each is to serve only as a guideline in helping to determine your selection for possible use in establishing a mood, scene, locale or time.

1. *Martial Music* is basically rhythmic, often varying considerably in tempo. This music suggests sports of all kinds, parades and campus life.
2. *Liturgical Music* includes everything from gospel tunes, hymns, liturgical chants to portions of operas or religious songs. It might be used to depict churches, cathedrals, ordinations, christenings, camp meetings or other religious gatherings.
3. *National Music* encompasses anthems, patriotic melodies, folk songs, music with identifiable national characteristics. These may

157

be used with patriotic events, rallies, ceremonies involving heroes and patriots or "scene setting" to indicate place.

4. *Popular Music* contains titles and styles which reflect time, place and situation through association with their titles and lyrics to help convey exact moods. Styles of performance are also used to indicate the types of music heard in places such as restaurants, social gatherings, dances, etc. A greater latitude is possible because of "stylistic" involvement.

5. *Seasonal Music* represents, through traditional use, various holidays and months of the year. Christmas, Easter and Thanksgiving music are familiar forms. Title songs such as "June in January," "Springtime in the Rockies," "Autumn Leaves," or "Winter Wonderland" also suggest seasonal music.

6. *Functional Music* is used at public or private functions, such as weddings, funerals, birthdays, games, etc. Actually all music is functional in one way or another, but this type represents (through traditional usage) specific types of functions.

7. *Period Music* identifies a certain historical era, such as the Renaissance, Civil War, World War I or II, the classical era, or modern times. Using music out of its known time spectrum is as anachronistic as putting a machine on the screen in a time before it was invented. Period music is represented by styles of performance.

8. *Geographic Music* refers to music which is used to define an area or locale specifically.

9. *Ethnic Music* is identified as being a part of the basic music of a race, a civilization, or a nationality through use of traditional melodies, harmonies, rhythms and instrumental characteristics.

10. *Nature Music* is descriptive of the function of the elements or imitative of the sounds of animals, birds, and insects. It includes sounds of storms (rain, winds, thunder, etc.), natural physical disturbances (earthquakes, avalanches) as well as realistic imitations of bird, insect and various animal sounds.

11. *Scientific Music* is imitative of electronic simulated sounds which presume to represent the action of some scientific apparatus. It is used to depict laboratories, experiments, space flights, undersea exploration and the like. A whole new world of electronic music has been created by "synthesizers" plus the use of telemetric signals which are used for this purpose.

12. *Big City Music* portrays skylines, crowds, traffic and other city activity. It is often represented by fast tempo, rhythmic and frequently strident music. There is almost a prototype of this style in

158

Gershwin's "An American in Paris" or Bernstein's "On the Town." Many times the effect is heightened by actually combining it with realistic sound effects.

13. *Small Town Music* has a nostalgic, sometimes satirical flavor, and is often slow in tempo and lazy in style. It is used to depict villages, hamlets or small towns. Western towns are usually portrayed in a more distinctive folkish flavor and often comedic music is used to depict the bumpkin, rube, or hick.

14. *Chase Music* is sometimes called "cops and robbers" or "cowboy and Indian" music. Its effect is to heighten action, generate excitement and lend credulity to the presentation. No action scene involving pursuit seems to escape this style of music with its fast tempo, rhymthic drive and note-filled excitement.

15. *Spooks and Goblins Music* is eerie, tension-filled, apprehensive, mysterious and suggestive of impending doom or fright. It is used in horror sequences, murder mysteries, detective and ghost stories, and reflects the general mood of being in the presence of the unknown.

16. *Travel Music* indicates descriptive and imitative sounds involved in almost all forms of transport including walking. It may be a transitional bridge to move a person quickly and logically from one place to another, or it may be a long section whose rhythms are that of the transport device. Customarily the tempo is involved with the normal speed of the carrying agent or imitative of its sound.

17. *Industrial Music* projects its mood by imitating or simulating the sound of machinery in motion. It usually has a mechanical sound, often having percussion effects, strong rhythmic pulse, discordant harmonies and angular melodies. It is used to depict factories, large industrial machinery or huge work forces in action.

18. *"Mickey Mouse" Music* the prototype of "cartoon" music, draws its name from a Disney-created character. It is customarily performed with small orchestration, depends a great deal on percussive effects and is very imitative of screen action. It is not actually limited to a single style at all. Instead it is a stylistic performance of anything that is needed to be a simulated "sound effect" commentary on the action.

19. *Ceremonial Music* is a standard type of music used in formal situations involving processionals, gatherings of dignataries, solemn events, dedications, etc. Customarily it is a broad, slow-moving melody supported by a simple harmonic structure marked with

strong rhythmic pulsations. This is much the same kind of music that is frequently used to portray broad panoramic effects (rivers, mountains, plains, oceans) as well as for long-range shots showing masses of people moving toward an important goal.

20. *Dramatic Music* covers a wide variety of moods ranging from tragedy, fear or violence to passion, romance, etc. However, it is more apt to be restless, pulsating and surging and should be reserved for a variety of situations which depict moments of great decision, danger, romantic fulfillment, heroic effort or any such other times of great magnitude. It is such a broad category of music that it is difficult to choose the cue to achieve a desired effect. In fact, it is much easier to know when you are wrong. The prototype of this music may be found in opera, drama or almost any kind of media presentation. Careful research in listening will provide clues to enable you to find the proper music for your use.

Such general categorization of music for mood, place, locale, action and transition might go on for several more pages. Any perusal of a sound track service catalog would disclose many additional categories broken down into tempo, length, mood, instrumental combinations and other serviceable characteristics. You might find listings under such content style as *agitato, tranquillo, dramatico, romantico, pastorale, mysterioso,* etc. as well as suggested uses for each to depict fire, storm, love scene, longing, etc. Similarly, a study of titles of standard music literature would reveal a wide range of possible uses to generate and sustain mood. Suffice it to say, however, that the foregoing list distinguishes a variety of traditional ways of achieving the desired effect.

Mood music, then, is that form of music which is to word and picture what color is to photography and art. While it lacks the capability to transmit actual information of itself, it holds the power of suggestion to evoke positive and definite emotional responses, to lend strength to picture and script and to stimulate learning and retention through association. As in the case of background music, it must be unobtrusive and nondistractive. Its purpose is not to dominate and overwhelm but to serve all other elements faithfully. Just as "a picture is worth a thousand words," mood music provides that extra dimension

160

which helps to unify all other components of a production by setting the emotional scene which is so necessary in achieving the goal of the presentation.

c. *Underscoring.* The term "scoring" a picture connotes providing music (background, mood, special effects, etc.) for a film, narrative or TV production. The term "underscoring" is used to denote a type of writing which virtually "sets the script" to music by using various forms of effect and commentary. When it is felt that an entire script needs this undergirding or that its materials would be enhanced by such techniques, careful analysis is made of the available possibilities. Once it is known which moods are to be reflected, what actions can be imitated, which words can be transliterated and the descriptive strength that can be brought to it, the music is written (or selected carefully by a music director and music editor) to provide these extra qualities. Most major commercial films are provided with music written or tailored to fit the exact mood, the nuance of speech, the scenery—in short, every element of the film is searched to provide the composer with clues to his appropriate action in every second of the presentation. In the hands of a skilled craftsman everything fits perfectly. This requires a skill beyond composition itself, for the creator must now direct himself toward the same goal as do the script and picture. Properly done the music is not incidental to the script and picture. In a real sense it is a major factor in the production, functioning in all of the ways that script and film cannot in order to create the illusion of reality. The procedure itself is much like that employed by a composer in writing an opera. He involves himself in every facet of the production, striving to unify all elements to produce a work of art. In electronic media the stage is a screen or a loud-speaker, but the results are the same as if he had used each bit and piece in the creation of art music.

d. *Transitional Bridges.* Transitional music performs a definite function: it changes the mood, action, locale or time from one scene to another. This is done as it emerges from behind the words to be heard momentarily as full sound before it fades back into its role subsidiary to the words. It is, apart from music used for opening, closing and special effects, the only time that music emerges to perform a function that is entirely musical. Bridges serve as quick transitions from one mood to another because music is capable of instantly changing moods. It may emerge to heighten or sustain a mood to allow for a sense of the passing of time or character change. Its tempo may quickly change from slow to faster tempo or suddenly resume its slow pace. In addition, the bridge can be used as a point of commentary, in which the music echoes a final phrase or word, may shriek with pain or tragedy, or it may respond to happy content with the appropriate emotional reaction. It is a device which, in the multiplicity of its abilities to provide the user with effective transitional passage, has no equivalent elsewhere. It has no definite characteristics of its own musically—only a function.

e. *Special effects.* In the area of special effects many elements may be considered. A scene may call for a man diving from a board into the water: the music follows his movement with descending scale and an appropriate musical splash. A space ship may blast off and the music explodes it into action and ascends in pitch as it achieves altitude, following it with telemetric-like imitations from various instruments. It is imitative or realistically descriptive music which forms most of the special effects, for music has the unusual capability of imitation, whether it be a bird song, baby cry, steam roller or stockpen filled with cattle. What it cannot directly imitate it can suggest and, as Strauss used the tympani to suggest the beating heart of a dying man in "Death and Transfiguration" and the combination of a variety of instruments to suggest the bleating sheep in "Don Quixote," so may any composer attempt to provide believable sound in his scoring of real life.

There are a number of special categories in this area, the first of which might be described as musical punctuation called "stings and stabs." These words apply to sudden musical outbursts of various kinds. A classical example of such use might be a scene in which a character says:

162

"Sandra, Harold is dead!"
At this point the music is heard in a sudden forcefulness which represents Sandra's reaction to the news she has just received. Another example could be a scene in which a character says:

"Stop, or I'll shoot!"
Then the music is heard suddenly to emphasize the mood resulting from such a situation.

"Stabs and stings" may appear to be cold (having no other music prior to their appearance) or they may be the outgrowth of a mood setting music which culminates in the punctuated emphasis. Many times, but not always, they burst forth and then quickly fade into the establishment or continuation of the mood.

The "tag" is another form of punctuation which indicates the conclusion of an idea or sequence. The music makes its comment (if any) and then is "up and out," ending with an appropriate sense of musicality.

Many producers like to identify characters with specific musical themes, much as Wagner did in his music dramas. Such themes are worked into the music when the character is on the screen, being talked about or is shortly to appear.

Some regularly heard programs are identified with specific music known as "signatures" or "themes." Most of the music one hears at the early part of a telecast, and also at its close, is "theme" music. If used often enough, its familiarity indicates to the listener that the show is about to begin or end. In motion pictures and television, opening and closing title music is used. This music represents a type of "attention-getting" sound which is heard fully and generally without script. It continues until the show proper begins or when it ends.

It would be wise for those who are contemplating extensive use of music of any kind to spend time listening for the types of music we have mentioned. Watching a few television dramas or documentaries would reveal frequent use of all types of background, mood, special effects and transitional bridge music. In the process of studying these traditional usages, one should be able to determine the effectiveness of the various styles as they apply to the production of instructional media units. Resources available for such research may be found in record catalogs or catalogs of production staff which have had experience in finding and using these tools in their work.

Before final selection is made, care should be used in avoiding copyright infringement. Performing rights societies will issue a license to use copyrights which they control and copyrights which have been assigned to them by publishers and composers. ASCAP, BMI and CESAC operate in this way, as do many of the music sound track companies which provide permission for use along with materials.

If there is ever any doubt about your right to use music in the preparation of media even for local use, investigation should be made, as publishers take a dim view of the inclusion of their music without permission. Purchase of the materials (tapes, recordings or even printed music) does not also automatically include the right to perform, and infringements can result in lawsuits or court action with penalties prescribed by law. This is especially true in the case of unauthorized use of music in media without explicit permission, for the copyright laws are so hazy about such things as closed circuit educational TV, systems performance of audio tapes, etc., that they fight hard to maintain the control granted to them by copyright laws that were made long before the advent of mechanically or electronically produced sound. While the field is difficult to police, one always risks being caught using materials that rightfully belong to others without that owner's permission to use.

Music may therefore be divided into three classifications in use: (1) Public domain—that music whose copyright has expired. (2) Copyrighted music—for which permission must be obtained either by license or granted by the composer or his legal representative or publisher. (3) Restricted music—that which is denied inclusion in any packaged form unless payment is made for the right to use it.

Any discussion of the "right to use" must acknowledge the fact that all music, except public domain or the rights to which you have purchased yourself from the creator, belongs to someone. Its use is carefully defined and illegal use of it is indeed

164

risky. Just as one would not blithely use another's car or home without explicit permission, so he should not use musical properties for which he has not obtained permission to use in advance—particularly in media.

When such permission is obtained, and the script has been analyzed to serve as a guide for every type of music required, certain terms are traditionally used to indicate its use. Several of these will be listed here: *BG* is an abbreviation for "background." The script writer may indicate solemn music to be "BG" for narration. *Sneak* is a term which means a quietly unobtrusive appearance of the musical sound. The script writer may say, "Sneak music BG here, hold under to Sandra's reaction on page 4, line 2." He may then request that it "stab or string," come up "full," or be "up and out." "Full" indicates music which is "in the clear," with no dialogue or narration to bother it. It may come up "full" and be held "full," or it may fade. "Fade to BG" is a term meaning the volume or intensity is diminished below the level of the other sounds.

No collection of words can aptly argue the case for the values in using music in instructional media. Each creator of media must decide these for himself, and each creator is obliged to study its potential or solicit help from experts in the craft. The least we can do is admit that if it has worked well for others, it can also work well for us.

CHAPTER IX

GRAPHICS

Mr. Webster's *New Collegiate Dictionary,* gives us a lot more information than we really need when we look up a word such as "graphics." He states that it is something "well-delineated, vividly described, of, or pertaining to writing, or to the representation by graphs or charts." He uses the term partially as "the art or science of drawing," and at one point refers to it as "the presentation of a striking or effective picture." He defines "graphology" as "the study of handwriting," but it doesn't apply to our study. This definition of "graphics" provides us a pretty good foundation upon which to build our discussion. The term is used synonymously with "writing which creates a visual image" and, for our purposes in media instruction we can as easily say that it may also indicate a visual image which lessens the need for writing. In addition, it may be something that well-delineates, vividly describes or, by using the art or science of drawing, strikingly presents an effective picture.

A graphic then is a visual representation of an object or an idea. In short, it is the representation rather than being of the "real." It is itself something physical, such as a graph, chart, line-drawing, transparency, map, cartoon, photograph, slide, information card or painting—any or all of which may be used in instructional media to convey information, emphasize and reinforce a point, project an idea, illustrate a concept, create an illusion or evoke a response. Of all these important uses, "evoking a response" is the most important—but more of this later.

166

A skeleton of a man viewed on TV would not be a graphic. A photograph or an artist's drawing of it would be, whether it were life-sized or reduced to a 35mm. slide. A vase or a shotgun shown "on camera" would not be a graphic, but a picture of either one would be. Anything presented visually instead of orally which represents but is not itself the real is a graphic.

It is our use of the visual representation of the real therefore, which defines a graphic as a "graphic." For example, a real thing, such as a copy of a magazine held in the hand of a person being viewed on TV would not of itself be a graphic. If, however, the person referred to the front cover or any of the magazine's contents, and used it as a visual representation of the subject under discussion, the magazine would no longer be a prop, it would be a graphic. No longer would it be real of itself, but now it would be used to represent the real.

If we were to show a photograph of a rattlesnake poised to strike, its impact as a photograph would not be as strong as seeing a live rattlesnake televised. If our decision to use the photograph were made in order to permit us to point at various areas of the snake's anatomy and discuss muscular and skeletal involvements in the act of striking, it would certainly be more convenient (and practical) to use the photograph rather than the live snake. But the impact of the live snake would more likely involve the viewer emotionally than the photograph. In either case, the viewer would bring to the scene some pre-conditioned responses to snakes—rattle or otherwise. So the "use" of the graphic, in whatever form they may be, is essential to our planning and creation.

Let us pursue the "striking snake" a point further in our thinking. Showing either an artist's rendition, a still or a motion picture representation of a rattlesnake striking a small child would produce an emotional response of tremendous power on the viewer. Yet significantly, no matter which portrayal is used, when it is transferred to the medium of television or film, it is no longer real. Depending solely upon their use, graphics become effective instruments in instructional media. If our rattlesnake scene were used by herpatologists, medical students or a group studying safety in wilderness exploration, each individual would bring a different set of pre-conditioned reactions to the graphic presentation. Therefore, the intention of the user and his knowledge of the use of the graphic presentation provide the bases for his determination of graphics. The fact that the use has been transferred to television does not lessen the real elements involved in the presentation, and most of our physical-emotional responses are brought into play as we empathize with the "non-real-but-representatively-real" situation. This is the "illusion" factor we mentioned earlier.

We may heighten the pictorial illusion several ways: (a) by using the sound of the warning rattle, (b) by selecting music which creates a "fear-tension" mood, (c) by utilizing varying degrees of emotional suggestion-intensity in narrator's voice or (d) by adding the scream of the bitten child. Such re-emphasis of the power of the graphic depends altogether on its intended use.

A visual representation of the real, then, may convey an idea, just as words conveying an idea may also create a visual image. A graphic may convey an idea which may be translated into thoughts. Recalling the thought recalls the visual. Recalling the visual recalls the thoughts.

Our hope would be to utilize the symbolism involved as a means of achieving concept. Just as the mathematician may achieve a concept of the method of determining the circumference of a circle by multiplying the radius squared by 3.1459265, and may reduce this formula to the symbol πr^2, so he may use that symbol to think (in respect to circles) with positive assurance. He knows that this formula applies to all circles not just one. In fact, he has a whole body of knowledge about circles compacted into a symbolism that expresses a universal truth. Truth resides in the concept, whether or not one is making the application to prove it. No matter what size the circle, or what its use, π times the square of the radius will give the circumference. Within all concepts, regardless of the precision of the symbolic language, there is latitude for the human equasion. It matters not how large or small the circle's circumference, but how the human mind utilizes them—and, we might also add "why."

We might use further examples of this type of symbology: computer language, shorthand, blueprints, codes or graphics which express ideas directly, allow concept and even provide thought patterns to be projected into the inner-mind or from it. The graphic assumes enormous power when it is used to transmit an idea from mind to mind. This power includes immediate perception and stimulae for retention.

Communication through pictorial representation is not a new idea. It was used by primitive man as he reported his victories in the hunt or battle by drawing pictures on the walls of his caves. The Egyptian priesthood used a picture script called *hieroglyphics,* and everyone is familiar with international traffic signs which have eliminated words by using symbols which represent the things formerly spelled out with words. In all three instances, pictures transmit ideas accurately, and we are limited only to our ability to understand what the pictures mean.

There is, however, a universality in most of the symbols which represent emotional expression: joy, happiness, sorrow, pain, depression, exhaltation, pride, humility. This universality is sufficient to allow for communication through symbolism. It is this capacity to convey emotion directly and to develop an environmental circumstance of receptivity which makes the graphic so vital to us in instructional media. It, along with its sister arts of music, mime and dance, possesses this universality factor and, as such, is worthy of being probed in depth to take advantage of the inherent values of utilizing the emotional characteristics as a direct teaching tool.

Shapes, colors and sounds are all meaningful symbols. The cross, for example, is expressive of a spiritual concept; the police badge, of authority; the swastika, of totalitarianism; the flag, of patriotism; a gravestone, of sorrow; a clenched fist, of defiance.

As indicated earlier, we believe that all learning is a result of an emotional involvement of the learner in the subject content. We also indicated that the graphic arts possess unusual capacity to transmit ideas symbolically and non-verbally. With this realization in mind, we should lean heavily upon the creative

169

usage of graphics to convey information in an environment consciously designed to evoke emotional response.

A case in point would be a portrait of Nathan Hale. This young American, two years out of Yale University, enlisted in the American Army and volunteered for a dangerous mission. Disguised as a schoolteacher (he had in fact been one before the Revolution), he was captured by British troops and summarily hanged as a spy. We could show Nathan Hale's portrait and at the same time provide factual material about him. Merely showing him on the screen represents the physical reality of the person. By portraying him standing on a rough-hewn scaffold with a rope around his neck a heightened viewer involvement is produced. Put a few red-coated British soldiers around him, allow his much-quoted, "I only regret that I have only one life to lose for my country," to be heard in a voice other than that of the narrator, and still another involvement dimension has been added. If one added appropriate music to invest the picture and words with the further dimension of sorrow, suspense and tragedy, the learning process would be quickened even more dynamically because emotional involvement has been evoked.

What we are talking about, then, is the creative use of graphics in which the graphic transcends the mere visual representation and becomes an integral part of the whole. Knowing in advance how reaction may be triggered in response to certain recognized conditions, utilizing all possible skills—we make them part of the total spectrum of psychological factors involved in the learning process.

Having defined the term and attempted an explanation of values, let us now discuss the various types of graphics and the options available to us. Graphics may be classified into three basic categories: those which require large display areas, photographic materials (excluding slides, motion pictures and filmstrips) and those which require small display areas.

In the first category we may include materials which utilize fairly large surfaces for effective display. This includes posters, wall charts, large maps, paintings, flip charts and chalk boards.

170

The last two are not actually graphics, but are used for the creation of what we may call "instant" graphics (the area in which the performer illustrates his material simultaneously with his oral presentation).

The second category includes photographic display materials such as enlargements or printed copies of enlargements. These, as well as some of the items listed in our first category, depend upon the mobility of a TV camera (zoom, pan, dolly, tilt) for effective usage. As a rule of thumb the larger the surface being photographed the less likely the effectiveness of the graphic will be. Photographing a chalkboard filled with math problems, for example, would not permit the viewer to be close enough to it to see the whole clearly. Once we have established the chalkboard, however, the mobility of the camera will permit us to see each section of the total picture in a close-up. A sixteen-by-twenty-two enlargement would permit the camera to take in the whole graphic in addition to searching out details that may be of consequence in the instructional procedure. This same technique could be used on large tear sheets, posters, newspapers or large wall maps and charts.

In the third category only smaller (8½" by 11") graphics should be considered. These would include all types of pre-pared materials or photographic reproductions of materials. This categorization of graphics into three general classes is loose at best, but it does permit us to have a general concept of the variations.

There are still two other general categories of graphics which we will touch upon later—one is called "illusionary animation," the other "electronically generated."

To demonstrate the fine line of distinction between a graphic and a set prop, let me illustrate with a scene requiring the use of a set representing the locker room of a police precinct station. On the walls are some 8½" by 11" "wanted" posters similar to the types seen in post offices, a large bulletin board with typescript notices thumbtacked to its surface and a large poster board announcing a benefit show involving police personnel. Each of these items could be a

171

graphic in the strictest sense of the term, but none of them are used in such a direct way. Instead, they are used to create an environmental representation of a typical locker room in a typical police precinct station. They are graphics to the point that they serve to establish the validity of the total scene. They would be graphics (in our definition) if they were involved in conveying the information relating directly to the show itself at any point in the show.

The set also contains other props likely to be found in such a locker room: a coat rack upon which is hung a uniform coat and a police hat, a domino table and a police manual from which one of the officers occasionally reads aloud. At the point the officer reads, incidentally, his words are seen as well as heard. This is done by photographing the contents of a graphic made to simulate the words on the manual page. As the officer picks up the manual, we see and hear him begin to read, then we see his words appear on the screen. By seeing what we hear, we not only have our learning process reinforced by the combination of aural-visual, we accept fully what we see and hear as the same thing which is contained in the authoritative source, i.e., the police manual.

Let's talk for a moment about these 8½" x 11" graphics. They can be anything: line drawings, cartoons, maps, portraits, symbols or word groupings. Sometimes we call word groupings "information cards" merely to separate their general usage from illustrative cards. In any event, the making of these graphics requires that the information and illustrative materials be positioned so that both it and the slide reproduction will conform to the limitations of the television screen. It is also necessary to know color values so that the intensity of the color signal generated by the graphic will be within the capacity of the electronics scanning it. So color values, as well as positioning, are vital concerns *during* the preparation of the graphics.

In information or word card graphics, many types of lettering may be used. These may be either drawn by hand, done with some variant of the art-type or press-type method, accomplished with one of the many forms of typeset

172

machines or stencils for raised letters, jumbo type or magnetic boards.

In a series of word cards being made for any consecutive use, the same general type size should be maintained throughout in order to insure a constant focal position by the graphics camera. Word graphics to be used for super-imposition should be done with white letters on black paper. These are used, for example, when a lecturer is stressing an important point and his point is emphasized or reinforced by the appearance of the word card on the screen. Such information may also be placed directly on clear slides by using very small press-type lettering.

The marketplace is filled with electronic equipment which assists the graphic artist in maintaining a creative flow of visuals. The only problems are that its use is restricted to television, that new equipment constantly supercedes last year's models, that its use is often for production techniques rather than relevancy of subject content, that its use is too often substituted for creativity, that it is used far too much (even electronic wizardry can become boring) and above all it is electronic rather than real. True graphic art is that which is created by real people for real purposes.

Just as electronic music is a by-product of equipment output rather than the result of the combined efforts of live human beings to generate sound, most electronic graphics remain in that category of effects representing non-real values. This does not imply that they are unusable and may not make a contribution. It only means that one needs to take extreme care, particularly in instructional media, that their inclusion enhances rather than impedes the mind to mind goal that is our ideal. The one exception is the character generator.

Sometimes when you are watching your favorite TV program you may suddenly see a series of words march across your screen—a weather bulletin alert, an election result, a program announcement or a police message. When you see this, you are seeing the character generator in action. It is a highly sophisticated piece of equipment which enables one literally to write graphic information on the screen without the previously-used process of handcrafting it. Some units are capable of inserting information from left-to-right, some can move it from bottom and top, and some even blink and flash. A device similar to the typewriter is used to place and store a signal in an integrated memory circuit which can be converted into a similar signal for display on the TV screen at a later time. The character generator may well eliminate the need for future graphic artists who spend much time handcrafting informational materials involving words. Until the magic of electronics completely takes over graphics, however, let's look at some examples of valuable materials we can prepare for use in media instruction packages developed for uses other than just TV.

The first of these is called the "overlay." These are created by the artist visualizing the total scene but developing it in successive stages, which make up the total scene when combined. The combination is achieved through a series of transparent plastic overlays placed over what is called the "art base." Overlays add other elements to the total effect.

Let us imagine the base art to be a living room of two colors. The first overlay would place a fireplace in the room with a picture above its mantle. Overlay two would add two chairs, and a final overlay a man with one hand resting on the mantle. The following figure illustrates this procedure:

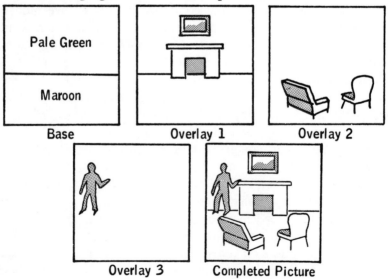

Base   Overlay 1   Overlay 2

Overlay 3   Completed Picture

174

Such plastic overlays are not very practical for use in the TV studio because they are difficult to handle perfectly under the pressure of actual production and the excessively bright lights in the studio tend to cause them to reflect (mirror-like) and thus distort the intent of the graphic itself. So for the most part TV overlays are built to be photographed for use as slides.

Still another type of word-card graphic may be classified as a pull graphic. It is achieved by dividing the graphic area into two parts, as illustrated below:

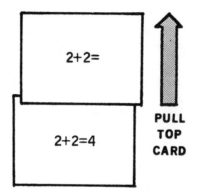

When the graphic is first displayed, only the top part of it is seen (2 + 2 =), the lower part being covered with another sheet of paper identical in color to the first. When the top card is pulled upward the second graphic (2 + 2 = 4) is revealed. When done in the studio, it can be the simplest form of the illusionary animation graphic, for the "4" seems to materialize before our very eyes. These two graphics may also be photographed individually and the slides shown successively, using a slow-dissolve technique to produce a similar effect.

Another form of simple illusion is made by setting up a stripping system by which letters seem to appear as the pull-away strips reveal information. Using the same mathematical problem we used earlier. Let's demonstrate this with the following illustration:

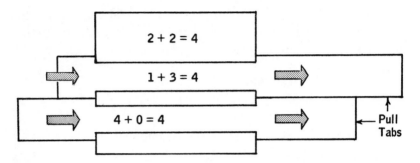

In this instance we have prepared simple slots through which a covering paper of identical color is pulled from the graphic below it. As we desire to show this information in a step-by-step procedure, the paper stripping is merely pulled to the side making it appear as if the information materialized from nowhere. This stripping technique may be employed with good effect in a variety of presentational situations.

There are other ways to do the same thing. Each one gets more complicated than the other and, of course, each has its distinct advantage. The first is a process involving the motion picture camera in which a series of frame-by-frame exposures are taken at exact time intervals. When the film is subsequently shown at projection speed, an illusion is created in which figures simply appear. This is a simple form of animation. Let's illustrate the various steps in the procedure involved by animating the word ANIMATION. We select the style of lettering we want, settle on a background design and then photograph the letters one by one until the entire word has been completed. Here is the procedure we follow:

a. Shoot 12 frames background
b. Shoot A, 6 frames
c. Shoot AN, 6 frames
d. Shoot ANI, 6 frames
e. Shoot ANIM, 6 frames
f. Shoot ANIMA, 6 frames
g. Shoot ANIMAT, 6 frames
h. Shoot ANIMATI, 6 frames
i. Shoot ANIMATIO, 6 frames
j. Shoot ANIMATION (hold as desired).

176

Depending upon the time and patience you have, the word or letters from it may be made to perform with all sorts of variations. If we do not have the facility for frame-by-frame motion picture photography, a simulated procedure would be possible by sequencing a series of slides, each containing an added ingredient of the information until the entire message was complete. Utilizing a fast drop-switch for the slide projection would give an animated effect.

Still another somewhat less complicated way of creating such illusionary animation uses a somewhat different form of stripping technique. Let us once again use the word ANIMA-TION as our example. The letters may be individually cut out of a heavy piece of construction paper. The original heavy paper is then placed on a sheet of glass and fixed in place. On the opposite side of the glass, the letters are put back into the areas from which they originally came. Once each letter has been taped with a heavy-duty, light-resistant, masking tape, a very bright light is placed behind the glass area. Be sure to check to see that no light shines through the glass when you have set the letters into place. As it scans the surface, the TV camera will read only the lighted areas that result when the letters are pulled away from the surface. It is a neat and inexpensive procedure.

One other illusionary animation type graphic is also involved with a pane of glass. This time, however, translucent paper is used and the lettering, picture drawing, or math-problem-working is done by someone behind that translucent area. Because the camera will read his writing mirror-like, it is necessary to reverse the polarization of the camera or to shoot into a mirror which reflects the actual writing. At the moment of viewing the TV screen seems to have writing or drawing appear instantaneously.

Variations of graphics for motion simulation may be achieved by using a device called a "merry-go-round." Shaped like a drum, it is a revolving display stand on which scenery, street scenes, etc. can be placed as a continuous graphic and used as a backdrop to create the illusion of motion. The drum can be built to any size, although one large enough to display 8½" x

11" graphics would serve most purposes. This same revolving stand could also be used to display a series of separate graphics. The mobility of the drum mechanism permits flexibility in display change, and such displays can be alternated with slide projections to make these changes smoothly. This mechanism has the added benefit that a number of individual graphics can be displayed and shot without changing the focal length of the camera. Using this device in conjunction with slides can create a realistic effect, as in the case where a continuous graphic representing a landscape or street scene is used as background for slides depicting a person walking. The slides, made from identical graphics except for arm and leg positions, are placed in the carousel on the film chain and activated with a switch that keeps them alternating at a fixed rate. These are superimposed upon the background of the revolving scenery to make an effective if not complete animation.

Another drum-like device can be made to revolve vertically instead of horizontally. It is commonly called a "crawl drum." Names are often moved upward or downward across the face of a TV screen by placing the information on a crawl drum and rotating it slowly in camera view. This effect can be made with long strip graphics for illusions representing upward or downward motion. Turntables covered with graphic patterns may also be effectively used for illusionary effect. As a matter of fact, a number of the excellent pseudo-special effects now achieved by generators may be simulated in this manner.

Thus far we have talked of graphics in the 8½" x 11" or long strip types as well as larger sizes for translucent or stripping effects. Since we have involved studio equipment for such display, we'll continue with this subject before going on to the other categories of graphics.

It is necessary to have a permanent graphic display stand built firmly enough so that it will not shake when bumped while the camera is focused on it, large enough to hold more than a single graphic and capable of displaying large graphic materials. An easel frame, such as used with large flip-charts would suffice. Flip-charts themselves may also be used to display graphics requiring sequencing for effectiveness. They

178

may also be used for making instant graphics as when the lecturer draws pictures or works problems relevant to his presentation.

The advantage of the larger display area should be obvious. It permits mobility of camera shots and techniques for examining the graphic materials in detail or as a whole. One should add a word of caution at this point. Studio space is usually limited, and unless some method of making large-scale display areas mobile can be devised the studio may soon get too cluttered for effective use by the technicians.

Thus far we have established the purpose of graphic use and explained some of the options available to the director, writer, producer and graphics artist for creating instructional media units. Thinking creatively with graphics is an exciting experience, for they can produce exciting and stimulating visual results which affect the total response of the student toward content.

Let me give you a couple of examples of creative use of graphics as we wind our way to the end of this chapter. In my initial days of producing a particular art series for media instructional units, color availability was limited entirely to the film chain. Although we could record in color with the film chain, there were no color cameras available in the studio. A series titled "Adventures in Art" was authorized and because of the limitation of facilities it was decided to do the series utilizing only slides and films done in 16mm. sequences. The result was a slide-tape-film-clip package. The tape itself was a pre-recorded mix of commentary, music and sound effects intimately co-ordinated with the visual portrayal of content material. The visual portion consisted of motion picture film and graphics of three types: straight information cards, photographs made of paintings, exhibits of art works and "Zelda."

Zelda was herself a creation, a prototype of students who might be viewing the series. She was a gamin-face to whom voice was given in script dialogue. She could even make frequent uninhibited and solicited commentary upon the art works, the artists and occasionally the teacher. Since we had no capacity to animate Zelda, a series of plastic overlays was used

179

to create the Zelda face. The face, with hair, nose and general contour, was the art base for this overlay series. Eight different mouth positions, ranging from sly grin to openmouthed amazement, were created, as were corresponding eyebrow expressions. The eyes were created separately in a dozen or so representative eye positions ranging from closed lids to open-eyed stare. In addition, Zelda was provided with various sizes, shapes and colors of hair-ribbons varying from excessively bright hues to patterned-designs to be worn in her somewhat-mod hairdo. Let me illustrate with this series of drawings the steps leading up to her "being":

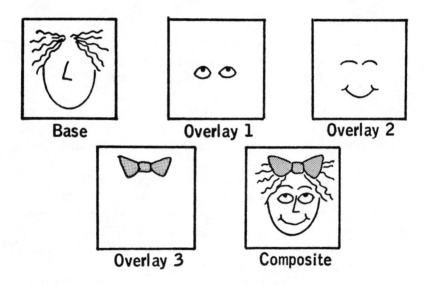

Base **Overlay 1** **Overlay 2**

Overlay 3 **Composite**

Zelda was used in sequences of slides to show reactions of various types: surprise, dismay, self-satisfaction, concentration, puzzlement, amazement, etc. Sometimes the slides were used in a dissolve mode, moving slowly one to the other. At other times they were flipped quickly into position as fast as the carousel would advance. On other occasions they were combined with a film segment we called the "swirl." This color swirl procedure created a dimension of animation, or at least of a non-static screen. The graphic Zelda, delivering lines in a quasi-Brooklynese voice, became a real person to the viewers of the series. It enhanced the presentation of the material, gave new dimension to the script, and provided a source of empathy by the students.

Let me give you another example of creativity in the use of graphics. This came as a result of an assignment in a media writing class, where students were to develop a pilot video-tape on "Punctuation."

Ideas for pictorializing punctuation marks individually with explanations and examples of their use were presented. The class decided to utilize slides (copies of graphics), small display areas and an illusionary animation device (the translucent paper procedure) in combination with a stereotype professor in the form of a puppet in cap and gown. They then selected an actor to represent the learner.

Two sets were designed: one, a simple puppet stage, the other a simulated study, complete with easy chair, end table and a few book props. After they had clearly defined the objective of the total show and its individual elements, they wrote the script.

Having written the script, prepared the graphics and the sets, they now prepared an audio tape. The audio tape contained the voices, music and carefully selected sound effects. This pre-preparation of the audio tape was done in order to facilitate the production of the video-tape. Two voices were used: one of professional quality to represent authority, and one representing the puppet-professor. The authority voice on the tape represented that phase of the material which was to be pertinent to the use of and recognition of the various punctuation marks. The professor's voice was somewhat less authorative and more in keeping with the puppet representing him.

The on-camera actor had no speaking lines. He portrayed someone working a crossword puzzle involving words denoting punctuation marks. He was in many senses a "living graphic" because of his reactions and facial expressions. His attitude in this non-verbal communication was as vital to the show as were the crafted graphics.

181

The crossword puzzle was placed on a large poster display board both before any of the words had been filled in and in its finished form. A number of translucent sheets were prepared using this same model so that the words could be written in as an illusionary animation during the show. They made a model of their puzzle in slightly smaller form and photographed it in a sequence, using white raised letters to make up their words. Their completed puzzle graphic is shown below:

Fourteen words appear in the finished puzzle and so the base graphic was progressively photographed as it was completed. Two sets of slides were made: one with just the puzzle (as we described it above) and the other framed with simulated newsprint to make it seem as if the crossword were in a newspaper or magazine. Unframed slides were used in the review or summary unit, while the framed slides were used during the progressive working of the puzzle. These were made white-on-black to facilitate supering the puzzle at will. Students made 8½" x 11" graphics as solution hints.

ACROSS

1. Encloses editorial corrections or
interpolations in quoted matter.

182

Each of these were made into slide format, and the solutions to the problems were prepared on pull card graphics:

Brackets [ ]

•••••••••••••••••••••••••••••••••▶

Encloses editorial corrections or

interpolations in quoted matter.

These were done with a rub-on lettering material. They were placed on display stands, the bottom half of the graphic covered and then pulled away at the appropriate time. As the learner in the set wrote the words into his crossword puzzle, so did the writer behind the translucent screen. Still another set of graphics were made with jumbo-sized type on a typewriter. These were placed on display stands to be exhibited as needed.

ENCLOSES EDITORIAL CORRECTIONS OR INTERPOLATIONS IN QUOTED MATTER.

Graphics were arranged on the crawl, display stands, slides and appeared instantly in the translucent form. They were used as the sole image on the screen and as supers over live action. In short, these visuals became an active set of characters themselves, playing against the characters represented by the puppet-professor and the learner. These visuals were not merely illustrative of show content, they were indeed themselves show content. All of the graphics were used along with the slides as part of the summary.

The show was difficult for students to produce, but it revealed an exciting way to transfer information mind-to-mind. It also proved to them that learning can be couched in an easy-to-view format that is enjoyable to present and to achieve.

The one form of graphic presentation we have not yet touched is the transparency and its use on overhead projectors in the classroom. They may also be used effectively in the studio as a prompter or substitute for cue cards. An entire script may be transferred to transparencies and projected to a screen placed beside the cameras, thus enabling a speaker to read copy without losing eye contact with the audience. It also enables him to move about as he reads his lines. Even if he is not reading from prepared script, an outline of his material plus reminder cues can be put on the transparencies to help him in his delivery. Using transparency rolls instead of individual sheets gives even greater flexibility to this format.

Still one other tool which could be brought into the studio is the microfilm and microfiche reader. Thousands of pages of potential graphics are available on various microfilm spools or microfiche cards. If the machine itself is not part of available studio equipment, print-outs can be made and used as visual display cards. Any print-out device which may be programmed in advance to supply information on cue (automated typewriter or typewriter activated to a computer terminal) is a valid, includable resource.

If you really want to see superlative use of graphics, con-centrate on the commercials. You'll be surprised at what you see and the creative way in which graphics are used. Keep in mind that if intelligent use of graphics is important enough to use in selling soap, it is important enough for us to incorporate in our selling of ideas, mind-to-mind.

CHAPTER X

RECORDING, EDITING AND MIXING SOUND

Preparing the audio track for a presentational unit, whether it is to be used solely as a reel-to-reel, cassette package or pre-recorded sound track for a video production, is a critical function demanding a variety of skills. The basic intention of this discussion is to indicate proper ways to record the spoken word, edit the tape and mix other sounds with it. We will be speaking altogether of monaural, single-track recording using 7½IPS. The steps involved in such a process include the following:

    a. recording the voice track,
    b. editing out extraneous noises and errors,
    c. adding sound effects if needed,
    d. adding music.

If the voice track can be done under ideal conditions, as in a good sound-proof studio using good recording equipment, the tape editor has little to do except remove false starts, errors in pronunciation, throat-clearings, coughs, lip-smacks, clicking false-teeth and such unwanted sounds such as paper-rustling, accidental bumping of the microphone, jingling of costume jewelry, engineering goofs, etc. We will assume that conditions for recording are at least those which will allow the reader to tape his materials without too many distractions. It is best always to have an engineer and an audio director rather than to permit the speaker to operate his own equipment. The presence of at least one other person enables suggestions and corrections to be made in a recording session. Instructions may be made on pacing, pronunciation or re-reading of faulty lines or paragraphs. Listening to and marking the script will

185

indicate that small errors have crept into the taping session and making corrections on the scene will provide a master tape which will save much time in the final edit. By all means, do not attempt to record over materials in which errors occur. Let the tape continue playing and keep on recording. The stopping, returning and erasing during a session tends to destroy pacing and adds to the probability that some needed materials will be erased. Most engineers and directors also advocate recording "room tone," the natural sound of the studio when all else is silent. Such room tone sounds are very valuable when, in the editing process, you wish to insert pauses or change the pacing slightly. Most studios have their own characteristic room tones and since such characteristics are variable, it is good to tape a minute or so of it each time you record.

When this master reel has been completed with all of the unwanted material edited out, the editor can lay in additional voices, sound effects and music by mixing the composite tapes together in a final track.

In the next few paragraphs we will examine a variety of voice tracks. The first of these is the single-voice narration. This is the simplest form of master to prepare and, depending upon the reader's ability, and the studio conditions, the least complicated. No matter how uncomplicated, however, editing still requires effort and skill.

As in all editing, the tape editor works with a script. He is concerned with obvious errors as well as details. Obviously some undesired sounds should be heard by the engineer or director during the session itself, and corrections should be made immediately. The narrator may need to re-record those sections. The script should be marked at the point of an error to assist the editor as he works on the editing process at a later time.

Such edit markings are usually made by placing the letter "T" (take) on the script at the point of the error. If an error occurs within a sentence and the sentence (or phrase) is re-recorded, the director marks a "T2" (or uses the number indicating the number of times the reader started over). Many editors refer to those extraneous noises and repeated sections, which must be removed from the tape as "garbage." This term will be better understood as you attempt the process yourself, for you'll notice your wastebasket filling up with scrap fragments.

At this point we will provide you with a script sample in which we will illustrate some of the markings the engineer or director places on his script during the actual taping session. Professor "X" is speaking:

Prof: At the very outset of this recording session, we must make (studio sure that the microphone is placed properly for the reader. Noise) We must also assume that the recording levels have been established prior to the beginning of the taping. (Noise)

T3

This is done by the engineer, either with a signal tone which he introduces into his equipment to calibrate his console amplifiers with his recording equipment—or he may ask the reader to speak in his normal reading voice while he watches his VU meter to see that there are not too many peaks or volume variables in the reading. He may even record a sample of the speaker's voice and play it back to check the validity of his work.

(Throat Clear)   T4

T2 On a cue from the director or engineer, the speaker begins to read the script and without thinking he clears his throat. This sound is, of course, recorded and must be eliminated (by editing) from the master tape.

(GARBAGE)

T3 But first, the sentence must be repeated in its entirety because at the point of the throat-clearing the narrator begins reading again at a higher volume level. Since the first part of the sentence and the second part of the sentence would not have matched in intensity, the entire sentence is repeated.

GARBAGE

T3 The first part of his next sentence is read correctly, but he stumbles over the word "hyperbole." Before re-reading he practices saying it correctly several times before repeating the T5 entire sentence. This practice material must now also be eliminated. The narrator again muffs the line containing the word "hyperbole." On the third attempt, it is done perfectly

187

and he continues. The director indicates garbage around this entire section of practice and repeated attempts, finally marking T3 to indicate the sentence is accomplished after three major attempts. The reading proceeds to the end on an easy basis except for a couple of (throat-clearings) and a slip of the *T6* tongue when the phrase "instructional media materials" is *Noise* read. The professor finally decides to re-arrange the wording to "materials of media instruction." He accomplishes all of this with a good deal of garbage and six takes.

Having thus recorded the script and marked the points of definite edit, the tape may now be put into final form.

To edit, one should have at least six items (beyond endless patience and a large wastebasket):

1. an editing bar,
2. a marking pencil or felt-tipped pen,
3. splicing tape,
4. white leader tape,
5. an extra take-up reel,
6. a sharp, single-edged razor blade.

The editing itself is done most effectively on a tape recorder where the playback head may be exposed enabling the editor to mark the segments of the tape to be edited. The head areas of a tape recorder looks something like this:

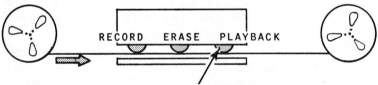

The concern of the editor is with the playback-head, the one on the right in the preceding illustration. The sound on the magnetic tape is activated here. The portion of the tape where the cut is to be made is marked on the tape precisely at the point it passes over the playback head, using the left side of the head as the exact point of marking.

Let us re-visit our sample script which has been recorded and the reels of which are now on the tape recorder for editing. The tape is in motion and you are listening to it. Our script indicated that there was studio noise before the professor actually said his first word. We let the tape play to that exact

188

point where his speech begins and stop the recorder. Making sure that we have the first word in view, we mark that point on the tape with pen or marking pencil. We may gently rotate the reels to check the exact point of editing, moving the tape slowly back and forth over the playback head until it has been determined that it is the exact spot. When this is done we pull the tape away from the tape head, place it on the editing bar with the marked area on the diagonal slot as here illustrated:

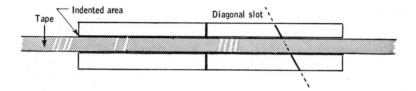

Take a sharp razor blade, hold the blade slightly at an angle and cut the tape diagonally across the slot in a "carving" not a "mashing" motion. Remove the discarded tape (containing the noise and errors) and, using some white leader tape, splice the magnetic tape and leader tape by placing the two ends together and over-laying it with about an inch of splicing tape across the cut area. Making sure it is placed precisely within the indented area of the editing bar, the splicing tape is pressed down firmly on the two joined ends. The tape is now ready to be checked by playing it.

We continue now to play the tape we are editing, looking at the script as the sound is heard. In our sample script taping, we notice that our next edit point occurs after the word "reader." There is a "T3" indicated here, meaning that the professor got it right after muffing it twice. We may either make the tape cut at this point and then move ahead to the beginning of the "T3" or we may decide to merely mark it and wait to cut it until we have found the exact point of the beginning of "T3" before cutting. In any event, this material is eliminated from the master tape and those two ends are then spliced together.

Be sure you allow a normal pause customarily given by the reader between the end of one sentence and the beginning of another, otherwise the effect will be jerky. If there is not

189

enough editing space possible, you may want to use a half-second or so of room tone to make the transition. You will also want to listen to breath intakes, for that also plays a part in our editing. Sometimes it is good to edit from the beginning of one breath intake to the beginning of the breath occurring immediately before the next take. In some cases it is better to edit from the end of an intake to the end of another. In either event, pay close attention to these breath marks. Take them out and you'll have your listener gasping for breath. And never ever have your speaker take two gasps to get one word started.

Always check the effectiveness of a splice before proceeding by playing back the edited section. Never throw the edited out portion away until you are satisfied with your work. If the tape is filled with difficult or critical editing points, you might splice all the out-takes together on a second take-up reel in case they are needed at a later point in your editing. Proceed step by step until you have finished the job. When you have put another length of white leader tape on your master tape, re-wind and then double check your work with script in hand. You may also wish to time the reading and mark the progressive timings in your script.

The procedure just described may be most effective in utilizing the techniques involved, but it won't do YOU any good at all unless you take time out of your busy schedule to practice editing a few voice tapes. Unfortunately we can't construct a book so that you can get the actual hands-on equipment practice you need. Unless you stop now to practice, or already know these simple principles, don't continue until you have gained enough practical experience to feel comfortable in the editor's chair.

Let's examine another sample script which introduces procedures such as sound effects, inserted "voice" quotes, and music cues:

SAMPLE SCRIPT

Narrator: We live in strange times, fear-filled times—yet they are not so different from the days of World War II when Franklin Roosevelt said:

190

Voice: We have nothing to fear but fear itself.

Music: Full for fifteen seconds, fading for:

Narrator: Those were noble words, echoing the sentiments spoken ⌐T2
            by that unknown Roman poet as he addressed the
            Senate in 306 B.C.

Sound: Crowd noises up, fade into background for:

Voice: Ye men of Rome, fear not the evils of this day. Rather ⌐T2
            fear the cowardly feelings that cause you to be afraid.

Music: Full for fifteen seconds, fading for:

Narrator: And in conclusion, I urge you to re-examine your
            T5 motives, take renewed faith in the courage of our
            national heroes and believe in Almighty God, for:

Voice II: (echo chamber) If God is for you, who can be against
            you? GARBAGE

Narrator: ⌐T5 With these words, I now declare this convention to be at
            an end.

Sound: Three gavel raps, sound of crowd, scattered applause.

Music: Up full to end title, out.

Our editing process is now more complicated because there are more components involved. First clean up the basic script materials done by the narrator as indicated on the script. Then, assuming that your insert quotions have also been properly edited and placed in correct sequence on another insert reel, splice each one onto your master tape at the point indicated by the script.

Please notice the music cue indicated after the first voice insert. At this point, use 15 seconds of white leader tape. In case you don't have a stop watch, each 7½ inches of tape equals one second, so measure out 112½ inches to equal 15

191

seconds. Splice the end of the white leader tape to the beginning of the narrator's next speech. Following it, a sound effects cue is indicated immediately prior to the Roman poet's quote. Measure off ten seconds of white leader tape between the narrator's speech and the beginning of the poet's speech. Another fifteen seconds music cue follows that speech. Insert another fifteen second length of white leader tape, splicing it to the beginning of the narrator's next speech. At the end of the narrator's last speech is a sound effects cue marked "three gavel raps." Insert these after the last word of the narrator, allowing a brief pause before they begin. Then fix a length of white leader tape to mark the end of the master voice reel. Mark the reel and after you have re-wound the tape, set it aside momentarily.

We now have the master voice reel. It consists of:

1. White leader tape.
2. Narrator's voice.
3. Roosevelt quote.
4. 15 seconds white leader tape for music cue length.
5. Narrator's voice.
6. 10 seconds white leader tape for sound effects.
7. Roman poet's words.
8. 15 seconds white leader tape for music cue length.
9. Voice II (echo) quote.
10. Sound effect: three gavel raps.
11. White leader tape.

Before we can combine (mix) this master reel with sound effects and music, however, we must first prepare another reel, the master sound effects and music reel. To do this, we select appropriate music and set up our components:

1. A music cue of at least 25 seconds, the last ten seconds of which fades into silence.
2. Sound effects of crowd noises of at least 20 seconds, the last ten of which will be fading into silence.
3. Second music cue, treated as above.
4. Final mix of sound and music for end title.

Preparing the first part of this reel is relatively simple. The final mix (No. 4), however, will have to be pre-mixed before it may be included.

Let's consider the techniques involved in doing this, following the directions indicated by the script, as we edit the master ending reel. We note that as the gavel raps, the sound of crowd noises (with scattered applause) begins. Then the end-title music begins and swells to full volume. Three steps are required: place the sound effects material on one reel, connect the end-title music into place with a ten-second leader tape, and place the scattered applause sound effect on another reel.

At this point we will need to discuss the mix process itself, for mixing sounds requires three tape recorders (two for playback, one for recording) and a mixing unit. Look at the following illustration:

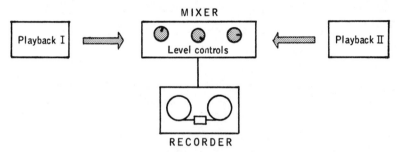

Playback units I and II feed into the mixer, which in turn feeds into the recorder. The small knobs on the mixer are called "faders." The small window indicates a VU (VI) meter, (see Appendix I), which registers the intensity of the output of any channel or combination of channels feeding into it. The mixer feeds into the tape recorder during our mixing process, recording the simultaneous output of the two playback tape machines feeding into it.

We will place the reel containing crowd noises on Playback I, and the applause track on Playback II. Having checked the playback levels on these two machines, we will activate the recorder to the "record" position. Start Playback I with its fader control set at the level you wish to record. At the same time start Playback II with its fader control set at zero. At the desired time bring the sound on Playback II to full level while fading the sound from Playback I. A cross-fading from sound of voices to applause results. After holding applause full level from Playback II briefly, let Playback I begin to fade in (beginning at zero level), doing another cross-fade until applause (from II) has disappeared. This same procedure is followed to mix and cross-fade the music reel with the sound effects reel. Having accomplished this blend between crowd noises and applause and then between applause and music, remove the tapes from the playback equipment, add white leader, and identify the composite or mixed materials reel as the master ending.

Having now prepared all three reels, place your master voice tape on Playback I and your master voice-sound tape on Playback II. The third reel (master ending) will be held in reserve temporarily.

For our discussion we will assume that the sample script is the final portion of a complete show and that the narrator's voice is going to be heard cold (without benefit of preceding music or sound effects). At the split second following the word "itself," when we reach the Roosevelt voice saying "but fear itself," we will start Playback II (music) at full volume. After 12 seconds we will begin the fade of the music so that it can be heard as temporary background to the narrator's next speech. We have separated the music from sound by a length of leader tape corresponding in length to the number of seconds involved between the end of the music and the beginning of the crowd noise. When the narrator says "Roman poet as he addressed the Senate in 306 b.c.," we will gradually open the fader for Playback II (music) to full volume for ten seconds, then fade it behind the Roman poet's words, before moving it directly into full sound after his last word. At the end of the final sentence of Playback I (gavel raps), stop the recorder and playback equipment.

Rewind all the tapes and remove them from the playback machines. Replace them with the mixed tape you have just recorded (Playback I) and your master ending reel (Playback II). Move fast forward on Playback I to a spot just a few seconds before the gavel sound near the ending.

Place a new tape on the recorder, set your master mix on Playback I and begin recording. At that point where the gavel raps are heard, start Playback II, fading in full sound immediately after the last gavel rap. Let the master ending tape play on to completion. Splice the new mix onto the end of the master mix, making sure that all elements of the tape flow smoothly and naturally. You may set all this up on a precise pre-timed basis or you may wish to do one segment at a time in a series of several takes. If you choose the latter, don't forget to edit the final mixdown by taking out the overlapping sections.

Let us now take another look at the script as it is set up for the final mix, first as a segmented basis and then on a pre-timed basis:

SAMPLE SCRIPT ON TAPE

REEL I, PLAYBACK I (voices, gavel raps)		REEL II, PLAYBACK II (music, sound)
1. Narrator:	We live in strange times, fear-filled times, yet they are not so different from the days of World War II when Franklin Roosevelt said:	
2. Voice:	We have nothing to fear but fear itself.	
3. White leader:	15 seconds	1. Music: 15 seconds
4. Narrator:	Those were noble words, echoing the sentiments spoken by that unknown Roman poet as he addressed the Senate in 306 B.C.	2. Sound effects sneaking in behind
5. Poet:	Ye men of Rome, fear not the evils of this day. Rather fear the cowardly feelings which cause you to be afraid.	the word "Senate" and fading behind the voice of poet:

195

6. White leader:	15 seconds.	3. Music: 15 seconds
7. Narrator:	And in conclusion, I urge you to re-examine your motives, take renewed faith in the courage of our national heroes and believe in Almighty God, for:	
8. Voice II:	(echo chamber) If God is for you, who can be against you?	
9. Narrator:	With these words, I now declare this convention to be at an end.	
10. Gavel raps		4. Sound of applause, music, end-title, sound fade in and up full.

After mixing in this form and tying the over-lapping sections together, we may then add the master ending (No. 4) and our mix will be complete.

In this segmented mixing procedure, we have recorded the narrator's and Roosevelt's voices, with the music fading out completely by the time the narrator says, "noble words." We stopped at this point because we want to use this as an edit point in the final assembly of our tape. Stopping both playback machines, we prepare for segment 2 by returning to the beginning of the narrator's sentence: "Those were noble words." This provides us with an overlap. While recording it, activate Playback II at zero output so the sound can be faded behind the narrator's words: "Roman poet as he addressed the Senate in 306 B.C." The sound is brought up full and faded after 8 seconds for the entrance of the poet's voice: "Ye men of Rome." It then fades out entirely before he reaches the final words of the sentence. We continue recording the voice track momentarily in order to have another overlap at our edit point.

Segment 3 begins with the poet's words, "Ye men of Rome," and continues to the end of his speech. Segment 4 begins with music from Playback II at full volume. Fading after 12 seconds, it is out completely by the time the narrator says, "re-examine your motives." Continue recording beyond this point momentarily for overlap. Segment 5 begins at the beginning of the narrator's last speech in order to get an edit point at the comma-pause after the word "motives." It continues on through the rest of his speech and the gavel raps. The final segment begins with the last few words of the narrator's speech, with the master ending mix fading in from Playback II during the gavel raps. Continue recording to the end of master ending mix. The next step is to assemble and edit these individual segments as suggested.

In preparing a pre-timed mix situation, we must first carefully time all of the segments. Having done this we will set up our playback reel as follows:

PLAYBACK I	TIMING	PLAYBACK II
1. Narrator and voice	:23	white leader tape
2. White leader tape	:15	music :18
3. Narrator	:10	white leader :04
4. White leader	:10	sound :10
5. Poet	:06	sound fades :06
6. Poet	:04	white leader :04
7. White leader	:15	music :15 plus :05 to fade
8. Narrator to gavel raps	:16	white leader :13
9. Gavel raps	:04	master ending to completion

If we could stretch out our two tapes (one on Playback I, the other on Playback II) it might look something like the following illustration:

```
        Narrator           Nar.      Poet         Nar.- Gav.
  I. |▨▨▨▨▨| Leader |▨▨| L. |▨▨| Leader |▨▨▨▨|     Leader
        23           15   7  10  6  4    15       16    4
       ⇒

                    Music       Sound      Music - Fade      End Title
  II. | Leader |▨▨▨▨| L. |▨▨| L. |▨▨▨▨|     Leader  |▨▨▨▨▨|
          23        18   4  10  6  4       15    5   13      26
         ⇒
```

197

This form of mixing is more practical for you at the outset of your experience than it will be later, for as you become more adept, you will not need exactly-timed pieces of leader tape. As your experience continues, you will rely more and more on a stopwatch and a running time or accumulated timing sheet. This simply places the various segments of your script in order with the accurate time for each segment as well as their accumulated time, as the following chart indicates.

ITEMS	TIME	ACCUMULATED TIMING
Narrator and voice	:23	:23
Music	:15	:38
Narrator	:10	:48
Sound	:10	:58
Voice	:10	1:08
Music	:15	1:23
Narrator	:16	1:39
Sound (gavel)	:04	1:43
End title	:26	2:09

With such a sheet, we need not rely on setting up our tapes with white leader timed to exact length. Instead, we can rely on the times shown by our accumulated timing sheet, knowing that the music would enter at the end of the narrator's segment at :24, that the narrator would begin again at :39, etc. The addition, by the way, is accomplished simply be adding the seconds together and, if they exceed 60, change the 60 to one minute.

We suggest that you do not proceed beyond this point until after you have taken time out to use a script segment and go through the entire recording, editing and mixing process until you are reasonably sure you are familiar enough with it to continue.

The preceding record-edit-mix experiences fall into the category of relatively simple operations. You are limited in your mixing capability only by your available equipment. You may be fortunate enough to have a six or eight channel mixer, or a tandem hook-up between two mixers. If so, input can be set up to feed into any or all six channels. Such a hook-up would be diagrammed as follows:

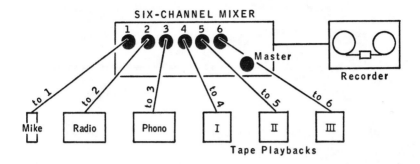

In professional recording studios where multi-track units are used, one can conceivably feed the output of an eight-track cartridge or reel-to-reel tapes by individual tracks or simultaneously to provide an almost infinite number of combinations. We will limit our treatment to the several channels feeding into a single-track recorder, however, since this will be the most commonly used unit for preparing media instructional materials.

Thus far we have demonstrated the use of two playbacks (with materials previously mixed) feeding into one recorder. In the illustration of the six-channel mixer, you can see the added potential of additional inputs (microphone, turntable, radio).

Another word of caution about mixing should be raised at this point. Sometimes you can get so far away from the original sound source that what started out to be a beautifully recorded sound is only a faint shadow of itself when compared to the original. These steps away from the original are referred to in dubbing-parlance as generations. When the master is dubbed it becomes the first generation. If the first generation (a copy of the original) is dubbed, it becomes the second generation. Be careful not to make that generation gap too wide, or the tape quality will decay enormously and you'll be hearing sibilants in the voice and high frequencies in the music. Look at the following illustration of decay rate in sound quality caused by dubbing from a dubbing.

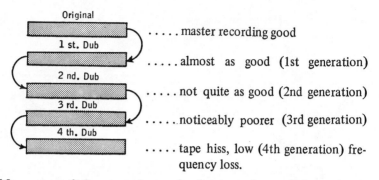

Move your faders evenly to obtain smoothness in bringing up or lowering the sound level. Always give yourself an "edit point" in mixes, even when you are dealing only in words. When mixing segments, allow yourself a re-recording of script materials beyond the edit point before mixing new materials. Provide yourself with an over-lap before continuing to the next segment so there will be sufficient space to join the two segments in a natural manner. Music is especially difficult to edit. Although an editor can take the "s" from a plural word and make it singular, or can edit in the middle of a two-syllable word, the skill needed for appropriate and un-noticeable editing of music demands practice and experience. Here are a few suggestions to help you.

In cutting from point to point in music, one may use the sound of a variety of percussion instruments, such as triangles, bells, drums, chimes and gongs. Cutting at the precise point of sound entry to another similar instrument or percussive sound (provided key relationships are not too jarring) will help you. Music also has pauses which can be used. Remember, however, never eliminate the room tone that follows such a pause. In addition, one may edit on a phrase-to-phrase concept—that is, musically identical phrases become editing points. It is also possible to connect two pieces of music by the cross-fade technique, particularly if it is to be used as background music. Key relationship and tempo are determining factors in the success of this procedure of editing music.

Let me add to your growing range of knowledge by telling you how to transfer phonograph recorded sound to tape.

200

Using a standard turntable, patch its output line into the input of your mixer. Then take the output of the mixer into the input of your tape recorder. Set your mixer levels with a mixer which has a built-in test tone, a test-tone tape or, if your ear is good, you may do it that way. With the VU meters of both the mixer and the receiving tape recorder indicating the same reading, you are ready to begin. Before doing a great deal, however, I would advise a recording check to let your ear determine whether the tape sound is the same as the playback sound from the turntable. Band each musical selection with leader tape and don't forget to let the normal room tone following the last notes of the selection also be heard or the music will have a "chopped-off" effect. Music recorded from low-level sources will invariably (as you raise the level on your tape) have a noise level that is incompatible for general use.

Another useful and practical bit of information is back timing. In order to have your end-title emerge at just the proper time following the last word, or to have specific music cues emerge at a split-second time in the script, one must learn to back time. To do this, you may mark the beginning of the cue with a long piece of splicing tape. This splicing tape is used only for your convenience in locating the exact spot on the tape in the event you miss it the first time. In the figure below, we show you a tape recorder with A and B reels. After you have marked the cue entry with splicing tape, reverse the reels so that the music will now sound backwards instead of its natural progression of sounds. Reel A is now put where Reel B was. The cue marking is placed at the playback head.

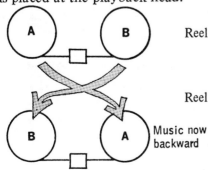

Reel A: normal playback mode. Cue has been marked with splicing tape.

Reel B: reverse direction of tape. Music will sound backward. Cue marking placed on playback head.

201

Having previously timed the segment of the script, knowing precisely where you want the music to emerge at full sound, and having planned the point in the script where you want the music to sneak in behind the words, you now press the play tab on your playback unit and let the music play backwards the exact number of seconds required. After stopping the machine, place another piece of splicing tape at that point where the tape is on the playback head (again, for your convenience). Reverse the reels to their normal play mode.

With your script materials on one playback machine, your music materials on another, start both machines and the tape recorder simultaneously. Your music track should be at zero level. At the point designated in your script to sneak in music, gradually turn your fader to hear music at its desired level.

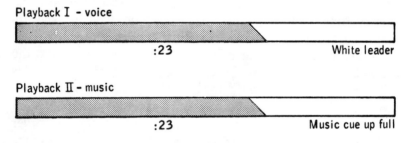

Playback I - voice

:23   White leader

Playback II - music

:23   Music cue up full

ZERO LEVEL - GRADUAL SNEAK

At the exact second on your stopwatch, or immediately following the last word of your script, turn the fader full volume to achieve the musical effect you want. If you have timed both script and music accurately, it will occur at the very point you wanted it.

The audio-tape editor is important to the production team, for he is responsible for a successful sound track. His skill demands a good ear, imaginative manipulation of the sound resources and much patience. If you are involved in any way with media, your success more often than not will depend largely upon the successful preparation of the audio materials.

202

Unless you are in an institution which provides such skilled staff support, or even if you're not, I would suggest you learn how to perform this vital task.

CHAPTER XI

THE MEDIA LIBRARY

There is an old axiom which goes, "If you have two of anything, you will not be able to find the one you want when you want it." This is probably exaggerated, but it serves to lead us into our discussion of how to take care of the components involved in the production of media materials—*after* we have produced them. They must be cared for if we don't want to work in a chaotic state leading to countless lost hours trying to find things or duplicating lost and mislaid materials.

For ideal service to your institution all media materials should be contained within your assigned storage and catalog areas. Many institutions allow departments to buy their own media collections. This is fine for those who do not utilize media beyond the classroom, but for any co-ordinated program of media instruction involving Learning Centers or Media Library Services, all such materials should be placed in a single collection. Until this gathering together is done, no unified program can succeed.

Ideally, this collection should be presided over by a resource person who needs to have had functional experience in the production of media in addition to library experience itself. While the collection may be a part of general library services, its specific use is primarily for Media Instructional Production services and only secondarily for classroom and library use. Therefore this writing will acquaint you with practical methods in arranging and cataloging media materials so that you may store them efficiently and retrieve them easily.

I. 35mm. Slides.

There are several existing systems for cataloging slides. Most of them relate to specific subject areas and have been developed by professional associations with emphasis placed on their particular subject matter. All of these work well enough to serve the needs of these special disciplines, but for the most part, they are collections of only a few hundred slides. Since we will be dealing with slides numbering in the multi-thousands, our suggested method utilizes a different approach: one developed at Dallas Baptist College by Carol Ann Mills under the supervision of the Director of Library Services, Margaret Gibbs. This plan, with some modifications, will be offered as a workable, efficient procedure.

It involves a basic cataloging system using combinations of four letters of the alphabet as its code: AAAA, AAAB, AAAC, etc., culminating with ZZZZ. This four-letter combination allows for almost 500,000 listings and doesn't (at least not too often) spell out such dirty words as DIRT. This letter grouping has nothing whatsoever to do with classification or categorization of slides, for it merely indicates the shelf position of the slide, which in this case is a tray. Classification and categorization of slides appear in the card index file as well as in a loose-leaf notebook which devotes a single page to each slide. Writing space on a 35mm. slide is very limited. Although additional classification systems can be placed on the slide, it is of dubious advantage. However, if such a system is desired, one might adopt a code comprised of such abbreviations as MUS (music), SCI (science), BUS (business), EDU (education), REL (religion), PSY (psychology) and ETC (and so forth). Further categorization may be added, such as HF (historical figures) and IA (Italian Art), but it gets complicated quite rapidly.

Under sub-classifications in the card file a listing of all slides representing historic figures and Italian Art, can be made, making sub-classifications of photographs, drawings, paintings, statues, etc. This is certainly more practical in the card-file and notebook than it is on the slide. On the slide itself the entry should be kept simple.

The assortment of letters and numbers in this illustration may be translated as follows: GFKP-2 means that the slide is filed in the tray holding GFKP items and the "2" indicates it is a duplicate of the original. HF-515 means it is the 515th slide in a series classified under historical figures, with a cross-reference classification number. In the long run, this additional information on the slide itself would not help locate it—so, at the risk of being redundant, let me adjure you to stick to the RITE (or four-letter) system.

You will need to make slide withdrawal and duplication forms. The following samples might be appropriate:

SLIDE WITHDRAWAL FORM

Issued to: _____

Slide Code: HCNP, JJOK, FFRR, MNDA, FOXY

Use: 494 in the lab category of science slides.

Signature: _____

Another form may be used for duplication orders.

SLIDE DUPLICATION FORM

Slides to be duplicated:

Date needed:

Copies of each needed:

Person or department charged:

Account number (if inter-department charge):

Signature of requesting agent: _____

Date slides ordered:

Processing company:

Date slides delivered:

Signature of receiving personnel: _____

The information in the loose-leaf notebook record should include the type, source, format, number and variations of copies available as well as the date, place, practical adaptability and other pertinent comments. In addition a black and white film strip copy of the actual slide itself should be pasted into the notebook as well as on the master copy of the script.

The corresponding file card should include the:

Catalog number:	
Type:	Art work, Blue Boy, Gainsborough
Source, Date:	Art Reproductions, Vol. II, p. 647
Description, usage:	Upper body view only.
Usage:	Adventures in Art, unit 3
	Western Civilization, unit 17
	Curtain Going Up, unit 34
Variations:	AABC, ABDN, SSPT
Photographer:	(date made)
For video use:	Yes ____ No ____
Video rights secured:	Yes ____ No ____

This information can now be cross-filed. The shelf card can be listed under Art, artists, nation, period, etc.

In such a system, for instance, the "Blue Boy" of Gainsborough could be listed under the general classification "Art," under alphabetical listing "Paintings," under "Painters," "English Painters," or "18th-Century Paintings." The more materials are cross-filed, the less time it will take to locate them when they are to be used and greater the assistance the catalog system will be to the media research teams using it.

The loose-leaf notebook should list all the cross references. A page on the painting we just mentioned might include the following information:

Catalog number:	AABA
Title:	Blue Boy
Artist:	Gainsborough
Source:	Art Reproductions, Volume II, pg. 647, pub. Jones Press, 405½ Peachtree Lane, Atlanta, Georgia, 1917. (Add General Library card catalog number.)

Rights:	Duplication rights secured for class viewing, closed circuit TV only.
Suitability for video:	Good. Color values and positioning okay.
Description:	Head and shoulders shot, upper body view.
Variants:	Full length study under AABC, face only ABDN, detail of right hand and sleeve area SSTP.
BW film reproduction:	(paste the print of the slide in BW.)
Use:	Adventures in Art, unit 3 (slide 13) Western Civilization, unit 17 (side 82) Curtain Going Up, unit 34 (slide 56) History of Art: 18th-Century English Art, unit 7 (slide 12)

Also included would be the photographer's name and date photographed, for whom the slide was originally made, and if the slide is on permanent loan to a slide-tape package and any other pertinent information the librarian chooses to add.

Let's take a moment to review:

a. Select the four letters of the alphabet to code your individual slides. Example: AABC. Add, if you like, the number indicating the copies of the slide you have available: AABC-3.

b. Shelve these slides (in trays) under the broad general classification suggested by the code itself. Example: AAAA to AAAZ 26 slides, then add tray marked AABA, etc., until ZZZZ is reached.

This provides 456,976 possible letter combinations. If it is insufficient continue by using five-letter codes beginning with AAAAA. This will provide (heaven help you) 11,881,276 possibilities.

c. Prepare a card file listing.

d. Prepare a cross-reference card file under general headings of subject, names of people, countries, eras, etc.

e. Prepare a loose-leaf notebook with one page devoted to each slide. It should contain complete information from all cross-reference cards and shelf card as well as a detailed description of slide and a small BW photoreproduction of the slide itself.

2. Provide a viewing area under staff direction to service the customer to reduce damage and theft.
3. When a slide is checked out for viewing or duplication, make a penciled card to indicate pertinent information. Example: AACD being duplicated, request Chm. Dept. English 9/14/89. This card can be taken out when the slide is again back in tray position.
4. Tag file cards for slides having restricted use.
5. Store your slides in a dust-free, humidity controlled area.

Slides are expensive even when purchased commercially. Customized slide production and cataloging costs still more. Keep your cataloging system up to date by insisting that all slide processing be handled quickly and cataloging done prior to use. Develop a number of handy forms for check-out, duplication and photography requests. In training staff to help meet the demands of the media library, insist on having one person who can be responsible for the task.

II. Scripts.

A script is the basic content of the media instructional unit in written form. In the event there are no written words, it is the detailed outline of the structure of the unit. A script as produced should be filed, with at least one duplicate in the Master Script File. It may be listed in the catalog under title, author, subject, catalog course and alphabetical listing.

In the card file and notebook information may be entered as follows:

Title:	Making of a Dictator, The
Writer:	Enstam, Elizabeth
Catalog course number:	History 123
Unit number:	7, Part I
File number:	42, drawer 3
Master Audio Tape:	A6015
Master Video Tape:	V3311
Master Voice-only Audio:	MV2170
Master sound-music mix:	MSM6735
Production notes filed:	File 62, Drawer 6 under Title: "Making of a Dictator"; Writer, Enstam; Script File 42, drawer 3.

Some organizations use mimeo script copies. If so, arrange a similar file for the master stencils by title, writer, subject area and alphabetical listing. Each script should be filed in a properly labeled manila file folder.

III. Production Notes.

Production notes are required for the unit. These notes should contain a complete report from the director. Production notes are valuable materials, particularly in the event of having to redo or revise the production. They should include his script, a list of his materials and personnel, the date and location of the final taping, a sketch or photograph of studio set, a list of props and costumes and a lighting cue sheet. The director's report should be rendered as fully as possible.

IV. Graphics

For filing and cataloging purposes, all materials used in visual sequences of media production (except slides and titled motion pictures) will be included as graphics. Anything defined as a media graphic should be coded, cataloged and stored.

If a graphic is photographed to make a slide or an enlarged print, each one should be cataloged: the slide as a slide, the photograph as a photograph and the original as such. Photographing a graphic should be done as a matter of regular procedure because of the time and money involved. Should the original be lost, the graphics artist could recreate it from a slide or photograph.

Since there are so many types of graphics, they should be placed in categories such as cartoons, transparencies, overlays, word cards, titles, etc. As with slides, a card catalog and a loose-leaf notebook file should be made. Here is a sample file card entry:

Graphic number:	Gr-207
Graphic type:	Line drawing, color BG, plus collage involving newsprint
Artist	McGee
Date completed:	6/24/71

Made for: Chm. Arts Division
Slide file code: HPBS
Photo-print enlargement:
Photo-print file code: GRP-600, Photo-file 25, drawer 3
Use: Career Investigation

This card may be cross-referenced into its several sub-classifications. In the notebook listing a more detailed description and strip print of the graphic itself may be provided.

Large photographs and photographic print-reproductions are commercially available in a variety of disciplines. Such collections can add immeasureably to the flexibility of the illustrative potential and should be acquired. This form of graphic should be cataloged and coded under either photo-print or photographic reproduction.

The basic principles of coding slides and scripts should be applied to graphics. Storage may be more complicated because of the lack of uniformity in size. Storage units other than the usual file cabinets are manufactured for this purpose and are listed in any standard equipment catalog.

V. Recordings.

In the good old days when records came in a variety of sizes, speeds and shapes (there used to be cylinders and heavy half-inch thick discs), recordings were a big bother to catalog and store. Now that the market has a two-size, two speed format it is still a bother, but not quite as big as it used to be. There still may be some 10-inch LP and some 78 RPM singles around of course, as well as multi-record boxed collections, but all-in-all cataloging and storing these is simple.

For analysis of the cataloging problem a 33 RPM recording has been selected. Its title is *Dvorak's Greatest Hits* and it contains only music by Anton Dvorak (1841-1904) of Prague. Already two things are noted: Dvorak may be listed under a broad category of composers and under a specific category of Czechoslavakian or 19th-Century composers. A further sub-categorization of the composer's works could include symphonies, operas, songs, overtures, string quartets, dances, keyboard works, religious works, solo instrument works and cantatas. Most likely, the majority of these categories would be placed under "Dvorak" in the composer classification.

Just as there is no real advantage in trying to arrange shelving space under specific categories of titles, types, etc., there is no advantage in developing a code number that includes categories. Since the slide catalog procedure works so well, it could be used again or a six-digit number system preceded by an R (meaning "recording") could be adopted. In the event separate storage areas are needed for 10-inch LPs and 45s, a different letter could indicate them, such as "T" for 10 inch and "S" for 45s. All this gets complicated, however, so the standard, six-digit system for all recordings is suggested. It includes all sizes, speeds and collections. It will also allow up to 999,998 listings.

These numbers should be placed on the front and back of the record jacket, label, card file and loose-leaf notebook. The following illustration shows how these entries are interrelated:

R-000001	
(Jacket)	

Cat. Code:	R-000001
Title:	Dvorak's Greatest Hits
Composer:	Dvorak, Anton
Record serial number:	Columbia, MS-7524
Library of Congress catalog number:	76-751006
Speed (circle):	33 45 78 Stereo Mono
Information on jacket:	Program notes, titles, times, arrangers, conductors, orchestras.
Tape copy made and code (circle):	yes no
Tape Box number:	TBS-413
Composition titles:	(see listing in notebook file)
Condition of record:	Good Fair Poor

In the loose-leaf notebook enter the code file card information and other pertinent data. Some of it could include details listed on that card, such as Side I: Performers, Times, Rights; Side II: Titles, Performers, Times, Rights.

The rights column is very important, for it would identify the holder of the copyright, such as ASCAP, BMI, CESAC, a publisher or PD (public domain). Even if the rights are PD, there may still be performance use rights which must be obtained from the recording company producing the disc. Do not forget to red-tag a record which has restricted use.

The information obtained from *Dvorak's Greatest Hits* shows the necessity of making cross references. There is additional pertinent information on the record jacket itself as well as data on design, graphics and illustration. This particular record jacket has an advertising blurb that indicates *Dvorak's Greatest Hits* is one of a series of a dozen or so similar albums of "greatest hits" by various composers. Such a series could be worthy of a special listing along with specialized subject area groupings such as poetry, drama, language, lectures, composers, performers, poets or dramatists.

Many varieties of cross-references are needed to use record holdings efficiently. Under normal use a record catalog would not need so many sub-classifications, but in dealing in media, it is essential that maximum information be provided to writers, directors and researchers. Do not hesitate to build sub-classifications in detail, such as various soloists, groups of vocalists, instrumentalists, orchestras, readers, dramatists, etc.

Recordings should be stored in a dust-free, humidity-controlled area. They should be stored on edge rather than flat. Under coding system suggested shelf space might be arranged as follows:

R-000001 to R-000025	R-000026 to R-000050	R-000051 to R000075

213

There should be at least two play-back booths for record auditioning. Appropriate withdrawal and restricted permission slips should be prepared. The record library should not be a classroom service, but be restricted to media personnel use only. When acquisitions are made, order a tape duplicate immediately and file it under proper TBX (tape box) number.

Recordings are like magazines: fresh off the press they are easy to replace if damaged or lost. As time passes they become harder and harder to secure due to the transient nature of the record business. Recordings must be cared for constantly, for they deteriorate rapidly whether or not they are in use. Check them regularly for any fungus growth and cleanse them with warm water and a mild soap before drying them with a chamois or very soft cloth. When a playing record becomes scratchy or filled with clicks and pops, withdraw it from the catalog for replacement (if possible with a new copy).

VI. Music Materials.

Although many music materials are actually recordings, they are discussed separately because they are as often tapes and do not fit into the regular connotation of normal compositional trends. Instead these materials relate to that body called "cue" or "mood" music. Procuring functional music materials for production is a never-ending task. Taped or recorded music libraries have, however, been created for this specific purpose and are available for lease or purchase, although one may make materials for himself by dubbing them from phonograph records.

Obtaining your cue music from a standard Music Track Library Service is the safest approach, for usually they also provide clearance privileges. Having a music library especially written for you is even safer, but far more expensive, of course. Be careful that your dubbing of music does not infringe upon the proprietary or performance rights of others.

These will include music for opening and closing titles, themes as well as pastoral and urban music, mysterious music, bright "travel" music, mechanical music, dance music, etc. In short, you will run the gamut of music types and moods, all of which should be indicated on the filing card of the media library.

If possible, individual music types should be gathered together into a single reel area. Each selection, with its playing time, rights and record source should then be listed in the notebook file by box content:

MUS-SOLemn, TBX-11

BAND NUMBER	TIMING	RIGHTS	RECORD SOURCE
1. Gloomy Day	1:53	Chappel, Inc.	R-243790
2. Dark Emptiness	2:07	Sam Fox, Inc.	R-001361
3. Morbid Mood	3:19	Ricordi, Inc.	R-222552
4. Blue Funk	2:27	Boosey-Hawkes	R-512321
5. Low and Lonely	4:11	Boosey-Hawkes	R-512321
6. Midnight Sorrow	1:15	Sam Fox, Inc.	R-001361
7. Solemn Mood	2:45	Boosey-Hawkes	R-512321

This material should also be placed on the inside of the front lid of the tape box, the reel and front cover of the box as well as the properly labeled spine. Each music cue would be banded by separating the cues with white leader tape for convenient location.

These classifications can be cross-indexed into categories such as "tempo" (fast, slow, medium), "mood" (sorrow, happiness, neutral), "rhythm" (bright, Latin, Spanish, martial), "dance" (rock, blues, minuets, bolero), "travel" (music which moves to indicate transfer from one point to another), etc. Coding can still be listed as MUS-Dance, MUS-Mood with a TPBX (tape box) number added. Some cue types would be cross-indexed in several various listings, such as "sadly, brightly, mysteriously," "brightly, sadly, excitedly," etc. These should be designated as "mood changers" and so classified. Short items such as stings and stabs punctuate suddenly and then fade into the background. These too can be separately listed along with their times and sources. Acquiring a sound-track library will help solve some of these category problems for their listings are generally described in detail.

Provide a listening area for the director or writer searching for cue music types. Give him a duplicate tape or record source rather than the original for use in his production. If he's orderly he'll make his duplications in the order he intends to use them in his unit and save time in the long run and you will still have your original source.

VII. Sound Effects.

We will discuss three general areas of sound effects: those created manually using sound-effect props, those commercially produced on records and tapes and those privately recorded on tape.

The use of sound-effect props may prove to be too limited to justify the expense of buying or building them. Nevertheless, they may be classified by their sounds and the props themselves coded under equipment times. Of greater concern is the vast body of effects available on record and tape.

Since these effects are generally of short duration, rarely exceeding a few seconds, it is good to review the entire list available before arranging them (by categories) to be stored on tape reels or among general recordings. Let's assume that a large assortment of a wide variety of sounds has been requested. You may choose to use tape exclusively in actual production, since recordings are difficult to handle. If so, transfer the material directly to tape.

Divide these materials into such general categories as animals, birds, human, automotive, railroad, aviation sounds, etc. Further categories, such as factories, street traffic, crowds, bells, clocks, screams, laughter, gunshots, etc., may also be used. Under each category list and describe the individual effect and timing. Under some categories there may be enough variety to sub-classify. For example, guns could be sub-classified, with one of those classifications being rifle. Under "guns" further descriptions could be listed to include a close up sound, single shot, repeat fire, richochet, multi-fire simultaneous (funeral or firing squad), and one could continue

216

classifying the sounds of M-1, Civil War, etc. Once the general classification, timing and description are arranged, these sounds should be placed together on reels within that classification. This is a time-consuming effort, but doing it initially will save time. A single reel may be used for each classification, with the code SE (sound effects) and a number. A file card would look rather simple, as illustrated here:

SE-1, Bells (20 varieties of bell sounds)

SE-2, Clocks (32 effects)

The corresponding listing for SE-1 would be more complete as the following example shows:

BAND NUMBER	TIME	DESCRIPTION	RECORDING SOURCE
1. Small clock alarm	:22	Alarm bell rings	R-223344
2. Large clock alarm	:25	Rings 4 times	R-200001
3. Fight area bell	:25	4 fast medium-distant clangs	R-223344
4. School Bell	:30	Large, fairly close, handbell	R-200017
5. School Bell	:30	Distant, Belfry type	R-200017
6. Door Bell	:20	"Avon calling" type	R-223344
7. Locomotive Bell	:32	Constant dinging intermingled with engine sounds	R-197230

How are sounds to be classified? First code letters and numbers such as SE-1, SE-2, are developed. These are followed by general sounds to be found on the reel: SE-1-Bells. Acquisitions made following catalog completion should be added to the end of the list.

Each box of sound effects will have its own card file, with an alphabetical file for each sound effect card. For bird sounds, for example, there would be a card entry on the sound, its time and description as well as its master box number and source. Having listed everything from orioles to whooping cranes under such an entry, and having them listed alphabetically in this classification, the researcher wanting a particular sound will be able to locate it quickly.

Having found its location, the tape box can be taken from the shelf. On its inside cover are listed all effects contained on the reel. Be sure the reel is labeled with the same number as the tape box.

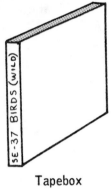

Tapebox	Reel (Label both sides)

Since all tape boxes and reels look alike, be sure to label each one clearly. Let me remind you again not to issue these master reels for production use. Duplicate the effect desired and transfer it to a show tape reel.

VIII. Master Audio/Video Tapes.

When a master show tape has been completed it should be catalogued and stored. In all instances cataloging should be related to title, series title, subject area and type.

The code can be a simple "A" for audio followed by a shelf-storage plus standard abbreviations for discipline or catalog curriculum number, series number and unit title. An example could be A-175, SCI-BIO-113-7: A-175 (shelf position) SCI-(science) BIO-113-(catalog course number, Biology 113) 7: (unit of series). An audio tape box spine has limited label space, but there is enough room for this information. A similar listing should be placed on the front of the tape box. Always make sure that the shelving number is cross-filed with the script filing position.

The "V" series, indicating video tape, would be coded in a similar way, containing the same information except that "V" listing in front of your number: V-175, SCI-BIO-113-7 "Invertebrates," Part I. Because video-tape containers are

218

larger, more detailed information can be listed if desired. Do not forget to label the reels with code number also. Shelving video-tapes requires more space than audio tapes, and because productions are completed piecemeal, they should not be stored by series. The shelf number alone is sufficient.

Let me stress once again the importance of providing information relating to master tapes and scripts. The script is listed in the master script catalog. The entry V-128, HIS-123-7, Part I "The Making of a Dictator, Hitler," would indicate shelving as well as several facts about the contents. Shelf space V-128 is assigned to the video tape containing History 123, unit 7, the introductory portion of the unit. The script file indicates this shelf position and the video tape master file indicates the location of the script file drawer. If there are hand-out materials, handbooks or required assignments, corresponding numbers should be indicated. Otherwise, such materials should be filed with the master script.

Each tape should also be filed under its author, title, discipline and its shelf location. As suggested earlier, do not hesitate to over inform in the loose-leaf notebook. Cross-file to the extent that intelligent research can be done. Provide the fullest service for identifying the master tape, ascertaining its content and locating its source materials.

IX. *Voice and Mix Tracks.*

In producing materials for audio and video use, master voice and sound-music tracks are involved. The first contains the voice of the narrator and others. The second refers to music, sound effects, special effects, etc. Sometimes film sequences are also placed on video tape for insertion into the master video tape. Our discussion here will be limited to the audio tracks of voice and sound-music.

These are important items to keep if only because they are difficult to re-assemble in the event the finished master tape is damaged or lost. A simple code such as AMV (Audio Master Voice) plus a shelf number (AMV-111) can be used for the voice track, an AMSM code and number (AMSM-154) can represent the Audio Music Sound Mix of the composite

219

sound-music reel. In both instances the code and shelf number should include reference to the finished production item. Thus AMV-111 would be followed by MV-2106 (Master Video 2106) and, if separate audio tape is available, A6015, HIS-253-9. The AMV-111, HIS-253-9 would refer to the master voice track used in preparing unit 9 in History 253, and AMSM-HIS-253-9 would locate the materials of music and sound effects used in that same unit.

The general procedures used in listing sound effects and music cue items should be followed to indicate the audio tape box and to label reels and boxes.

X. Film Loops, Filmstrips, Film Clips, Titled Films.

Many media libraries contain a wide variety of subject areas in packaged units called film strips, loops, clips and complete motion pictures produced for educational purposes. Most of these are obtained from commercial packaging agencies. Frequently rights may be secured to transfer them to video-tape for use in closed-circuit TV. Those for which rights cannot be obtained must not be included in media packages involving video-taping.

Filmstrips are collections of transparencies designed to illustrate a subject area. Film loops are also generally issued in series. These are made up of films arranged in a loop sequence so that rewinding is unnecessary. These convenient insert items are mostly silent and the majority are BW. Film clips are selected segments from other films which are taken out (or purchased as such) to serve as specialized visual illustrations. Out-takes from newsreels or segmented sections from discarded motion pictures can also be classified as film clips. Motion pictures include the broad spectrum of either 8, super-8, or 16mm. films produced commercially or personally cover a large area of instructional materials.

Storing such materials creates an unusual problem because the packaging in each instance is so different. Film loops and strips are normally packaged in small boxes of dissimilar size, while film clips and regular motion pictures are packaged in film cans. All film cans are not the same size, varying with

220

the size of film. There is, however, a general similarity in cataloging these items. It begins by selecting letter codes representing each, and follows that by a shelf-space location number: e.g., FL-17 (Film loop). If this were part of a specialized subject area such as baseball, the cataloging might read FL-17, Phy. Ed-113-BB-1, "The Pitcher." Another film loop series representing World War II in several separate units could include such titles as: The Eastern Front, The Luftwaffe, Dunkirke, Normandy Landing, Submarine Warfare, Dachau, The RAF, U. S. Convoy to Minsk, Pearl Harbor, The Atom Bomb: Hiroshima, etc. Obviously a filing system which reflects titles is needed, as is information on the product source (distributor or producer), running time lapse and the discipline for which it was obtained. A filing card might have the following information on it:

Catalog Code:	F1-227, HIS-253-WWII-a, The Eastern Front
Time:	7:05
Description:	scenes involving refugees, dive bombing, battle areas, tank fighting, horse-drawn cannon, Russian troops in retreat, bivouacs, weather. For scene-by-scene description, see notebook file: FL-227.
Source:	American Heritage, Code WWII.

This information can be translated to indicate that the first unit of the World War II series, "The Eastern Front," was stored in shelf space 227. It is seven minutes and five seconds in duration and a full description of its contents can be found in the corresponding Code number of the Notebook File. A separate card should be used for an alphabetical listing of subject titles.

An identical file procedure could be used, coding filmstrips as FS, film clips as FC and motion pictures as MP, adding a number indicating whether it is 8mm., super-8, or 16mm. Such a listing for a super-8 film might be coded simply as MP-S8-112. The key to successful cataloging of these materials is the detailed analysis of their content to provide that information for the researcher. Motion picture producers will occasionally provide a scene-by-scene breakdown of the film, but not often enough to depend on it. A detailed analysis of the film in each instance (keeping a running time in seconds or footage) will prove most valuable.

XI. Check-out Packages in Media.

Sometimes media libraries are asked to maintain and issue additional instructional units. These generally include cassette audio tapes, cassette video tapes, video tape units and slide-tape packages. These should be listed as separate items in the card filing system and identified with their original sources. For example, a slide-tape package is built, using the same materials which were used to create a video production of Biology 113 unit 3, "The Respiratory System." This package would include a carousel tray of slides to be displayed as well as an audio cassette or reel-to-reel tape. A general code could be built to cover all these items using AC (audio cassette), AV (audio-visual), ST (slide tape), VC (video cassette) or VT (video tape) with the holding and shelf space number added. A sample card entry could include the following:

Catalog Code:	AVST-29
Media listing:	A217, V3726-English 113-1
Title:	The Dallas Baptist College Learning Center
Pulse-sync (circle):	yes no audio cassette only
General subject area:	Orientation to Learning Center
Authorized for use:	classroom, library, public meetings
Authorized personnel:	faculty and staff only
Detailed description:	see Eng. 113, V3726

From this we learn that there is a slide tape package available for checkout to faculty and staff which is a carousel tray with slides and audio cassette tape (previously pulsed to automate the projector). It is part of Audio series A217 and Video V3726, having an orientation feature for students and visitors to the campus. This item was prepared as part of English 113. It is stored as item 29 in the AVST package shelving and a detailed analysis of its contents may

222

be found under the unit description of Eng. 113. Finally, it may be previewed as media item V3726.

Shelving may become difficult in slide-tape packages if reel-to-reel tape is used, so audio cassette playback units are preferable because they may be included in the carousel tray box. Video cassettes, individual audio cassettes and individual video reels are also dissimilar in size and shelving may be a problem. All such checkout packages should be cataloged under the general heading of AV and cross-filed alphabetically under title, type and curriculum course number in the previously described materials.

Many schools will provide a complete set of audio or video tapes required for student hearing or viewing. These units are often complete with handbooks, exams, handouts, etc., in those areas were individualized instruction is the keystone of the educational progression. These may be handled in the general library area, but are developed and issued by the media library. All four types of checkout packages are included, generally in multi-copies.

Since the AVST packages require slides that should be on file, be sure that these AVST packages consist of duplicate slides, appropriately numbered. This also applies to other packages. Under no circumstances should the master be issued for use. Sometimes scripts are also required, when the pulse sync has not been put on the cassette tape for AVST. In this instance, make sure that the script has been marked at each point where a new slide is to be shown.

XII. The General Library.

The media library can be of utmost service to the general library by servicing check-out packaging and providing master card files of all audio-video units used in media instruction. The first function is important, the latter indeed is vital. Media holdings now become a central factor in any library dealing with instructional methods in any phase of media beyond print. Duplicates of the AV card file may be on hand at the checkout desk, but centrally designated area should be provided for the important master media file card system. All audio and video units should be listed by title, general topic and use. Any institution advocating correlated teaching will find this system invaluable. For example, a Biology teacher may well want to have his students view a unit made for History in order to get the feel of the era which produced certain biological advancements. Perhaps a music teacher may want to integrate his general teaching of music of the Greeks with a History unit on Greek Civilization. A sample card with this information could include the following entries:

Title: Learning Center Orientation

Code: A217, V3726, AVST-29 (also available AVVT in 1", ½" and ¼" tape).

Made for: English 113, unit 1 (see deatiled description under English 113-1), script on file Media Library, cabinet 47, drawer 3.

Possible use: All students, all teachers, all visitors, public viewings with AVST-29.

Number of copies: A217 (3), V3726 (4), AVST-29 (3).

Time: 27 minutes, Color AVST, BW-video.

Synopsis: Visitor is taken on tour of the Dallas Baptist College Learning Center, shown the location of the principal facilities, taught function and use of operating carrels and visits production centers.

Object: General orientation prior to live tour of center with guide.

Production process: (for all except AVST) video tape using motion pictures, slides and pre-recorded sound track.

Note: Video tape transferred to 16mm. film (color) available to recruiting personnel and public TV.

A recap on the advice given to this point can be reduced to three words: accuracy, diligence and creativity. The library must service the needs of its clients. It can do this best when an accurate accounting of what is in the collection and where it is located has been placed within an easily-understood set of filing statements. To comprehend the purpose of the library, why it was founded and what use will be made of its holdings, overlaps accuracy and gets into the diligence. The librarian needs to understand the processes involved in bringing about creativity in its holdings. With this trio of impetus-factors, the gigantic jig-saw puzzle will neatly arrange into a completed whole.

The curator for such a media library should, in addition to being schooled in library science, have training in media. Hopefully this will be in a functional way as a part of production crew. The librarian must be an imaginative and creative person, capable of a communative relationship with all personnel with whom he comes into contact. He must be one who is content to serve two masters: the Director of the Library and the Director of Media Instruction. Above all, the media librarian must be a person of infinite patience, for the work demands much to fulfill 'the endless needs of media production. Given a proper budget, space, facilities, staff and time, the media librarian will command a position once occupied only by gods and heads of states. The media librarian is the one from whom all "boons" must be begged, if indeed there is to be any production at all.

Try it on as a career potential. If it fits, wear the mantle proudly, for you will serve the media arts well by making it possible for them to function efficiently and creatively. Never forget, if there are two of anything, you—the media librarian— are the person who knows where the other one is.

225

CHAPTER XII

TELEVISION PHOTOGRAPHY

Photography for television and motion pictures for instructional media is a specialized skill requiring special photographic equipment and extensive training. In addition to his adeptness in all facets of general photography, the photographer must also be sensitive to the demands of the television format and movie production. This chapter will be devoted to a brief discussion of the equipment and requirements for both types of photography will be examined. First let's look at TV photography, later in the chapter we will look into motion pictures.

There are two basic types of photography used in television: photographs used in the studio on an easel and 35mm. slides used in film chain. Almost any camera which can produce enlargements of 11 x 14 inches with adequate sharpness and contrast will suffice for studio work. Careful work with a 35mm. focusing camera can produce results acceptable for studio enlargements. As noted in the chapter on Graphics, care must be taken when photographing materials for black and white television use. There must be enough contrast in the color values to provide good subject-background separation. Filters may be needed to render certain colors lighter or darker for good gray scale separation. Certainly the format or size of the photography must be kept in mind when preparing visual materials for television. The television camera produces a picture which has a 3:4 aspect ratio; that is, it is three units high and four units wide. Since the 35mm. format is 3:4.5 and 2¼" x 2¼" or Instamatic formats are square, allowances must be made in printing and mounting them. Either the

226

mounting board must be large enough to provide a border to adequately frame the picture for the television camera or the picture must be printed with the frame cropped to a 3:4 ratio. Past experience has shown that mounting the pictures on oversize boards provides the best results, since not all pictures can be cropped to the 3:4 aspect ratio and maintain their compositional impact. Photographs should be mounted in a dry-mounting press. White or rubber glue does not provide a lasting bond and may have disastrous side effects. They may fade, buckle and peel off of the mounting board. Pictures should be printed on a non-gloss surface to prevent glare and reflections in the studio. If possible, the mounting boards should be gray or some color other than white. Television cameras do not process a stark white very well.

Photography for the television film chain must be of the 2 x 2 inch transparency variety. Commonly called "slides," they may be 35mm., 4 x 4cm. (superslide) or Instamatic. The 3:4 aspect ratio still holds for film chain photography. In all of the above-mentioned transparency formats, some loss of picture material will result and this must be taken into consideration during the photographing process. While any camera producing a 2 x 2 inch transparency may be used in a film chain, the 35mm. camera has gained wide acceptance as standard. The requirements for a 35mm. camera to be used for television transparency photocopy work are as follows:

1. single-lens-reflex (through-the-lens viewing)
2. 50mm. to 55mm. macro lens capable of focusing to 1:1 reproduction
3. interchangeable or easily accessible viewing screen.

Another photographer might make many other requirements depending upon special needs and personal biases, but these three appear to be basic.

The single-lens-reflex camera provides through-the-lens viewing which eliminates all parallax error; that is, the picture seen through the viewfinder is identical to the one projected upon the film plane. Rangefinder cameras which have separate viewing ports above the lens do not register the same picture on the film. As a result, they should not be used for critical

227

photography work. Much photography for educational television work is copywork. Charts, graphs, words, photographs in books or magazines and other small-scale work require a close-focusing lens designed to photograph flat-field subjects with a minimum of linear distortion. The best lens for this purpose is a macro-type lens of the 50mm. to 55mm. focal length. Macro lenses enable the photographer to focus close enough to produce a 1:1 image size. A 1:1 image means that the photographed image is as large (on the film) as the subject is in real life. Many normal 50mm. lenses focus very close and by adding extension tubes or close-up lenses they may focus to a 1:1 image size. However, the resulting linear distortion, especially at the edges, renders them inadequate for television film chain work. The interchangeable viewing screen is not a must as long as the screen is accessible for marking. As noted earlier, the television camera produces an aspect ratio of 3:4. The 35mm. camera has a 3:4.5 ratio. For the most accurate results, the viewing screen should be removed and marked by drawing a 3:4 frame in the viewing area which corresponds to the area processed by the film chain camera, as indicated in figures 1A and 1B.

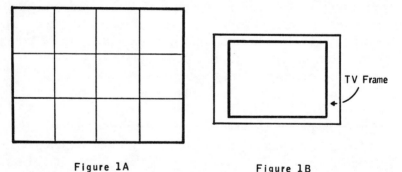

Figure 1A   Figure 1B

There are many additional accessories which make picture making for the television photographer much easier. One of the most important of these accessories is a good, professional-quality light meter. Many of the newer 35mm. cameras have built-in metering systems. While these light meters are adequate for general photography, they are not good for copy work. They are easily fooled by large areas of white or black and produce incorrectly-exposed slides. Nearly all of the built-ins are integrating meters and read all areas of the picture alike. This means they will lighten an area of black to a medium gray and darken a white area to a similar gray. A few of the latest built-in meters, such as Nikon's FTN and Minolta's SRT-101, are 60% center-weighted and are supposed to compensate for large masses of white or black. Experience has shown that they do in fact compensate rather well, but there is nearly always a change in overall density in the final transparency. This affects the film chain adversely because the TV camera can compensate to only a small degree for variations in light transmission caused by differential slide densities.

To maintain a standard density and correct exposure an incident light meter, such as the Seknoic L-28c, should be used. This type meter measures the light falling upon the subject rather than the light reflected from a subject. Variations in large masses of light and dark areas have no effect upon the final transparency. The slide has the same tonal scale and in the same relationships as the original. A reflective-type light meter can be used with the same effect if a Kodak 18% Gray Card is placed over the subject and light measurement made from it. The Gray Card provides an even gray color reflecting 18% of the light falling upon it. It approximates the average of all of the tones normally found in materials to be photocopied.

It might be appropriate at this point to mention shutter speed and f/stop combinations. Select a shutter speed which will produce motion-free slides and choose an f/stop in the mid-range of the lens. The mid-range should be used because the lens is generally sharpest at this point. Experience has shown that 1/125 of a second is a good selection. It is fast enough to stop most vibrations caused from the camera itself yet slow enough to allow an f/stop of about f8. Approximately 125 to 500 foot candles of light are necessary with most modern color transparency films and these shutter speed-f/stop combinations.

A second valuable accessory is a copy stand. Copy work can be done from a tripod, but it is very inconvenient. The stand must be easily adjustable in height, sturdy, have a large flat base (16 x 20 inches) and have a good camera mount. The main criticism of most copy stands is that they are too unstable. Parallelogram mounts are the most unstable. One of the best copy stands available is the stand made by E. Leitz.

Since most copy work is done indoors and there is seldom enough available (ambient) light for photocopy, some type of additional lighting will be necessary. Photofloods are the most commonly used and serve the purpose well. The lamps should have ceramic sockets as the photoflood bulbs will create an enormous amount of heat and eventually ruin the plastic sockets. To maintain the correct color balance, photographic photoflood bulbs should be used. They have the correct red and blue color balance for use with type A film emulsions.

There are many transparency films on the market which may be used in photocopy work. Most professional studios use Kodachrome II Type A film for copy work done under photoflood illumination. While some of the other transparency films may work this film appears to have the best natural reproduction of all colors, consistancy in film speed, color and grain structure. Some color films may be processed by the photographer, but Kodachrome requires commercial processing which is probably why the product is so consistent. It may be purchased in 35mm. size only on 20 or 36 exposure rolls.

Every photographer has his own special desires for extra equipment. The following list suggests a few of those which are helpful to the TV photographer:
1. cable release,
2. extra lenses: 35mm. wide angle, 105mm. medium telephoto, 200mm. telephoto,
3 lens hoods,
4. filters for black and white and color,
5. additional camera bodies.

Since no text is available on television photography, information must be gathered from numerous sources and compiled for the beginning photocopyist. This section will discuss briefly some of the procedures and pitfalls of this vocation.

Shooting black and white film for enlargements to be used in the studio is a demanding task and great care must be taken in all aspects of the process. A high-speed film such as Kodak TRI-X (ASA 400) should be used. This will allow a medium shutter speed of 1/60 to 1/250 indoors. Very few photographers can hold the camera still at 1/30 second or less. Any blur caused by camera motion will be magnified in the enlarging process resulting in an unsharp picture. Photographs taken out-of-doors require higher shutter speeds and thus eliminate any camera motion. Pictures taken indoors under available light may produce thin negatives and prints having low contrast. If low contrast situations are encountered, the film must be processed very carefully and printed on a higher contrast paper. Great care must be taken during the enlarging process to eliminate dust specks and to ensure adequate sharpness. Information about processes of film development may be found in many photo texts.

Color transparencies for the TV film chain must be of the best possible quality in all ways. Density should not vary beyond one-half f/stop. The image must be sharp and centered within the 3:4 aspect ratio area. Some of the slides may be pictures of large subject areas, people, etc. The photographer must remember to frame the subject carefully. Use a marked viewfinder screen when photographing anything which will ultimately be used on the film chain. If the camera does not have a marked screen, allow 1/8 inch on top and bottom and 1/4 inch on either side of the screen for film chain cutoff and center the subject within these boundaries. Photographing materials from books, magazines, and artwork requires use of the copystand. The camera must be mounted on the movable copystand arm parallel to the baseboard (see Figure 2).

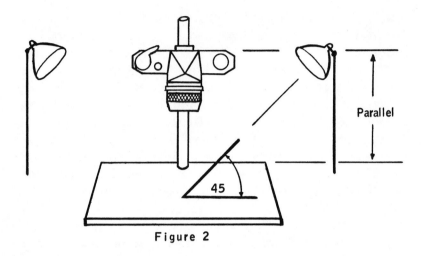

Figure 2

The two photofloods, located on either side of the copy-stand, should be adjusted so that the baseboard is evenly illuminated. The center and both sides of the baseboard should be accurately measured to check both the even distribution and level of the light. The light level is measured by placing the exposure meter in the center of the copy work and activating the meter's indicator. The shutter speed and f/stop combination should then be transferred to the camera's controls. Include only the important subject matter within the 3:4 ratio frame marked on the viewfinder by moving the camera up or down the copy stand pole. The lens should be focused very slowly and accurately to ensure a sharp image. Care should be taken in making the exposure so that no vibrations are induced or that the camera is moved from its parallel position. The result should be a perfectly-exposed transparency.

There are some special problems which may occur. Large books or magazines, which have a tendency to bend when spread out for copy work, can be flattened by placing a clean sheet of glass over the page. Photographing acetate overlays (sometimes called cells) also requires glass to flatten all of the pages; otherwise, a double image or shadow will result. Placing

232

glass over the material causes unwanted reflections. These may be minimized by using a large piece of black cardboard with a hole cut in the center the same size as the lens. The cardboard can be fitted over the lens to act as a large shield blocking out reflections from the metallic parts of the camera. The photographer should stand as far away from the copy setup as possible, and a cable release or self-timer should be used since the glass may pick up his reflection too. Care must also be taken to see that the photofloods are not reflected. It may be necessary to move them from their normal position.

Another problem which television photographers encounter is the problem of photographing odd-sized and vertical pictures on transparency film for the film chain. There are two solutions to this problem. The camera can be moved in on a piece of copy so that the area included in the final slide is a horizontal with 3:4 dimension ratio. This means that some of the original picture will be lost in the final slide. The second solution is to cut a mask from colored art paper so that the entire copy may be photographed with adequate, neat-appearing borders. Using masks also requires a glass cover to hold the mask flat against the copy.

In summary, television photography is a complex skill which combines the exactness of science and the feeling of art. Expensive equipment is not a necessity, but the basic demands of the television format must be met. In general a 35mm. single-lens-reflex camera with a 50mm. macro (close focusing) lens should be used for photocopy. The viewfinder should have the 3:4 ratio mask marked within the frame. Care must be taken in making exposure-measurement calculations to ensure a constant density of all slides. The photographer should be aware of the gray scale produced by the black and white television cameras. Large prints used in the studio should be of the best possible quality. All the developing and enlarging processes must be completed with care.

Photography can add another dimension to television. It can bring the viewer many visual stimuli which would not be available any other way. Television photography is demanding but rewarding, as is the use of motion pictures. Let's now turn our attention to their role in instructional media.

The objectives in this brief survey of motion pictures and their use in instructional media are to (a) explore the advantages of including such materials in the body of the unit either as total video transfer of a film or segmenting scenes from it; (b) discuss the use of super-8, single concept film loops, 16mm. films, filmstrips and 8mm. films, and (c) offer some practical hints in planning and making films specifically for television use. At the outset it is suggested that you procure Kodak's *How to Make Better Movies*, Nikon's booklet on super-8 photography and as many film resource catalogs as you can obtain. Consult Appendix II in this book for suggestions on obtaining information about film availability.

In any comparison between motion picture and still photography, the results seem obvious: one moves, the other doesn't. Actually, neither of the pictures (individually) move, but the rapid projection of individual pictures on a reel of motion picture film traveling at the rate of 18 to 24 frames per second are interpreted by the eye as continuous motion since it cannot translate the rapid start-stop into individual still pictures. This is important to know only in that most of the basic discussion related to picture composition, contrast, color values, focal lengths, shutter speeds, lens openings, film speeds, lens types, photography angle and aspect ratio in the section on still photography apply also to making motion pictures. It is also important to remember that much instructional TV is still in black and white, and films selected for TV should be carefully screened via TV transmission to make sure that the color values of the film itself are not ineffective. Thus the material on the gray scale will apply to film selection as well as in film making when black and white TV is the mode of delivery.

Before discussing how to make films, however, let's review how to use the ready-made motion picture in televised instructional packages. Films may be converted to video tape either in whole or in part. This may be done in the studio by photographing a screen with video camera or by projecting materials directly into a film chain. Video tapes may also be converted into film. If this is contemplated, basic TV production techniques should follow closely-related film-making techniques in the planning and execution of the production.

Since it is largely 16mm. films which will be available for use in the film chain, you must devise other ways of introducing 8mm. or super-8 into your video units. These, along with film loops, filmstrips, or even 35mm. slides, may be projected within the studio on standard screen, white cardboard in a shadow box. Frequently a white cardboard (14 x 14) is used for projection with the video camera tightly focused on the area. This method produces better color values than either the normal movie screen or shadow box. Ideally all such filmed materials should be introduced through the film chain. In the case of all except 16mm. (with some possible super-8 equipment now available), however, studio projection into the video camera must be used if other films are employed.

Remember that in any motion picture projection where the equipment is not designed with a TV-shutter, a fluttering effect will be noticed on the TV screen. This flutter is caused by the fact that video tape moves in a continuous flow of signals while film is a series of stop-start sequences. Some super-8 equipment makers (among them Bolex) have marketed a comparatively low-cost projector for super-8 with a TV shutter. There is no such convenience (at least at this moment of writing) available for film loops and 8mm. projection. This, however, should not keep you from involving them. A comment in the script will advise the student of the situation—most film loops (made from relatively ancient newsreel and vintage photography) need no such explanation. The mere fact that they contain values otherwise unattainable is justification for their inclusion.

When a director wishes to insert several film sequences into a TV show, he may find himself in a strait unless he has physically removed film segments from the original movie and sequenced them in the order they will be used. This is caused by the fact that normal rewind and reset times of the projectors often make it impossible to put a substantial number of film segments into any given program. One may combine studio projectors with film chain projectors or sequence the film needs on pre-recorded video tape at the desired spot in your production if your studio is equipped for drop-in or edit-in of pre-videoed segments. This actually provides a more flexible method of insert and makes it unnecessary to cut your film to make a series of film clip spots.

Many producers have a feeling that the visual aspect of TV needs a constant variety of illustrative materials. This often results in the screen being busy and frequently conveys a hodgepodge of materials of peripherally-related matter. Thus film materials must be selected with care and used only if there is no other way to illustrate the subject content.

For those who are particularly interested in utilization of film materials, I would suggest an examination of the resources available on the single-concept film loops. These are generally in 8mm. black and white but offer an infinite variety of commercially available materials on many subjects. Examination of film loop catalogs will reveal the potential they offer in helping you plan and illustrate your media instructional units. Unless you have a skillful technician who can provide a TV-shutter for your film loop projector, however, you will have to accommodate yourself to the resultant flutter effect. Flutter or not, such materials provide viewing experience available in no other form.

My personal belief is that super-8 equipment is the best choice in motion picture photography for instructional media. It is already widely used in mass media news coverage and there is an abundance of highly-sophisticated equipment on the market to enable its use on commercial TV. The cost factor in super-8 as compared with 16mm. results in considerable savings (always a good thing in school budgets). Except that the editing is somewhat more difficult to do, the results are effectively (especially in transfer to video tape) the same. Just as 16mm. photography has almost altogether replaced 35mm. use (even by major production companies), so 16mm. is being supplanted by super-8 in many areas of TV and particularly in materials designed to be used in educational media centers.

During recent years, advances have been made in the development of ultra-high speed films for super-8 photography as well as cameras which do not require the expertise of either 16 or 35mm. There are a number of super-8 cameras on the market which have automatic control capabilities which predetermine the lens-diaphragm opening in ratio to available light, and which have a variety of lens options, fixed focal length, and a variety of special effects. The film itself, responsive to available light (minimum usually 60 to 80 light candles) is packaged in cartridges of 50 feet (about three minutes shooting time). Its use eliminates the need for expensive and cumbersome lighting equipment. There are black and white as well as color films available. Although color negative (for use when multiple picture prints are desired) is not yet widely available in super-8, firms providing film duplicating service reproduce it with amazing fidelity.

Super-8 is also limited in its ability to provide motion pictures with lip-sync sound (except in the most expensive equipment). No double-systems sound facility has evolved in the average price range. In 16mm. double-system sound, tape recorders of the Uher or Nagra types permit the eventual blending of picture and sound onto a simultaneously projected film using either magnetic or optical sound, thus permitting "sync" of picture and accompanying sound. In super-8, the film processer is asked to add a magnetic stripe to the film so sound may be added. Having transferred the sound to the magnetic film stripe, a super-8 sound picture results. This process should be carefully rehearsed and timed before final recording. There are a number of brands of projectors which provide this recording capability. Many film makers using super-8 involve tape recorders during the filming process in order to permit the addition of as much natural sound as possible onto the completed picture. A good recorder with synchronous motor should be used for this effect.

Editing equipment is available for super-8, but it is more difficult to accomplish than 35mm. because of the size of the individual frames and the limited space between frames. In 16mm. film editing is done between the frames but in super-8 editing is smoother when the top half of one frame is joined to the bottom half of another. In professional TV many directors have super-8 footage transferred to video tape before editing because it is quicker and easier to edit than the small frames.

One basic rule to cut down on editing time is to plan well before shooting. Ninety percent planning and ten percent shooting will automatically improve your film making, no matter what millimeter size you use. Not only will this help you with your editing problems, it will improve the overall effectiveness of your product.

A motion picture, be it industrial, theatrical or educational needs a purpose for being. It is a whole which is divided into a series of components called scenes. The sequence of scenes makes up the total film and one plans a motion picture to fulfill its objectives and purposes. Once the idea is conceived and the statement of purposes made, the film should be analyzed into its scene-by-scene progression. Sometimes this is done with a full-scale scenario in which the writer describes the scenes in detail. At other times, only a basic outline is made in the form of a story-board. In this format the scenes are outlined in sequence and illustrated with pictures (many times only crudely drawn stick figures) which show relative positions of people and scenery. These processes may be as elaborate as you wish. They may indicate the types of angles and shots or suggest costumes and body movement. You should always indicate the approximate length of the scene. With super-8 cartridge you are limited to 50 feet of film, which means a maximum of 3 minutes. You should never include a scene that is shorter than five to seven seconds, since the human eye cannot translate the meaning of environment much more quickly than that. Sometimes black and white photos or Polaroid shots can be utilized instead of drawings. These should be pasted or pinned onto a board along with notations involved with each sequence.

Another planning method would be to prepare a series of 3 x 5 inch cards numbered in sequence with the film analyzed from its opening to end title. These would include a full description of camera work, action, etc. Sketches of each scene may also be added to the cards.

From either the story-board or the 3 x 5 cards, make a shot sheet. After you have thought carefully through each scene, make appropriate notations and you are ready to begin shooting. Prior to filming, however, have another rehearsal so you will know that each element you have planned is indeed in the scene. As each scene is completed, indicate the deviations from original plans on your card, or, re-shoot the whole scene if necessary and check it off your shot-list. Then proceed to the next sequence. It is also always better to re-shoot a complete scene than to attempt to match up partial sequences later. Likewise, it is better to over-shoot and edit out than to find yourself in the editing room without enough film to tell your story properly. At all times know where you are in the shooting sequence.

Since we suggested earlier that a motion picture is simply a series of still photographs, it is important that the viewing of the pictures not be done constantly from the same angle. Viewing from a fixed position is similar to sitting in a theater to watch a play. You are locked in position, your viewing angles vary only as the actors move. Of course you can move your head as you follow the action, but you are limited to the amount of maneuvering you can do personally. You are also limited in your ability to move close to see the actors' faces. Not so with a motion picture when you use the camera for your eyes. Here you have dozens of variants in your viewpoint and you may zoom right in on a whisker. In planning your scene, review the options and select the frame of reference which will tell your story or teach your lesson best. Where the angle of viewing needs to be the same throughout, as in a scientific experiment, or when the viewer would be distracted if camera angles were suddenly changed, single-angle filming brings better results. As a great pianist has options to play loud, soft, fast, slow and is able to select works which best reveal his technical abilities, so the cameraman should use his camera as a creative tool to fulfill his intentions in film making.

Establish the environment, make the action flow smoothly, plan and execute artistically and then edit carefully. Always keep in mind that a good motion picture should be able to tell the story with pictures alone. Narration, sound and music are tremendous assets, but they are only extensions of the picture. Your responsibility is to maintain a continuity of thought with pictures sequenced so the viewer gets the message without further explanation. Difficult? Yes, and although somewhat exaggerated in challenge, we should film with such care that should no other factors be obtained the film will still do the job.

Some movie makers take a small portable video camera along and actually video tape a scene after rehearsal and prior to its filming. This is a tremendous asset for it allows them to verify judgements and permits them to make changes based on the video test of the scene. It also involves extra expense and equipment.

Film speeds are now such as to allow color motion pictures to be made without additional lighting equipment. If one feels that only direct lighting is desired, then by all means involve extra lighting. But don't overlook the values created by varied lighting within a scene. The use of lightbars attached to cameras, sun guns, reflectors, etc. may create more problems than benefits. For the beginning film maker, we suggest depending upon the built-in advantages of automatic camera controls and super-sensitive film rather than hastily trying to acquire expertise as a lighting authority. When more available light is necessary, use it to increase the general illumination of the rooms, by directing your lights toward the ceiling, rather than to the specific areas being photographed.

While photographing, use a tripod as much as possible. Hand-held cameras more often than not produce jerky results. Make your panning movements smoothly. Some photographers pan as if the camera were a garden hose and they were watering an acre of flowers on a dead run. Moving a camera from side to side will produce nothing but a blurred effect if done too rapidly. Rapid panning and uncertain camera motion is something like visiting the National Gallery at top speed. You may see pictures, but you get very little benefit from the experience.

Making movies for TV use, whether for instructional purposes or general viewing, must take into account that the screen upon which they will be shown is much smaller than regulation theater or home movie screens. With the advent of projection TV, it may not be as necessary to take into account the reduced viewing area, but until then make sure that what you will be showing on the TV screen will be offered with clarity. Keep in mind the aspect ratio between the film proportion and the TV screen. Make sure that your important action takes place in the screen areas that will not be cut off in the border areas. Make sure your informational graphics and illustrations are done so that they may be read on a small screen as well as on a large one.

The awareness of dimension will affect your shooting concept and eliminate most wide angle, distant shots in favor of medium close-up shots. Keep in mind that the greater the area you are attempting to show on a large screen, the greater will be the loss of detail when it is reduced for TV showing. Movie makers who produce film for video conversion are extremely careful to take this limitation into account.

Other options are available in addition to camera movements. They are all in their way valid tools and should be utilized in proportion to their effectiveness in transmitting the message, however, and not as effect for effect's sake.

Film speed is one such option. Silent film speed is 18 frames per second. At this speed all action appears to be normal and natural. Slow motion is accomplished by increasing the number of frames per second to 40 and above. Some highly specialized photography is done at 500 to 1000 frames per second, resulting in a multi-figure representation. Most good models of super-8 do provide for slow motion. Fast action motion is accomplished when a smaller number of frames per second are allowed. Shooting at 8-12 frames per second results in a scurry-like effect. If you know what special effects are available in your TV control room, it is possible to utilize many of them during the conversion from film to tape. This imposes an extra

241

set of conditions in planning, but if your studio potential is greater than your camera capability, it is good to utilize them.

Another effect is single-frame shooting, since most cameras have the ability to shoot a single picture as well as a series. In this instance the camera is usually mounted securely on a copy stand when overhead photography is used, or on a heavy-duty tripod if the materials being photographed are on a display stand or wall. We may photograph a flower opening (time lapse photograph) by shooting 4 to 6 frames at each stage of the bud opening, or we may photograph a chess game and cause the pieces to appear to move of their own accord (in a form of animation). Machinery or equipment may be assembled bit by bit and seemingly grow part by part. In short, there are numerous ways to use single-frame technique. Combining the single frame with various other techniques can result in interesting photography. For instance, music and photograph materials may be selected in short sequences so as to match the rhythm of the music with the shots. This sort of photography takes much time to accomplish, but if well-planned it is an effective addition to your repertoire.

In summing up this brief discussion of films and their effective use in TV, you are reminded to secure copyright permission before transferring any film (except that which you make yourself) to video tape. Use of film on TV would include complete films, excerpts from films for insert into the body of the show, and in addition to 16mm. commercial availabilities, 8mm., super-8 and film loops are worthy items to consider. These latter probably will have to be projected within the studio through shadowbox or screen. Much study should be done in selection of films to be excerpted for inclusion in video materials. Do not use film just to have effect on your screen. It, like all other elements of your video unit, should. serve a maximum purpose or not be used at all.

For making film, select your equipment with care. Make sure you know why you are buying specific cameras, editing and projection items. Take time to learn to use this equipment so that you may acquire skills that enable you to work

242

creatively. Super-8 is suggested because of the availability of high-speed film, automatic diaphragm controls and particularly because of cost-factors. Use a tripod, plan your films in detail, prepare a story-board, use either a card file or shot-sheet system and allow yourself the luxury of much rehearsal. Practice with your camera until it becomes an extension of yourself. Above all, let your picture itself transmit the message you want to get across. When you have done your planning, learned to use your equipment, rehearsed your action, then—and only then—should you indulge yourself in the age-old pleasure to hearing the call:

"Places everybody . . . lights . . . camera . . . action!"

CHAPTER XIII

THE ROLE OF THE DIRECTOR
IN INSTRUCTIONAL MEDIA

The most important person selected by a TV producer is the director. He functions as the catalyst-authority in both broadcast and instructional media. In this chapter we will offer basic observations about his duties, his creative opportunities, and his unique role in educational circles as a teacher of teachers. We will discuss his working relationships with his crew and staff, as well as offering advice in his association with faculty members with whom he becomes professionally involved. We will summarize his position as being to instructional media creation what the academic dean is to curriculum and administration. And we will include an analysis of individual units and unit series with regard to the position of the director in the successful fulfillment of his task.

Most instructional programming includes a producer, in this case the academic dean, who is responsible for administrative decisions about curriculum to be placed within media, assignment of teaching personnel to create or perform, allocation of time and money to the project and directed use of media products when they have been completed. The producer function within education is largely administrative and, as with all good administration, operates best when delegating authority and responsibility to the personnel performing production activities. Administrators have to be ever-trusting people, wise in their ability to select the best personnel for a task and wise enough to let them alone while they are doing it.

No matter how many team members there are, the time comes when only one person may be the final authority in

244

judgment. As Mr. Truman once said, "The buck stops here." The "here" in educational media instruction procedures is the director. Directors as a breed are individualists and each has his own pet methods of staging a production. Because he has final authority however, does not mean that he must not be flexible, for his performers and various members of his creative and technical team are also individualists. Although he may guide and direct, he must remain open to suggestions and creative technical ideas. Otherwise he may deprive others of initiative and himself of a great deal of creative assistance. Hopefully, he is in command of a team of creative personnel from whom he should get optimum assistance. In the final analysis, each production decision has to be made in the light of the program as a whole. That is the director's responsibility.

During the production rehearsals, the director determines the camera movements necessary to cover the action. Also during these sessions, he continually checks on lighting, sound, picture composition, and the overall effect of the presentation. In short, every part of the performance that fits into the mosaic that is a TV program comes under his final direction—acting, camera work, visuals, music, script and revisions, sets, wardrobe, makeup and special effects.

In the control room the director follows the outline of the program closely, anticipating each performer's moves so that he can have a camera ready at the right place at the right time. He closely observes the monitors in the control room and selects the picture which is to go on the master tape. Through an intercom, he is in constant touch with the camera operators and helps them anticipate their movements.

The director of a TV or other media package is much like a chef. Presented with a formidable array of ingredients, he must select and then combine them into success recipes in order to unify the whole into a usable product. Basically, the director's needs (as with the chef) include a knowledge of not only how to make the product, but for what purpose it is being made. As chefs do not often spend their time building gourmet dishes for the mere joy of having them on display as examples of their genius, neither should a director indulge himself in the creation of materials whose finished product has no more purposed meaning than evidence of his directing skills. He is, above all else, a creative functionalist with a designated purpose: to deliver a finished product which will fulfill its role as a medium of instruction uniquely.

His tools are cameras, microphones, audio and video-tape equipment, sound effects, lighting, scenery, music, visual-effect equipment, script, graphics, media resource materials and performers. His helpers are various crew members (the number depends on his minimal requirements and budget) who perform designated duties under his direct authority. Among such helpers we will find audio engineer, video engineer, assistant director, technical director, floor manager, lighting director, sound-effects man, conductor, writer, scenic designer, video effects director, graphics director, media librarian, music consultant (or composer), instrumentalists et al. Before you think I am fantasizing in this number of needed personnel, I am actually being very limited in my listing. This, of course, relates to the people required in a television production. Other forms of media packaging may require fewer people.

With all of these tools and people using tools, the director becomes an administrator himself as he selects and then designates duties. He may feel more like a master juggler as he controls the multi-faceted details involved in production, since all of them must be simultaneously and perfectly controlled at the point of final taping. It is a precision business with the pre-determined demand of success. And success is defined as a production in which maximum efficiency and creative effectiveness can be obtained from all components involved in the production effort. In this effort he is a major domo, the chief artisan of a highly skilled team of artisans who are his to command. It is a team effort with the director acting as captain.

Because of the responsibility assigned and the power given to him, it is fundamental that the director must have a working knowledge of the capabilities of the various areas

246

involved in the production. In short, whether it be audio effects or scenic design, the director must know the how, what and why of all of the potentials of his available tools and people as he is planning his production methodology. He can only perform his function as catalyst to the exact ratio of his knowledge and understanding of the physical elements and of his own ability to achieve maximum delivery from his people and tools.

In professional television, an assignment to director status usually follows a number of months or years in many of the previously-mentioned work categories. He may have served as floor manager, writer, cameraman, assistant director and in some instances as performer, or perhaps he had concentrated in-service training at a technical school or college. Thus, the director comes to his position with practical and functional experience.

With this knowledge and authority he controls those functions necessary to the production in an administrative-executive-performer capacity. He is an organizer who identifies needs and sees that the tools are arranged to meet those needs. When he has done all of this he combats human frailty, endeavoring through rehearsal and cajolery to achieve what is needed from the humans serving him. The secret of a director's success is in this seemingly impossible, complex and detail-filled task.

In educational media we do not enjoy the luxury of individualized skills assigned to work only within a specific area. On the other hand, neither are we limited by union directives circumscribing work areas. We do not have facilities or personnel to work with the same latitude as do commercial TV productions. So, in educational media it is even more incumbent upon the director to know his resources and production capabilities intimately. He must act as a creative force in contriving effective substitution for unavailable resources and limited talent by his ability to manipulate equipment and people to achieve his goal.

In educational media the director's resources are not only his tools and the people who operate them, they also include the faculty and administration, all of whom may be compared to the talent and producer functions of professional TV.

Ideally, faculty and administration should be experts in media education, i.e., they should also understand and utilize the potential of the various media tools available to them. This does not suppose professionally-trained hands-on operating skill, but it does mean that their training in the art of media instruction has included functional experience in the tool-using processes. In situations where this is not true, I feel that it is the director's added responsibility to organize workshops to enable the faculty to experience these production processes in detail. Administrative personnel also should participate in this in-service training, primarily because of their responsibility to make decisions about the materials to be included in the curriculum as media units. Many of the problems existing in academic media relate entirely to status rather than to time and cost. Not only do many faculty members come reluctantly to media, they come with an attitude of superiority-by-virtue-of-degree toward the media staff. As long as faculty members regard media staff as nonpersons (because of their lack of degree quality), or until faculty members themselves can perform the role with equal expertise, it will continue to be a problem. Media personnel are also often at fault. They are prone to belittle the multidegreed academicians as being less important in media than themselves as practical-experience people.

Even if the attitudes of the faculty and service personnel are the highest toward each other, we still must admit that one of the major failures in instructional media attempts is caused by a lack of administrative understanding of the time required to create materials for media and the cost required to produce them. Faculty assigned to create media are, more often than not, given little release time to do the job properly. Once it is recognized that classroom procedures and media procedures are altogether different, administrative understanding and respect for the time factor could alleviate the problem. In this dissimilar situation, administrators need to recognize that time is not only of the essence, it *is* the essence.

As for money, most administrators are willing to spend vast sums to acquire the gleaming, shining tools and sophisticated hardware, but restrict the budget which would allow for their proper use. Owning the hardware itself, no matter how sophisticated, does not imply that its operation is as simple as driving into a service station with the latest model automobile and saying, "fill it up." It is almost like buying a collection of Stradavari violins for a 4th-grade string class.

Administrators thus become an integral part of the director's responsibilities just as he becomes theirs. He must make them aware of the time-money, attitude and the goal factors of media instruction. This is not meant to be a negative attitude toward administrative policies as they have existed. Rather it is designed to help make administrators aware of their role in the ultimate success of their quite expensive, very time-consuming program. In addition, hopefully, it should make the faculty aware of their responsibilities of the use of such tools in order to help fulfill their own roles of teacher-creators in media instruction. Perhaps faculty and even administrators will want to solve all problems by becoming so facile with the tools and knowledgeable about the procedures that each can become his own director. Until this happens, the director himself is entitled to wear the electronic purple heart as he accepts the bruises of faculty and administration alike in order to get their tasks completed for them. In the meantime, he must be diplomat, teacher, captain, chef, major domo, leader and boss.

For a moment let's examine a hypothetical situation within an educational system and examine some of the problems he must solve. Let's say for the sake of our discussion that the director's administration and faculty are committed to make a media production. Let's say too that he has been given better than average production facilities. His studio is equipped with a color film chain, a good control room for sound and picture equipment and more than adequate production space. Let's provide him with two studio cameras with mobile availability and one fixed position camera as well as an excellent chief engineer who is willing and co-operative.

249

It would seem that he had everything. And he does, mostly—except that he has no trained personnel to operate cameras, TV switching, sound equipment, nor to serve as trained floor managers, boom operators or scenic design-construction people. He has limited graphic support and equally limitedly sound-support in mixing, editing and recording. His studio is limited in that he has no color cameras, although he does have a color film chain. Finally, he has no special effects generator nor tape editing equipment.

After reviewing his advantages and disadvantages, he generates a program of training personnel to be studio crew generally, to build sets, handle lighting, cameras, sound and act as technical and assistant directors. He is a good teacher and accomplishes his task of making non-professional, inexperienced student populations into dependable crew material. This takes time, but he does it because he *knows* how it should be done. Because he knows, he can show them how to do it. Knowing the limitations of his studio he plans for their fullest use by doing without where reasonable substitutions cannot be created. He is actually working within the framework of administrative misjudgement, for no media instruction program should ever be contemplated, no piece of equipment purchased nor facilities designated *until* the administration has determined its goals and then, having stated those goals, provided the necessary equipment to enable their accomplishment.

Nevertheless, it is still the director's responsibility to use whatever facilities he has to achieve the very best he can while he enlightens (educatively of course) the administration about the needs and urges them to add the equipment that will enable him to do a better job. His training of a crew must be thorough, for his success depends upon the individual members to function efficiently at the critical moment they are needed.

For the next few pages let's put the director into a role of actuality in a media instructional situation. Since we have already explained the terminology related to production

250

activities, we'll begin with the role of director in an audio cassette tape production.

The title of the series is "Great Men of Music." The stated objective of the series is to give the student an overview of the composer's life, offer illustrations from his writing, correlate his life with other activities coincident to it in science, politics, art, religion and discovery as well as motivate the student into further exploration about the composer by suggesting additional materials which he might use. The units are to be self-contained, that is, each unit is to be complete in itself in establishing the composer and his position within the galaxy of compositional stars. The creator of the unit is assigned to research writing and select music is to be included. The recording, mixing, editing and final preparation of the master tape for transfer to cassette is assigned to the director.

The director determines the format with the individual units of various lengths to be included as part of a series. He determines that each program is to open with a familiar excerpt from one of the composer's better-known works. He determines that the script is to be written in as easy-to-listen-to style. It is to be accurate, factual and motivational to students. In short, the unit is to be complete enough within itself to enable the student to have a meaningful experience with the composer's life and music, and to whet his appetite for more. Although the units are part of a series, they are self-contained and need not be used as a series. The audience in view is general rather than being a single age-group or discipline.

The director's activities include research and familiarization with the script. Simultaneously with script preparation, he checks the availability of music to be used. When this is done and the script is completed, transfer of samplings of the composer's music is made onto a separate sound track for introduction into the show. The script is then recorded, voiced by the director in this instance, and edited by the director until a clean voice track is obtained. The final mix-down of voice and music is then completed, edited and the master voice-music track transferred from reel-to-reel tape to audio cassette tapes for individual use by students.

In this instance, the creator and director are the same individual. He performs all of the functions necessary to the packaging of the show except the engineering required to do the audio taping of the script. He acts as director in the fullest sense of the word, doing precisely what I think all faculty should be able to do. He has responsibility and authority and, because of his knowledge of media tools, he creates the media to do the task.

Our next example concerns a brilliant young media man named Jerry Plemons, whose chapter on Television Photography makes a great contribution to this book. He conceived the idea of a unit on Abraham Lincoln. He decided on a presentational form of slides, script and a prepared music track. These were combined into a slide-tape video unit. He researched the photographic materials and did his own photography. As director he proceeded to write the script, relating his words to the available photography. He decided to use a number of quotations from Lincoln and assembled some talent for a taping session. Handling the recording himself, he directed the actors on the stylistic delivery of their lines. He then selected a narrator for his script, recorded and edited him, finally cutting-in the other voice tracks with one or two sound-effects to make his master voice-effects tapes. He prepared graphics of opening and closing credits, photographed them and arranged his slides in the carousel trays. He had a music track prepared from available taped materials to reflect the mood and action of the script content. After hearing the available options he selected what he wanted and then assumed the task of creating the final mix-down of music and script. This completed, he went to the studio and, utilizing the film chain, directed the activities of the production. The finished production was almost entirely the result of his own personal involvement in creating the video materials or his efforts in working with people to direct their activities to achieve what he desired. This is another example of being-able-to-do in order to create instructional media.

A third example is a video-tape production directed by Mrs. Lynn Young, a member of the production staff at Dallas Baptist College. The unit title was, "Physical Education Concepts," based on exercise and the heart. The teacher, Mrs. Verona Stevens, was also a performer in the video-production. She and her student researcher, Mrs. Young (as director) and the Director of Media Instruction met with other members of the production staff to explore available resource possibilities, design a format, declare informational intent and estimate costs, work loads and potential use of the unit.

Subsequent meetings involved graphic artist and photographer. As a group they examined available resource materials including slides, film clips and possible display items. When these were selected and the perimeters were outlined for the unit, the script was assigned. Before this had happened however, the entire unit was outlined in a story-board style and mutual decisions were made regarding the delivery of information to the students.

The main body of the show was to be a drama, preluded and followed by appearance of the teacher who was to state the basic objectives of the unit, discuss a display model of the human heart and speak briefly of the cardio-vascular system. The unit was then to move into the presentational content format, one which included two characters: a man, who represented his thoughts in mime rather than spoken lines, and a puppet shaped like a conventional heart and endowed with human facial configurations. It was he who would do all of the talking in the drama itself.

When all of this had been decided, the script was written. The writer imagined a monologue to be spoken by the heart in which he would complain against his master for refusing to take care of himself by proper exercise, diet, rest, etc.

Since it has been decided that two playing areas would be involved, the director set about arranging a puppet stage and a set which would represent a very messy dorm room. These were constructed under her supervision. The multi-list of props needed for the dorm room (including coke cans, dirty ashtrays, food scraps, books and clothing) were arranged and secured by the director. The acting, costume and make-up requirements were discussed. In the meantime, the director and graphics artist were busy designing and creating an appropriate puppet for the lead role. The director was also engaged in supervising the creation of additional graphics, requesting photographic assistance in slide preparation, selecting appropriate music and casting talent for the part of the puppet-heart.

The script, prepared with full knowledge of the details just mentioned as well as the studio possibilities and limitations, was delivered. Equipment needed would be a film chain for slides and 16mm. film, audio and video recording gear, two mobile and one fixed camera position. Having been informed by the director of her general camera angle shots, the script was written to co-ordinate these factors. Actually some modifications were made after the script was delivered, as the director exercised her authority to change script to fit possibilities and limitations of the studio.

The puppet's voice was recorded and edited, music background supplied and a final mix-down completed under the supervision of the director. Sound in the production was both prepared sound track and live mikes. The director made crew assignments and arranged to discuss their routines.

The production crew, including cameramen, assistant director, film-chain assistant, video-engineer, floor manager, *et al.*, assembled in the studio following preparation of the set. Film footage, slide sequences, display objects and word cards were in place and a previously arranged rehearsal schedule was begun. The director supervised the rehearsal of the puppeteer, checking various camera positions she thought necessary. During rehearsal she changed some of them to give greater latitude in operation. She then directed the mime activities of the actor, also rehearsing the camera crew for appropriate video possibilities. The teacher was then rehearsed to open and close the show. Finally a run-through, step-by-step rehearsal of the show sequences was done. In all instances the director made final decisions about all components of the show. The assistant director made appropriate annotations on the script about cue information for the director. This would serve as a memory refresher during the actual taping of the show.

When the director had satsified herself that the components were functioning as planned, she called for a dress rehearsal to be video-taped. The director and staff examined the results of the effort, some minor changes were made and on the following day the unit was completed.

Mrs. Young, as director, had the following personnel under supervision: video-engineer, audio-engineer, two cameramen, lighting and design personnel, assistant director, audio and edit specialists, script content researcher, teacher, graphic artist, two floor managers, production co-ordinator, photographer, performers and writer. When the seventeen-minute unit was completed, it had involved activities by twenty people whose combined efforts had consumed well over three hundred hours. It is a tribute to the director's efficiency that the result was an acceptable product which became a permanent part of the video-taped materials to be used in the "Concept" series of the Physical Education Department.

A final example of what the director does concerns the creation of a series of video units entitled, "Adventures in Art." In it I acted as the director and assigned myself to be writer, photographer, sound technician, music consultant and graphic artist. In this project I had the valuable assistance from two faculty members, graphic artist, from various others who helped prepare graphics as well as considerable assistance in cinematography and final video-tape transfer.

Even with all of that assistance, the series took almost a year to produce. It was a valuable year in projecting production techniques to be studied by colleagues as well as the fulfillment of stated objectives for creating the series. Twenty units directed to general audiences were planned and completed. Each segment was self-contained although primarily designed as part of a series for Art Appreciation. Nevertheless, its greater use was on an individual unit selection basis by various other academic disciplines.

The broad goals for the total series were stated and included the following:

a. convince the viewer that he knows a great deal more about art than he realizes,

b. provide a basic vocabulary of art terms and the proper pronunciation of artist's names,

c. show how art may be used to explore history,

d. give an over-view of the history of art,

e. simulate tours of the world's great art centers,

f. take simulated visits to galleries in the Dallas area,

g. provide examples of campus creativity and electronic art gallery exhibits,

h. make the viewer aware that he lives in a world whose function is dependent upon art,

i. show that art is a billion-dollar business with career potentials,

j. provide a pleasant viewing experience throughout, making it possible for the viewer to learn about art whether he consciously wanted to or not.

In the capacity of writer, I planned presentations to include narration, dialogue, ad-lib interviews, dramatic interludes and long sections of voice silence where music and graphics would be used to convey information. Recognizing the need for additional voices, materials especially suited to drama students were written.

As writer-director I created a format involving 35mm. slides, a few 16mm. segments and prepared an audio track. The audio track was prepared and mixed, with particular emphasis on musical underscoring for dramatic effect.

As director-researcher, my visuals were selected from among hundreds of available slides, supplemented by materials done specifically for this project. A Nikon-F copy was used for this photography. Most graphic inserts other than pictures were made by using various type fonts. Since the series was in color, special care had to be taken in assessing color values and their response to the equipment.

As director I set about developing a general format for each unit, allowing myself flexibility in making frequent changes. I decided to use the slide-tape technique with film clips to be transferred to color video-tape.

Being in charge of planning a complete series brought the advantage of flexibility in choosing the visual materials for the whole series. One photocopy session could produce pictures for sequential units, a research period could produce much useful information for the script, a recording and dubbing session could include several hours of material and an editing session could involve work on a half-dozen or so units at a time.

As director I performed most of the· functions normally assigned to others. This enabled me to experience complete control over and responsibility for all content materials in their own screen representation. It also allowed me to create production models which might be emulated by others. Thus, as in "Men of Music," the video series became a dual project. Its primary use was for Art, and its use for Media Art was in technique study. With all components of the show series planned in advance and being assured of the available visual-audio resources, the scripts were then written.

In bringing this series into being I functioned with many hats. As writer, I was responsible for content accuracy, following behavorial objectives and keeping a consistent environment. As producer-director, I supervised the details of filming, graphic production, casting, and of making final decision in acceptance or rejection of all elements. Nevertheless, it was as director that I functioned with the ultimate authority to change, eliminate, re-arrange, re-photograph or accept the totality of individual components which made up the series.

Perhaps as you have been reading, you may have felt that both the duties and responsibilities credited to the director may have been over-exaggerated. On the contrary, the involvement presented is an understatement, especially if we add to it the ability the director needs in order to utilize all of the people and equipment required for media production. If the director is unprepared, leaves things to chance, fails to take precautionary measures or gambles on the ability of the crew to function without knowing precisely what and when to do it, the results will be chaotic.

257

One might sum up this experience as being the unique effort of one individual performing many tasks, but it is not. It is rather what I hope ultimately may develop among teachers as a general experience. Not that the teacher *must* perform all of the individual functions of production single-handedly, but that he *may* be able to do so. Having that capability, he can assume the dominant role within media arts just as composers conduct their own works, playwrights stage their plays and choreographers create ballets and direct their performance. In the last analysis, this is how media instruction becomes great. We needn't worry about replacing the director by the knowledge we develop in our understanding of media tools, for the more we know about them, the harder he will have to work to bring ideas which will generate to creative fruition as art in media instruction.

Academic participation related to content-oriented directorial function translates the spoken materials of the classroom into visual-audio materials media. The director's role as a teacher of teachers during this transition from faculty to media creator is to create a concept which will best express content materials. He often finds himself in an untenable position of attempting to be the catalyst between the faculty and the TV screen when decisions have to be made which are more properly within the province of faculty. This is because the faculty itself doesn't really know what it wants done. It is to this point that we have repeatedly counseled that the faculty must act as the vital and responsible agent in being able to direct the entire process from concept to system delivery.

Until that time, however, planning meetings may be only unhappy committee sessions. In media planning between faculty who are insufficiently attuned to the media and media people who want to get the show on the road, the result is more often an instructional white elephant instead of the proverbial camel put together by a committee planning to build a horse. And no institutional budget is Maharajahish enough to afford that for long.

Without question the director is king of media-land. His kingdom will flourish only if he by effort, knowledge and design wins every battle he fights. Winning in instructional media means the fulfillment of an academic dream: the unit and series thus delivered presents its message so perfectly that *every* student learns.

CHAPTER XIV

INSTRUCTIONAL MEDIA AND THE CHURCH

Historically the church has been centuries ahead of everyone in the employment of media to instruct, for graphic arts and music (two of the most potent media forces) were used at the outset to teach great masses of people. These masses for the most part were unable to read or write and they depended upon such teaching aids as tunes whose words were scriptural, stained glass windows, statuary and paintings for information about biblical characters and events. Later, drama was employed to enact biblical stories. These elements, plus the work of the clergy from the pulpit, combined to transmit information about Christianity to countless millions. Until the advent of printing and the growth of literacy, they were the only ways to Christianize the western world beyond a one-to-one telling of the gospel story. Based on this historical tradition and the heritage of countless thousands works of art which were created about biblical figures, events, stories and doctrines, it could well be that the church will again assume a leading role in the creation of instructional media.

This is already apparent from the number of listings in the catalogs of denominational publishing houses declaring the availability of all sorts of teaching devices and aids such as audio cassette cartridges, filmstrips, recordings, slide packets, musical materials, display charts, etc. In addition to film there are instances of available video-taped sermons, lectures and Bible studies.

Many catalogs advertise these wares along with their printed materials. Several of them even sell the hardware with which to use these materials. The emphasis in advertising has been toward use of these materials in Sunday school classes, vacation Bible schools, discussion groups and home study courses. Some publishers have even produced multi-media packets, and evidence reveals their recognition of the trends of the times. Certainly both education and industry have adapted themselves to the media age and they are beginning to seek to implement, if not replace, their printed study materials with a variety of other media elements.

While few seminaries and Christian colleges have begun to offer courses leading to degrees in this particular church-related field, some have fostered it and advocate its continued use. There is much conversation about incorporating media instruction within a ministry of "music, art and drama" rather than in the traditional province of the director of religious education. The transition to new methods is as natural for this century as it was for the older times to move from non-print into print as technology advanced to make it all possible.

Many churches own numerous audio-visual equipment items, such as carousel slide projectors, 16mm. and super-8 projectors, various types of tape recorders, recording playback units and some overhead projectors and filmstrip units. Some churches have begun building libraries of media materials. Few churches have established media learning centers or invested heavily in more sophisticated video reproduction equipment. This will unquestionably come, for the value of the idea in educational service will cause it to be included in any well-organized system of teaching occurring within and for the benefit of the church.

While the principles involved in the creation of media materials for religious instruction are basically the same as for any other teaching areas in media, this chapter provides suggestions and examples for the organization, execution and use of such media in various church training programs. It also suggests ways that these techniques can also be used within the worship service itself.

Since there is a parallel between the minister of a church and a teacher in public schools and colleges, the success or

261

failure of a church program in media instruction will depend on his willingness to allow it to happen. Just as the teacher is frequently "classroom-only" in his attitudes, the minister is frequently pulpit-bound and often fails to see that the congregational gathering is not the all-end-all potential of his influence. Granted that the church has long used radio and television to extend its pulpit activities to home and community, but more often than not these have been merely reportorial functions with little evidence of an awareness of the potential use of the media itself. Many denominations have commissions in radio and televisions whose mission is more directed toward public reception than in church training use. It will be well to remember that these commissions do exist, that they have developed first-class materials and that they should be called upon to help furnish and develop materials for individual churches.

These statements about the ineffectual use of media by the individual church are not meant so much as criticism as they are a reminder that only those who know media equipment and its potential can achieve a creative level of development or use. Unless church leadership takes this into account and adjusts its attitudes toward media as the means of establishing a one-to-one relationship which adds to the church program, then it would be better not to begin using media at all. The classroom syndrome and the pulpit concept are much alike in that they relate to individuals who do not choose to recognize the challenge. In both instances success or failure of the total program will be the admission that their present arenas are not limited to the classroom or the sanctuary, but that there is a world of people whom they cannot reach except through media. Whether the product is only a taped reproduction of a lecture or sermon or a full-scale media production, it is the creation of enduring influence rather than the influence of the moment to be used with a captive audience. In one instance the school bell terminates the performance, in the other the benediction ends it all. In the electronic procedure, the ending of a lecture or sermon is only its beginning in its potential influence on an audience that never enters either the classroom or sanctuary. One's influence lasts only in human memory, whereas the other endures in the instant replay of media.

It is to the pastor and his professional staff that our efforts are now directed, for they will be able to extend their influence and deliver the now into the future by use of audio and video playback units. An outstanding pastor or teacher may now be able to teach in his own church, homes, hospitals or in other churches which do not have their own media production programs.

Perhaps the greatest encouragement for the pastor or teacher comes from the fact that he will be dealing on a mind-to-mind basis with his listener-viewer in media. His audience is not a sanctuary-filled congregation, it is a single individual who voluntarily tunes him in via electronic gadgetry. This volunteerism ought to make the pastor or teacher work even harder to hold his one-member congregation. If he can hold him his student will return time and again, to hear and re-hear until understanding and learning take place.

In media, then, there is a privilege for those who wish to teach (whatever their gospel may be) not once, but enduringly. As if this reward were not enough, the live audiences will increase rather than diminish as a result of his electronic ministry. That alone should be worth the effort.

Organizing a media instructional program in the church has another important effect, it involves people who have special talents which are never utilized in the church activities. I refer to the artists, writers, photographers, composers, painters, actors, poets and those skilled in crafts such as design, lighting, printing, costume making, electronic technology, etc. If a church becomes serious about utilizing media, it should analyze its potential human and physical resources, investigate commercially available media materials, determine its objectives and allocate time for problem and value study, appropriate an adequately studied budget for financial support, prepare workshops for all personnel involved and apprise the whole church of the contemplated program through a well-organized sales campaign. Above all, no church should even attempt such a program unless it realized that it may be losing much more by not doing it (however great the financial cost) than by doing it.

Let's turn for a while to a review of each of the factors involved in the church's use of media. Many people are needed in media production, among them the media librarian. Although many churches maintain a standard print library, few have established a media library as such. Since the chapter on The Media Library describes in detail how to build and maintain the library, we suggest that the church design and maintain its media library following those patterns. It can be maintained entirely separate from the general library and the music library and will not necessitate staffing by personnel who have had professional library training. The librarian and assistants should be selected because of knowledge both of the equipment and resource materials used in media. If the present church library already contains media material, it should be transferred to the media library. If this isn't feasible a close cooperation between the two librarians should be maintained, for media people will need to make use of pictorial and research areas of the general library.

It is in photography generally that the greatest number of helpers can be recruited. Although their worth varies, there are many church members who have abilities which can be utilized. Some expertise is needed to do particular work in photography, including copy work, enlarging, printing and editing work. Feel free to involve as many of the amateurs as you can, including their collections of photographs and slides, depending more on professionals for assistance in production areas.

The preparation of graphics has been presented in another chapter. It provides information to help in determing what kind of people should be mobilized to help in this all-important aspect of media. While many graphics are relatively easy to learn, there may be need for artists, illustrators, cartoonists, designers, teachers and other qualified personnel who have had technical and professional background. In addition, "idea" people, those who can see visual potential but

264

who do not have the technical capacity to execute it, will be needed. Such people are also very valuable to writing staff and research teams. Don't bypass anybody at all in graphics—not even the doodlers and tracers. Even the cut-out experts and pasters will come in handy. Anyone who has ever done any display advertising or magazine-newspaper layout work is also important. Employees of print shops who know type fonts, paper qualities and sources also contribute positively to graphics production.

A number of possibilities for participation are available in audio recording. Anyone who has had experiences as outlined in the chapter on "Recording, Editing and Mixing Sound," can assist in this area: equipment crew, the recording engineer, tape editor, tape duplicator, public address sound systems people, maintenance experts and individuals who can serve as script assistants. These are all very important people and they will feel important when they do their task in production. Look for people who know how to take care of equipment, build various audio components, operate multi-channel mixers, make cabinets, do electrical wiring and assist in converting a room into a sound-proof studio.

All media presentations have need for people who are handy with tools. If there is already an active drama department within the church, these craftsmen may already have been enlisted to build sets, paint scenery, handle lights, make costumes, collect props and work backstage. They may also be valuable in co-ordinating the needs in instructional media. Treat them well, for what they do makes it possible for media to function.

If the church develops a video production program of media instruction (or only uses it in teaching), it may need a video crew of engineers, technical directors, maintenance personnel, cameramen and directors. Although some of this equipment may be operated reasonably well by unskilled personnel, a rule of thumb would be that the more complex and sophisticated the equipment, the greater the need for skilled operators. Check the church census to see if any members are TV repairmen, work in any of the TV stations or deal with video in public schools or colleges. If an expert can be found, set up a training program so that he can help develop a trained crew.

In the future the church may use closed-circuit TV systems to serve teaching areas. These could be connected to a central video-audio distribution center. This probably will not take place, however, until the use of such equipment (along with the program content called software) justifies the investment. There is no reason, however, not to believe that, given the equipment and organized education program, church facilities would be used more advantageously than customary. Whether closed circuit develops or not in your situation, the use of portable video tape recorders, cameras and playback equipment can be used in a variety of places—including hospitals, jails and homes of shut-ins. When news gets about that a church is doing video work, people will be attracted to it in order to be a part of it all.

In most instructional media situations, it is in the area of writing (scripting) that the greatest shortage of personnel is to be found. This is odd really, for there are great numbers of people who engage in creative writing of one sort or another. It may be that those who do not shrink from attempting poetry, novels, short stories or plays may fear to try their hand at scripting. Script writers can be trained, however, and a concentrated effort should be made to enlist their efforts in the church's behalf. Research teams may also be developed to dig out informational materials from which writers can work. To these a list of helpers, including typists, mimeo operators, etc., may be added.

Instructional media can use a wide variety of voice types in narration and dramatic presentation. If your church has a good drama department, it is well ahead of the game in finding talent. If not, encourage auditions. During these auditions a roster of voice types can be built. A large number of people don't like to record but many others do. Some good stage actors are impossible on mike, and conversely many good voices have never tried out for theater because they do not like public appearances. Whatever the particular problem,

266

it can be solved with diligent and persevering effort. When video equipment begins to be used for other than ministerial teaching sessions or video-taped sermons, this catalog of usable voices for reading, narration, acting, dialect, assorted age groups and panel discussion experts will find many uses.

Now for a few words about mobilizing the music potential in the church for media instruction. In church-related subject areas the spiritual power inherent in music must be involved deeply in teaching in what is, after all, a spiritual subject. Beyond the use of the church choir, soloists and instrumentalists, few churches have extended the range of involving their membership in a music program. There are many people in the church who play instruments other than those customarily used in the worship service, but these are seldom used. Before a media program is undertaken, it would be well to take a census of this potential. And not just among performers either, for there may be composers, conductors, arrangers, copyists, specialists in music literature (of all kinds), and recorded music as well as already existing folk groups, vocal ensembles and entertainment units which have gone unnoticed by the music staff. At one time or another, all of them could be useful to the media instructional staff. Not just for the program itself, but as a part of people involvement in the arts in the church.

Instructional media can use live performances by the choir, instrumentalists for background and cue music and small ensembles (wind or brass) in the background and underscoring areas as well as for opening and closing titles. It can use composers to write materials, music specialists to make the writer-directors aware of resources, record specialists to locate already-recorded sources, arrangers and copyists to service composition and groups of all sorts to provide needed music. In short, all this music potential can be used, so mobilize them and make them an active part of the media operation.

Let's turn now to discuss *physical resources* involved in a church's media production. A basic media program will require cassette audio and reel-to-reel recorders, turntables, overhead projectors, microphones, speakers, 16mm. and super-8 movie projectors, audio and editing film and splicing equipment, film-

267

strip projectors, amplifiers, mixers, speakers, dark room facilities, projection screens, copy cameras, lights, carousel slide projectors, slide dissolve units, slide-tape programmers and perhaps 16mm. motion picture cameras. The TV route would also require video tape recorders and playback equipment, cameras, monitors and some basic electronic materials such as duplicators and editors. Should a studio be set up, some quite refined and sophisticated equipment will be necessary. Since the initial investment is so great we will forego a discussion of the studio equipment and discuss the equipment which the membership owns and which may be borrowed or given to the church. Begin a campaign to locate it and get it involved in the media program one way or another. It will be at this particular point that you will sorely need maintenance people, for many gifts may be provided which are slightly on the blink but which deft hands can put back into working order. These items can become part of the permanent equipment pool.

Those items which cannot be borrowed will have to be purchased, but a resourceful churchman can always engage in a fund-raising enterprise. As a matter of fact, unless properly budgeted, films, light bulbs, tape, splicing equipment, reels, video tape and other needed expendibles may have to be obtained by fund raising.

While slides, film footage and recordings are not truly equipment in the generic sense of the term, they should be sought as the equipment is being gathered. They should be given to the media librarian for cataloging and classification.

Somewhere along the line begin to seek information concerning material available for media instruction. A number of such materials may be found in "Appendix II: Resources in Media Instruction." Many varieties of free and low-cost rental materials are listed there. The local public library may also have a media department. If so, use it to the best advantage. Film catalogs, tape and video cassette listings and record catalogs will reveal an over-whelming amount of already-existing materials. Someone will need to procure, evaluate and suggest the use of these materials. Perhaps so many are available that you won't need to develop your own. However, if you don't you'll be missing that great chance to involve people, and part of all of this concerns that special involvement of the presently-uninvolved.

The objective in doing all this is virtually pre-stated: utilization of media to do what the church already does anyway. Only this time it will be done more efficiently to serve those who can't possibly be a part of the congregation as well as those who are a part of it. Our purpose too is to create enduring materials, usable time and time again to allow a one-to-one relationship between teacher and student. Accomplishing this it will put new vitality into the church by involving many in a common cause. A good beginning to demonstrate the values of such a program might be to set up one teaching room involving audio-visual equipment. Make sure that it is equipped sufficiently to play tapes, show motion pictures and slides as well as to use turntables, reel-to-reel tape recorders, overhead and filmstrip projectors.

Thus far we have discussed the primary values inherent in a media instructional approach to the church, stressing the immediacy of possible techniques, the availability of materials and the benefits accruing through involvement of membership in Christian service. The rest of this chapter will be divided into two parts: a plan for creation of multi-media (on electronic equipment) and as media support for live performances. Some script samples and hints for preparation of religious instruction materials are included to show how to create in media.

We speak of dual use in preparing materials to be used on electronic playback equipment as well as for media support of live performances. Acknowledging that few churches have thus far involved themselves in the latter concept beyond dramatic presentations of plays, tableaux and pageants, we propose to indicate how media materials can be used within the framework of a worship service to involve the total congregation. Frankly speaking, this is difficult because church architects have not designed the sanctuary for much else than a

269

gathering place for people to come to hear preaching. Perhaps the church building of the future can be more adequately designed to utilize what is now the pulpit-choir area as a production area for media—complete with appropriate devices for lighting, staging, projection and use of instrumentalists. Until then, using existing facilities and utilizing moveable equipment will have to suffice for multi-media involvement. Possible exceptions to this dual use concept might be pastoral sermons, lecture series, etc., but it would be of benefit at the outset to conceive instructional materials to be usable in more than one way.

Let us say that we are preparing a series of units on Bible Heroes, designed to teach people of all ages the basic facts about the life of such men as Moses, David, Daniel, Peter, John, Paul, *et al.* A script should be prepared for each "hero" involving narrator, assorted voices and appropriate Scripture references. Either selected or composed music, created art work and photography are used to produce the whole of the components into a slide-tape show to be operated in an automated mode by programmer-carousel equipment. This would constitute its most frequent use and would remain the essential reason for having created it initially. However, a live performance of the script materials (in costume with scenery if desired) using the slides, live music performance and appropriate lighting could be done most effectively. Not only would it bring an innovative element into the worship service or fellowship group, it will also induce interest in the package itself. In addition, it would involve several customarily unused people in its production.

We could use such a media-supported live performance package within the worship service—in place of the anthem, for instance. Having developed a media series involving meditative narration on stories of great hymns put on slide-tapes, we may now easily use the media elements as part of the public performance. Following exactly the same format as in the creation of the taped-slide package, we now involve the basic performance elements live instead of pre-recorded. In the live performance the church choir, organ, piano and other

270

instrumentalists supply the music portion; the narrator and actors are positioned in the pulpit area; the slides are projected on cue. Whatever else is desired in the nature of special effects in lighting, costuming and sound can be easily arranged.

Other simple-to-produce media-supported ideas use projection of Scripture passages as the pastor reads the Bible. A pastor could even utilize slides or an overhead transparency projector to show maps, stress sermon points or select appropriate pictures to illustrate his sermon. All of this takes time but results in a new congregational involvement in what he is saying. Other simple ideas would include projecting the words of hymns or Scriptures to be used in responsive reading. This is particularly valuable in musical presentations to enhance the spiritual qualities inherent in the music.

The key to all of this is the pastor. If he can see that tradition-bound techniques can be improved by this exciting and dynamic programming, he will not only involve more people in the total effort, but he may well bring more people into his service. Perhaps this is no place to editorialize, but I am frequently shocked at the reluctance of the ministerial leadership to innovate in any way, much less deviate from the time-honored format of the one-man show surrounded by never-changing involvement of relatively unplanned music. If the Lord is to be well served and if the worship services are to be designed to bring all worshippers into a oneness with God, it behooves church leadership to take advantage of all possibilities to accomplish this. And media, is, without question, one of those possibilities.

Some script samples to help you develop dual materials for use in media instruction can be presented at this point. Two of them are my own creation (words and music) and the other is an adaptive presentation using a Psalm.

The first is titled, "Let us Pray." It involves a narrator, a teen-aged boy, various one-line actors (usually drawn from the choir), choir, orchestra, slides, motion picture film, scrim-set, pre-recorded tape effects and lighting. Dramatic action is provided for costume and set in several tableaux. The whole

271

work plays for about 45 minutes on the general subject of prayer. It is in every respect a sermon, although not delivered in the traditional manner. Although it involved writing an original musical score and script, similar presentations could be developed using existing music with a narrative thread of inter-connecting Scripture passages.

Another example uses a Bible text altogether. In this instance, it is the 23rd Psalm in the King James Version. As we examine the text for visual materials, we see obvious items: shepherds, green pastures, still waters, evil, rod and staff, table, etc. Literal visualization (photographs) could be used or combined with art work designed to utilize symbolism as well as realism in interpreting the meaning of a word. It is often easy to do this by using only faces. If a collection of faces is not available among your slides, build one using people of all ages and races. Hands are another good symbol: hands in rest, in prayer, in anger, intertwined, etc., have marvelously reactive impact on the viewer. They can be used effectively many times more than art or artistically-created symbolism. Slides of verses of Scripture, or prepared graphics can also be used, employing quasi-religious lettering (ART-Type 135) that can be made by simply rubbing the letters from a plastic sheet directly onto any other surface. It can be placed on clear plastic sheets and used as an over-lay above a photograph or a scene. The whole of the 23rd Psalm could probably be placed on graphic paper and prepared for transfer to slide by photography in less than an hour.

Having decided on slides consisting of scenes, faces and words, the script itself, with the exception of the opening line, has already been prepared. The remaining components involve music, simple lighting and, if we wish to be more dramatic, costuming and set for tableau. The music may consist of an original score, an adaptation of hymn materials, a re-arrangement of existing setting of the 23rd Psalm or a composite of all. In a series entitled *The Living Word,* a number of familiar Bible texts have been arranged for similar presentation. The particular format that follows is excerpted from that series:

PSALM 23

Components: Slides, narrator, solo, vocalist, chorus, instrumentalists, and congregation

Time: Approximately 5 minutes

* * * * *

MUSIC-VOICE	GRAPHICS
Music: (Up full, fading for voice)	
Voice: Hear now, the Living Word of God	1. Word card: "The Living Word of God."
Music: (Up full, fading for voice)	2. Slide or word card: "The 23rd Psalm."
Voice: The Lord is my Shepherd, i shall not want.	3. Art work or photograph: shepherd.
Solo Singer: The Lord is my Shepherd, I shall not want.	4. Flock scene.
Congregation: The Lord is my Shepherd, I shall not want.	5. Word card: "The Lord is my shepherd, I shall not want."
Choir: The Lord is my Shepherd, I shall not want.	6. Slide: shepherd or another pastoral scene.
Solo Singer: He maketh me to lie down in green pastures.	7. Slide: pleasant pastoral scene.
Voice: He maketh me to lie down in green pastures.	8. Slide: similar scene.
Congregation: He maketh me to lie down in green pastures.	9. Slide or word card: Scripture text.
He leadeth me beside the still waters.	10. Slide or word card: Scripture text.
Choir: He leadeth me beside the still waters.	11. Slide: lake or placid water scene.
Voice: He leadeth me beside the still waters.	12. Art work: outstretched hand with water in background.

273

Voice: He restoreth my soul.

Congregation: He restoreth my soul.

Solo Singer: He leadeth me in the paths of righteousness for his name's sake.

Congregation: He leadeth me in the paths of righteousness for his name's sake.

Voice: Yea, though I walk through the valley of the shadow of death ...

Solo Singer: I shall fear no evil ...

Congregation: For thou art with me, Thy rod and thy staff they comfort me.

Voice: Thou preparest a table before me in the presence of mine enemies.

Congregation: Thou annointest my head with oil.

Voice: My cup runneth over.

Choir: My cup runneth over.

Instrumental interlude: 25 seconds for slides

13. Slide: figure in prayerful mode.

14. Slide or word card: Scripture text.

15. Photo: stained glass window.

16. Slide: open Bible.

17. Slide: faces of people listening to sermon.

18. Slide: face of Christ.

19. Slide: Scripture text.

20. Slide: Scripture text.

21. Slide: cemetery.
22. Art work: crucifixion.

23. Slide: child's face, eyes looking upward in trust.

24. Slide: Scripture text.
25. Slide: Scripture text.
26. Slide: The Last Supper.

27. Photograph: refugee child receiving food from soldiers.

28. Slide: Scripture text.

29. Slide: golden chalice ... dissolving into

30. Slide: cup in hands.

31. Slide series of people
32. of all ages in helpful
33. gestures. These are

	34. shown at 5-second
	35. intervals.
Voice: Surely goodness and mercy shall follow me all the days of my life.	36. Slide: cradle scene.
	37. Slide: wedding.
	38. Slide: funeral.
Congregation: And I will dwell in the house of the Lord forever.	39. Slide: church spire.
	40. Slide: Scripture text.
Voice: And I shall dwell in the house of the Lord	41. Slide: sky, clouds, sunset.
Choir: Forever.	42. Slide: stained glass window.
Voice: Amen.	43. Slide: hands in prayer or face looking upward.
Choir: Amen.	44. Slide or word card: the word "Amen"

* * * * *

This presentation could be done in a more simple fashion, or with another selection of slides. Even film clips of a storm, funeral procession, tragic accident or an "evil" incident could be used. Or perhaps pictures of nearby familiar scenes or faces of people from the congregation. The script is yours to adapt in any way you choose, or it could be used as a sample to prepare another. The possibilities of using it as media support in a worship service as well as into a media package to be used over and over are unlimited.

A third example is based on a script and music titled, "His Name was John." This work was designed primarily for public performance by narrator and orchestra. The script concerns the last few moments in the life of John the Baptist. It is a sample of creative adaptation of a Scripture story combined with music to intensify and underscore its emotional and dramatic elements.

In this instance the original script will be adapted into a dramatic form, that is it will involve more people than just the narrator. We will describe the graphic possibility (visuals), suggest some way of creating them and indicate types of music which may be provided.

The principal characters in this script are John the Baptist, Elizabeth (John's mother), Mary (the mother of Jesus), Zaccharias, the executioners and a crowd. Created representations of these people must be found or made. Real or some pictures will need to be shot or suitable pictures from existing works reproduced.

In this particular script the following scenes will need to be depicted:

    a. John with his executioners,
    b. a dimly lit cell row with three figures at one end,
    c. a wilderness (without people),
    d. Zaccharias and the boy John,
    e. Mary and Elizabeth together,
    f. a small group of listeners in the wilderness,
    g. an assortment of faces with various expressions,
    h. the face of Jesus,
    i. the Baptism of Jesus (including dove).

From this selection of illustrations one should be able to make twenty-five or more individual photographs to serve as visuals needed in a presentation. Also make some word cards containing the passages of Scripture indicated by the script. Some additional word cards indicating script title and closing credit titles will also be required; e.g., "Narrated by Rev. William Cornwall," "Music by Richard Johnson," etc. The components involved for a public production include the following:

    a. slides (two carousel projectors with slide dissolve unit, preferably rear screen projection),
    b. music (special score composed or arranged),
    c. lighting (pulpit area only),
    d. microphone (narrator and cast mike),
    e. special effects (an echo effect on the voice of God and recorded tape of crowd noise, derisive laughter, etc.).

An enterprising production crew skilled in cinematography could enhance the materials with motion picture film segments of a scale model of Herod's castle and a Judean

276

wilderness scene. Using the same techniques suggested in the multiple use of the major graphics, a certain mobility-effect could be obtained by using motion picture techniques on the still picture. Don't try this, however, unless you do have skilled photographers willing to experiment. Now, let's turn to the script itself.

* * * * *

HIS NAME WAS JOHN

MUSIC-VOICE	GRAPHICS
Music: 25 seconds of music in a quiet mood (somewhat suspenseful but not jarring)	1. Word card: "...church presents..."
	2. Word card: "His Name Was John."
	3. Word card: "Narrator: Rev. William Cornwall."
	4. Word card: "Music: Richard Johnson."
	5. Word card: "Time: midnight the day John the Baptist died."
	6. Word card: "Place: the dungeon of Herod's castle."
Music: Fades to background for voice.	
Narrator: They stood* above him, two giant men of Herod's dungeon guard...the larger of the two with heavy ax in hand, awaiting the command to kill, the other tightly clutching hair to force John's head more firmly to the block.	7. Slide: giant men. 8. Slide: man with ax. 9. Slide: hand in hair. 10. Slide: John's head on block.

*Note: The underscored words in this script indicate points where slide changes occur.

There was no sound within the
room except heavy breathing
as the men above him readied
for the act to end his life.

11. Slide: complete shot
of scene.

Dragged from his cell at midnight, his hands and feet
securely bound, thrown to the
floor with fierce contempt, the
man called John the Baptist lay
there, knowing that in seconds
his life would end . . . and he
thought:

12. Slide: corridor with
three dim figures.

13. Slide: John's head on
block.
14. Slide: John's face, eyes
closed.

John: (Awedly) So this is what it's like
to die.

Narrator: He closed his eyes and waited
for the axe to fall.

Music: Suspenseful, moving to a more
placid pastoral.

Narrator: He seemed to hear a voice . . .
it was his own in Judea's wilderness.

15. Slide: John preaching
to multitude.

John: Repent Ye! Repent and be Baptized.
The Kingdom of Heaven is at hand.

16. John's face exhorting.
17. Slide: head and
shoulder shot of John.

Narrator: He remembered those days in
the wilderness as he went about
preaching the baptism of
repentence for the remission
of sins. He recalled the days of
his youth spent in the desert,
living from the land, eating
locusts and wild honey, studying the Scriptures, searching
for the truth of his life's purpose,
trying to solve the riddles that
made his life a mystery.

18. Film clip or slide:
wilderness.

19. Slide: young John in
wilderness.

20. Slide: John reading.

21. Slide: John in a
meditative mood.

278

Often had he pondered his
father's words. They were to
be believed, he knew that for
his father was <u>Zaccharias</u>, the   22. Slide: Zaccharias.
priest.

Music: (Up briefly).

But they were <u>strange</u> words,   23. Slide: John as a boy.
particularly to the ears of a
young lad.

Zaccharias: Thou, <u>my son</u> . . . my child   24. Slide: Zaccharias and
whom I have named John,   John.
shall be called a prophet and
thou shalt go forth before the
Lord to prepare his ways,
<u>to give</u> knowledge and salvation   25. Slide: Zaccharias.
unto his people by remission
of their sins. And thou shalt
go before the God of Israel
in the <u>spirit</u> and power of   26. Slide: John looking
Elias to turn the hearts of   up at his father.
the fathers to the children,
and the disobedient to the
wisdom of the just; <u>to make</u>   27. Slide: the Tabernacle.
ready a people prepared for
the Lord, to give light to them
that sit in darkness and in the
shadow of <u>death</u>, to guide our   28. Slide: the face of
feet into the way of peace.   Zaccharias.

Narrator: It was indeed strange talk for   29. Slide: the face of John.
a <u>child</u> to hear, almost as strange
as the story told him by <u>Elizabeth</u>, 30. Slide: Elizabeth.
his mother. Many times she had
told it, how her cousin <u>Mary</u>   31. Slide: Mary.
had come to join her in the sixth
month of her fruitfulness, and
<u>when</u> she had heard Mary's voice, 32. Slide: Mary and
he, John, had leaped for joy   Elizabeth.

279

within his mother's womb,
knowing even then that Mary
was to be the mother of the
Messiah. His <u>mother</u> had said   32. Slide: Elizabeth.
that she had been filled with
the Holy Ghost that day and
had cried out:

Elizabeth: Blessed art thou among women.
Blessed be the fruit of thy
womb.

Narrator: And <u>Mary</u> had replied: 33. Slide: Mary and
Elizabeth.

Mary: My soul doth magnify the <u>Lord</u>   34. Slide: face of Mary.
and my spirit hath rejoiced in
God my Saviour.

Music: (Mood change).

Narrator: He was not yet <u>thirty</u> when he   35. Slide: John in the
knew from God that it was he,   wilderness.
John, who was to proclaim to
all that the prophecies had been
fulfilled and that the time had
come for the Messiah to appear.
And <u>so</u>, in the wilderness out-   36. Slide: face of John
lands of Judea, he began to   preaching.
preach, saying:

John: I am the <u>voice</u> of one crying in   37. Slide: John and the
the wilderness, Repent Ye, for   crowd.
the Kingdom of Heaven is at hand.

Narrator: Again and again he cried out:

John: <u>Repent!</u> . . . I am the voice of one   38. Slide: John's face.
crying in the wilderness. Repent
and be baptized.

Sound Effects: (sneak in the sounds of
laughter and derision).

280

Narrator: They <u>laughed</u> at him, of course, and reviled him. Many thought him mad as he stood there, ǵaunt and bearded, dressed in <u>animal</u> skins, burned almost black with sun, his eyes shining brightly with the all-compelling need to cry his words:	39. Slide: the face of crowd member. 40. Slide: John's face.
John: Repent and be baptized. Repent Ye, for the Kingdom of Heaven is at hand. I am the voice of one crying in the wilderness. <u>Repent</u> and be baptized.	41. Slide: crowd faces.
Narrator: And when they stopped to <u>question</u> him, to ask what they should do, he told them fiercely:	42. Slide: John's face.
John: <u>He who</u> hath two coats, let him gave to him who hath none and he that hath meat, let him do likewise.	43. Slide: Scriptures.
Narrator: <u>To the publicans</u> he said:	44. Slide: crowd faces.
John: Exact no more than that which is appointed to you.	
Narrator: <u>To the soldiers</u> he commanded:	45. Slide: John's face.
John: Do violence to no man, neither accuse any man falsely.	
Narrator: <u>When</u> the Pharisees and Sadducees came to scoff and taunt him, he cried out:	46. Slide: a group of men.
John: <u>O Ye</u> Generation of Vipers, Repent and be Baptized!	47. Slide: Scriptures.

281

Narrator.   And when they asked him if he,   48. Slide: John
            John the Baptist — as they called
            him — were himself the Messiah,
            he pitied them that they under-   49. Slide: crowd.
            stood not, saying gently: 50. Slide: crowd.

John: There cometh one mightier than I   51. Slide: John.
            after me, the latchet of whose shoes
            I am not worthy to stoop down and
            unloose.   52. Slide: John and the
                                      crowd.

            I have indeed baptized you with
            water, but he shall baptize you
            with the Holy Ghost.   53. Slide: Scriptures.

Music: (Sad, pastoral).

Narrator: The weeks and months passed.   54. Slide: the wilderness.
            At times he paused to wonder —
            was he indeed mad or demon-   55. Slide: John's face.
            filled as many said . . . to spend
            his days proclaiming that the
            Christ had really come? He   56. Slide: the wilderness.
            shrugged his doubts aside. His
            voice now coarse and rough,
            croaked its message with a
            fierce and desperate urgency.   57. Slide: John and the
                                          crowd.

            And then one day, he sensed
            a stir among the crowd and   58. Slide: crowd.
            watched them part and give   59. Slide: crowd faces.
            way before a tall and slender
            Nazarene. He knew the moment
            had arrived, for looking deep   60. Slide: crowd.
            within the Galilean's eyes, he
            felt the awe of one who stands   61. Slide: John's face.
            within the presence of the Lord.

John: Behold! Behold the Lamb of God!

Narrator: A hush fell on the multitude . . .
            and Jesus spoke: 62. Slide: the face of Jesus.

Jesus: John, I have come to be baptized.

Narrator: John knelt before his new-found   63. Slide: John's face.
Lord and gently was he lifted up.

John: But Master, Lord, I cannot. Thou   64. Slide: John looking up.
art the annointed one. I am not
worthy.

Narrator: The words came once again,   65. Slide: Jesus head and
softly, but in strength.   shoulders.

Jesus: I came to be baptized by thee.

Narrator: Trembling, John took the out-
stretched hand and led him   66. Slide: one hand reach-
into the river. And when they   ing for another.
had come up out of the water   67. Slide: the baptismal
he at last knew the reason for   scene.
his being. The mystery, once
unsolved, was made plain this
day as from above the heavens   68. Slide: sky and dove.
opened wide and he saw the
Spirit of God descending like   69. Slide: baptismal scene
a dove alighting on the heaven-   with dove.
sent Messiah.   70. Slide: the face of Jesus.

Music: Surging full, 10 seconds, then
fading behind as screen fades to
black.

Narrator: And now . . . this.   71. Slide: Herod's dungeon.

He who had baptized the
King of Kings lay with his   72. Slide: John on block.
head upon a block.

He had no fear.
He seemed again to be warm   73.. Slide: Elizabeth.
and safe within his mother's

	womb, to feel once again that ecstacy of joy as <u>Mary</u> spoke:	74. Slide: Mary.

Mary: My soul doth magnify the Lord.

Music:	Tensely for 10 seconds, during which we see:	75. Slide: the dungeon. 76. Slide: the executioners. 77. Slide: the ax. 78. Slide: John's head held down.

Music: Underscores with tenseness:

Narrator:	He heard the quick intake of <u>breath</u> and he knew the death-ax had swung high . . . and in that swift and dreadful moment, he <u>heard</u> again the voice that spoke that day beside the <u>Jordan</u> River where he had baptized Jesus.	79. Slide: the face of executioner. 80. Slide: John's face. 81. Slide: River.
God's Voice:	<u>This</u> is my Beloved Son in whom I am well pleased.	82. Slide: dove.
Narrator:	He heard the voice and was content. He had seen the <u>Lord</u> and had believed.	83. Slide: the face of Jesus.

Music: Sudden sting of apprehension.

Narrator:	The <u>great ax</u> fell (quick succession of slides: bright red, purplish yellow, black).	84. Slide: bright red. 85. Slide: Purplish yellow. 86. Slide: Black.

Music: Violent motion then suddenly slow.

Narrator:	And John the Baptist knew no <u>more.</u>	87. Slide: face of Jesus and cross.

Music: To quiet finish with last slide a combination of the face of Jesus and cross.

* * * * *

284

If your imagination is triggered into both aural and visual awareness, I am sure you saw pictures, heard the sounds of voices and music and imagined a performance of this—or something equally as potent which you yourself, might create. If so, the inclusion of "His Name was John" was indeed worthwhile.

Let's take a few moments to summarize some of the things we considered important in this chapter. We said that a media instruction program for a church is important because it involves people in the service of the church, it is an effective and enduring teaching process because it reaches out beyond the church itself. We said that the program need not be overly-expensive if both equipment and people are mobilized for use and a program is developed in the church which takes advantage of commercially available media items.

A program should not actively begin until resources have been investigated, authorized, budgeted, organized and personnel trained. Above all determine the objectives and lay out a definite program of development and use of media. The whole church should be involved in understanding the program, that it be made available for use in training organizations (Sunday school, Bible school, home study) and that it also become a part of the worship services. In order to accomplish these goals a media library with appropriate working and shelving space needs to be developed in order to co-ordinate the media program with all other organized activities of the church. A multi-media center, with equipment designed to be operated easily from controls at the speaker's rostrum, should be created and made available for all to use.

Media is not, of course, the all-end-all. But it is the greatest of the functional tools the church has encountered in generations. With the rest of the world becoming involved in them for reasons much less valid, it would be foolish to bypass opportunities to develop ways to communicate the gospel mind-to-mind, soul-to-soul.

APPENDIX I

THE VOCABULARY OF MEDIA INSTRUCTION

A

AC – Alternating current.

AD – Assistant director.

Ad lib – Latin for "at liberty." It identifies remarks made by commentators, narrators or actors which were not included in the script.

AFTRA – American Federation of Television and Radio Artists.

Ampex – A brand name for various recording and playback audio-video electronic equipment.

Animation – A term used in photography for individual frames of motion picture film which are used to create the illusion of movement in otherwise inanimate objects. Each picture is photographed in sequence, separate pictures having been altered slightly to enable each succeeding photograph to show a forward progress of the motion involved.

Announcer – One who is appointed to announce. Abbreviasions used in scripts are "anncr." or "ann."

Apenture – Lens opening size (f-stops) on a camera.

ASCAP – American Society of Composers, Authors and Publishers.

Aspect ratio – Proportionate size of TV picture such as (3/4). See chapter on "Television Photography."

Assistant director – The assistant director in a production crew relates directly to the director and may perform a variety of functions designated to him by the director. He may also serve as technical director on a production to give cues and direct camera action.

ATR – Abbreviation for audio tape recorder.

286

Audio – That which applies to "sound." Frequently used terms are "audio-visual," "audio engineer," "audio track," "audio tape."

Audio engineer – The individual operating the equipment to record or playback materials that have been or are being recorded. He may also edit, mix, dub tape or maintain equipment to operating standards. He is the "ear" of the production. He works in what is called a control room or control booth. In studio work he functions on cue from the director. He places microphones, controls sound intensity, operates tape recorders and turntables during productions and "mixes" sound.

Audio tape – Material designed to record electronic impulses which are translated into "sound." The physical material is plastic tape which has been coated on one side by iron filings. The impulse of sound as the tape passes over the tape "head" (an electro-magnetic device) rearranges the molecular structure of the coating into microscopic "sine waves" representing a "picture" of sound itself. When the tape is later passing by a playback head the sound pictures are read electronically and are converted into sound.

Audio visual aids – Any material utilized by the teacher in the classroom which assists him in imparting information. It would include such a wide variety of items as film, slides, filmstrips, maps, displays, etc.

B

BG – Abbreviation for background. It is applied to background music, background noise, etc. For instance, a writer may indicate "Music up full, fading to BG behind speaker," or "Crowd noise BG" in the script.

Black – A unit may open abruptly with picture or it may come into picture from a black screen. Going to or from black merely indicates going to or from a picture. Terms such as fade to black indicate a slow lessing of light values until the picture is no longer visible.

Blend – An agreeable composite of any two or more components in audio or video. It is a combination of factors which has no distortion, such as combining a voice track with music or sound effects in which the results seem natural. The blending from one video sequence to another may result from a dissolve or the combining of two factors. The visual blend is successful if such a combination enhances the effectiveness of the presentation.

287

Boom mike – A form of extension rod or pipe on which a microphone is placed. It is operated by a crew member who follows the action by keeping the mike within range of the required sound source. The boom mike may also be stationary, and it is generally used in video sequences where the appearance of a microphone would shatter the desired picture illusion.

Break up – The failure of a picture in video caused by malfunction of equipment or decay in picture response of video tape is called a "break up." The effect is a distorted rearrangement of picture components.

C

Camera – There are a variety of cameras—still photography, super-8, 16mm., 35mm., video cameras. Terms such as "voice off camera" would indicate that we hear the voice but do not see the speaker. "On" camera would indicate that the object or person involved would be photographed.

Can – The term probably originated from the fact that motion pictures are customarily stored in metal containers, thus the "can" adaptation for video materials which are similarly pictoral. It refers to units which are completed and ready to be screened.

Carousel slide projector – A 35mm. projector which gets its slide feed from a carousel. The projector may advance and reverse, operate automatically on a pre-set timing device or be linked to a number of more sophisticated dissolve and pulse sync units. There are also random access projectors which operate single-slide advance or reversal.

Carousel tray – A circular device to hold 35mm. slides for projection on a carousel slide projector.

Cassette – A term connoting "package." It applies to audio and video tape, as well as film. These packages are self-contained and are usually designed for easy availability and operation. The principal advantages of cassettes are the easy availability of the playback units, the simplicity of the operation of equipment and the portability of the required equipment. One principal disadvantage is that the cassettes are difficult to change or modify.

Checkout packages – Any item or combination of items which have been prepared for listening or viewing, which may be obtained from a librarian for private use either at home or within a library, may be called a checkout package.

Composite — A composite is a combination of things. It may be a tape of mixed sounds, a graphic which is a combination of items or a combination of live action and film clip. It might also be called a montage.

Crawl — A crawl is a device on which informational sequences may be placed to be photographed. It is generally a large drum-like apparatus which is rotated to bring the information into camera view.

Credits — In some instances it is necessary to acknowledge the use of materials or the appearance of individuals. Such acknowledgments are known as credits.

Crew — The individual or group of individuals who operate the equipment and direct the activities for studio production. A video crew will normally be composed of a director, assistant director, technical director, cameramen, floor manager, audio and video engineers.

Cross fade — A technique involving the simultaneous increase of intensity from one source while decreasing the intensity from another. This is frequently used in going from one music cue to another to avoid abrupt changes of volume or style. It can also be used in blending from one voice track to another. Cross fading is not often used as a term in video but the same principle applies.

Cross talk — A technical malfunction which puts more than one signal into a single circuit. Illustration: while talking on the telephone you are able to hear another conversation on the same line.

Cue — An all-purpose term which may be given by any number of pre-arranged signals. It means simply "go" or "begin."

Cue card — Any form of large, easily readable card held in view to convey information either to performer or crew. These cards are sometimes called "idiot" cards.

Cue sheet — A page listing the sequence of cues involved in producing an audio or video tape. It is prepared to double check materials and equipment to be used. Normally the director does a last-minute check of all cues to be involved in the show as part of the production preparation.

Cut — This word is used in a variety of ways. If studio work is in progress and something goes wrong, it would mean to "stop." On an LP recording, the individual numbers are sometimes called "cuts." The word is also used for tape sequences which are usually identified with white leader tape. "Use cut 3" would mean to play the third of the banded sequences. The term is also used for a recording session, such as

289

"cutting a record" or "cutting a tape." It may also be used to indicate a deletion from a program segment or script. A program whose opening is omitted is sometimes called "up-cut."

D

Definition – Detail in TV picture.

Depth – The third-dimensional effect achieved in photography through depth of field relationships.

Dial access – The capacity of dialing a signal for a system to respond to a coded cue which sets it into operation. When the correct information is sent to the retrieval room via telephone circuit, the machine responds by activating itself to enable the program to be heard or seen.

Dimmer – A technical device which controls the brightness of lighting.

Director – The director heads a production crew in all its technical and artistic elements. He is in charge of people and components required to create a unit. The extent of his authority ranges from unit concept to final completion and is only limited by the operational restrictions placed upon him by the producer.

Dissolve – A movement from one sequence to another in which one element fades while the other comes into view. This may also be called a blend. We have capacity to "dissolve" from one camera shot to another, from camera shot to slide or motion picture, or between any elements that may be put into the show. Slide dissolve is fast and pre-set, but camera dissolve is more flexible in timing.

Distortion – A disturbance involving clarity of sound or picture caused by equipment malfunction or over-load of equipment capability. In video such distortion is noted in break-up or color bleeding generally caused by overloaded or defective equipment.

Dolly – This can be either (1) the apparatus upon which the camera is mounted, usually a moveable, wheeled device or (2) the process of moving the camera physically from one position to another. In contrast to "pan" (which is a left-right motion of the lens), "dolly" is a physical movement of the camera itself forward or backward.

Down Stage– In theater it means toward the apron (footlights). In TV it means toward the camera.

Drop — Can refer to (1) a decrease in the level of something or to (2) any canvas used as scenery (whether "fly" or "flat"). A "cyclorama" may also be called a backdrop.

Drop in — When portions of a previously-taped segment are inserted into a new show. It might also apply to dropping in an effect not included in the original version.

Drop out — Picture or sound loss.

Dubbing — The process of transferring a sound or picture source from one audio or video tape to another. Whenever possible it is a duplication process from a master to a copy.

E

Echo — An effect created to give the illusion of the sound being heard in a large hall, cavern, etc. Echo can be created electronically or by a device known as the echo or reverberation chamber.

Edital bar — A metal block used to cut and splice tape. The bar is grooved to hold tape in place while it is being cut with a razor blade either across a diagonal or vertical slot.

Editing — The process of change in recorded materials. Audio tapes may be spliced or cut and the materials re-arranged, eliminated or inserted. Video tape editing is done electronically.

Electronics — That branch of physics which treats emission, behavior and effect of electrons as in vacuum tubes, photo-electric cells, transistors, etc. Electronic systems are involved in TV, recording, radio, computer circuitry, etc.

End title — The final picture or sound. Usually music builds up to a final ending which is coincidental with "The End," as the screen fades to black.

ETV — Educational Television.

F

Fading — To lessen the intensity of audio, video, light, color or whatever, an engineer uses "faders" (sometimes called "pots") to alter the potential of a particular signal. The audio engineer may do a board fade by moving the fader to lessen the intensity of the sound input. The video engineer has a similar control of the picture signal, as does the lighting technician who may dim or fade the lighting. There are many variants in the fading technique.

Feedback – Sound generated electronically under several conditions. It is most commonly caused by the proximity of microphone to loud-speakers. Sometimes it results from an error made in the use of equipment. Faulty equipment can also produce the feedback, but it can generally be ascribed to human error.

Film chain – An instrument designed to introduce photographic materials into a videotaped production. The chain consists of a video-camera, slide and motion picture projectors. Output of these projectors is focused onto a mirror or prism which is seen by the video-camera. Usually film chains are remotely operated by the console engineer. Newer chains often include slide drums instead of carousels and super-8 projector capability along with 16mm.

Film clip – A segment of film. Sometimes this segment is edited from the original film and re-leadered for more convenient handling.

Film loops – Strips of film designed to be projected as continuously as desired. They are usually contained in a film cassette which requires a special projector. Film loops may be introduced into a video system by either direct or rear screen projection. More frequently they are projected into shadow boxes which provide for greater clarity.

Filmstrip – A series of photographs developed on a strip of film requiring a special projector to screen. Filmstrips may be shown one frame at a time silently or they may be coupled with a tape or recording sound source. The latter is sometimes "pulse synced" to enable automatic operation of the machine.

Filter mike – A microphone whose input is fed through a "filtering" device which removes the low frequency portions of the sound. A voice using a filter mike would resemble the sound of a person speaking over the telephone. Music fed through filter can give the illusion of distance or of music having been recorded prior to the development of extended-range recording potential.

Flat – Any scenery built with a frame upon which canvas or other materials have been stretched and representatively painted.

Flipchart – A series of title cards or graphics placed on an easel, the top of which is connected for easy flipping with loose-leaf notebook rings or similar fasteners.

292

Flutter — A condition resulting when materials are recorded or played back on malfunctioning equipment, interferring with the smoothly accurate passing of the tape by the playback or record head. The sound is easily recognizable as being jerky.

Fly — Scenery hung from above the set.

Format — The outline or pattern for a production. Example: The format of an interview show is billboard (opening information of show title, star), introduction of guest, interview, wind up, closing and credits.

Frame — There are two uses of this term in production: (1) framing the picture to achieve a balance in the scene being photographed, and (2) the individual frame of a motion picture film.

F-stop — Camera lens opening sizes. The larger the f-stop number, the smaller the diaphragm opening and vice versa.

G

Gain — Another term for intensity, volume, light, etc., applicable to audio and video.

Glitch — A fabricated word translated "picture disturbance." It refers to any sudden interference with the video picture.

Go — Sometimes used as a cue to begin. A show may be ready to go when all components have been determined and the rehearsal completed.

Gobo — A silhouette device placed in front of the camera lens in such a way as to create a framing to produce special effect for the scene.

Graphic — Any illustrative or decorative material that requires preparation in photography, line drawing, map and chart making.

Graphic artist — One who prepares illustrative or decorative materials.

H

Headset monitor — Earphones.

Hi-fi — Short for high-fidelity, which indicates a wide frequency range in the sound spectrum.

Hiss — A sound from a tape or loudspeaker, generally the result of a malfunction of equipment or the presence of high-frequency sound. It is most commonly detected on tape.

293

Hot – When a piece of equipment is turned on and ready to be activated, it is hot. An open mike or a camera feeding the picture tube is hot. A picture is hot if it contains distortion because of sudden brightness arising from reflection or sudden color intensification.

I

ID – Station identification. A picture signal is sometimes called "sig" or "logo."

Information card – Implies a graphic containing only words designed to be used on a display stand or photographed and used as a slide. It is also called a word card.

Intercom – A two-way telephonic system by which control room and studio personnel may communicate. These are usually worn on the head and may have one earpiece and a mouthpiece.

IPS – Abbreviation for Inches Per Second. The term is used in audio tape recordings where the tape speed may vary depending upon the equipment used. It indicates how many inches of tape pass by the playback or recording head every second.

J

Jack – A jack is a device used to connect circuits within electronic systems. It identifies connecting wire tipped with various input-output devices, such as phone jack, minature phone jack, pin jack, cannon male-female jacks, etc. The recepticle receiving the input jack (such as on a tape recorder) is called "female"; the tipped-end of the patch cord or connecting cable is the male. A jack is also a brace used to hold up flats.

K

Kinescope – A form of recording done by 16mm. film camera focused on the picture tube of a TV set. It was an early form of production recording in the years prior to video-tape.

L

Lavalier – A term derived from a "necklace," used to identify a cord or strap used for wearing a microphone.

Leader – A plastic or paper tape used to prelude the actual picture or sound or to connect segments. Sometimes the term "leadering" is used to signify the process of splicing such tape to the main body of the show or of connecting segments of show material together.

Lead time – Signifies the number of days (or hours) given for the preparation of a unit.

Level – Signifies intensity in sound or light source. Insufficient light or sound is low level, excessive is high level. The camera or microphone needs a minimum standard of intensity in order to properly function. Sometimes the term is used synonomously with "volume" and "gain."

License – Permission to use materials, equipment, etc.

Lip sync – A process of having speaker or singer syncronize his sound with a pre-filmed or pre-videotaped picture, to make it seem that the voice on the screen is actually uttering sound at the moment his lips move.

Live – Human (or animal, reptile, etc.) participation in front of a studio camera would be live in contrast to a series of slides or a film being video-taped. A live production is one which is done at the moment with the participants present.

Log – A detailed description of station broadcast schedule or of work-hours involved in a production.

LP – Short for "long playing." It is used to describe a type recording whose speed is 33 1/3 rpm.

M

Magnetic track – A strip of magnetic tape fixed to the edge of a film opposite its sprocket holes.

Main title – That information or identification which appears at the beginning of a film or video-audio taped production. Main title music is generally attention-getter material which acquaints the listener with the program being presented.

Makeup – Cosmetic materials used to create character in a dramatic production. A "flat" makeup may be used to reduce shine or reflection caused by facial response to too much light.

Master – The original source of sound or picture from which copies are made. When a unit is video-taped a master and one copy are generally made at the same time. The copy is used on the retrieval system, the master is retained for additional copying if needed. The same procedure is done in audio-taping. The copy made from the master is referred to as first generation and additional generations are numbered with each succeeding copy of a copy. The master-to-copy reproduction provides the best results.

Media – The plural of "medium," which means "method" or "manner." Media connotes all methods of communication, such as newspapers, magazines, microfilm, microfiche, textbooks, chalkboard, etc. In instructional media the term indicates all forms of communication tools, but more specifically it indicates instant call-up type, such as film, recordings, prepared graphics, filmstrips, film loops, transparencies, audio tape, video tape, slides, etc. In the last analysis any device used to communicate, from primitive smoke signal or drum beat to billboard or computer, can be included within the meaning of the word.

Memorex – A brand name for audio and video tape.

Mike – Short for "microphone."

Mixing – It is possible to combine more than one sound simultaneously on audio tape. Music may be added to voice or other sounds with the input intensity determining the perspective. Mixing is the process of combining two or more separate sound tracks into one. The process is also sometimes called a "mix-down." The audio engineer's console is sometimes called a "mixer" because he has the capacity to control the levels of several inputs simultaneously.

Mono – A short form of "monaural," meaning one sound track. Audio tape recorders are often built with multiple sound heads and several tracks may be recorded and played back from the same tape. Multi-tracks do not necessarily imply "stereo," for in stereo tape heads feed into separate amplifiers and from them into separate speakers.

Montage – A combination of things happening simultaneously whether in a picture or sound. It is a telescopic effect which gives an impression of several things happening as a unit.

N

NET – Abbreviation for National Educational Television or network.

Nudnik – An interferer, interrupter and otherwise undesirable person who "knows it all."

296

O

Off-camera (off-mike) — Action in TV where a voice is heard but the person speaking is not in the picture. Off-mike is a term used to mean "distance" from a mike's normal "presence" pattern.

Optical track — Photographic representation of sine waves made either directly on or imbedded within a film which is reproduced by photo-electric cell.

Overhead projector — A device designed to project materials, usually transparencies, onto a screen.

Overload — The result of trying to make the machine do more than it is capable, thus causing distortion of various types.

P

PA — Public address sound system.

Pan — A word used in motion picture and video photography to signify a camera movement during which the lens of the camera swing around an axis. It is not unlike the movement of the eyes when the head turns or moves up and down while looking straight ahead. The "pan" will be a successful technique if the cameraman and his equipment can make a smooth motion slowly enough to comprehend the scene.

Playback — The listening to or looking at parts of a completed audio or video recording. Sometimes in video-taping a short segment will be taped and then replayed while the engineer and director check the various values obtained. The same procedure is often done during a recording session.

Potentiometer — A "pot" or "knob" or "fader" used to control volume level in audio equipment.

Preview — To "look at" prior to decision to use. A teacher may "preview" a film before showing it to a class. A producer may "preview" materials he is contemplating putting into his show. In the case of the video console in the studio, the technical director may "preview" the upcoming slide or camera shot before deciding to use it.

Print through — An electronic phenomenon occuring when sounds on one section of a tape are absorbed by another section as a faint echo effect. This is frequently caused by tape being rewound too tightly and stored that way.

297

Pulse sync – Indicates high or low frequency tones recorded on magnetic tape. The tone itself is inaudible but it has the capacity to activate the mechanism of a machine that is tuned to its frequency. The tone itself is the "pulse"; the syncronous action it causes in operating another piece of equipment is the "sync." A tape containing pulse sync may be used to activate the mechanism of a carousel projector, making it possible for the slides to be screened without an operator.

Q

Quote – The use of material created by others. Obviously there is no way to put "visual" quotation marks around a quote, although the narrator may use the familiar phrase, "and I quote." As he is quoting, a reproduction of the material he is quoting from may be shown, or he may desire a change of voice rather than say the "quote" himself. Unacknowledged quotes might be considered plagarism.

R

Read out – Information conveyed by various electronic instruments related to picture or sound.

Rear screen – Projection on the reverse side of a translucent screen when the projector is set behind the screen rather than in front of it. This has distinct advantages in studio work because one sees neither the projector or the operator. Sometimes a device known as a "shadow box" is used to contain the picture within smaller dimensions. Rear screen projection is possible for all forms of projection units, but is particularly effective in slide and film loops.

Remote – Indicates program components recorded or video-taped outside the studio.

Reverb – Short for reverberation, an audio-echo effect. It may be obtained electronically or by placing a mike in front (at a distance) of a speaker feed and re-introducing the sound back into the system. In the past rather elaborate echo chambers were built to produce these effects. Now most echo is achieved electronically,

Rolling – Designates that the audio or video tape machines are operating up to prescribed speed.

Roll-over – Describes the picture on the video screen as it moves out of its "locked in" position into a rocking motion.

Rundown – Jargonese for "taking a look at" or "a listen to" elements within a production or a synthesis or synopsis of procedure.

S

Scotch – Brand name of various types of audio, video, splicing and leader tape.

Scrim – A theatrical curtain made of light weight, coarsely-woven, mesh-like materials (much like cheese cloth). It is hung and heavily weighted to stretch tightly, thus allowing action played behind it to be seen (when lighted from the back). It is also capable of serving as a backdrop when lighted from the front. Its principal function is to create illusionary settings. Its use in TV is somewhat limited since the development of the chroma-key, but it may be used effectively. Certain types of scrims may be used also as projection screens, although the effect is not as clearly defined as on a standard screen.

Sequence – Sequence has limited use because of its conflicting meaning. To some it signifies a series of units which make up a course content. To others it is a series of information bits which when combined make up a unit. It has been used traditionally as the sequence of shots, slides or motion picture inserted into the main body of the studio production.

Set – A staging device depicting an environment. To be effective, the designer-builder must try to achieve a credible realism. A set may also be the situation in which the subject is photographed. Sets need not be elaborate—two comfortable chairs, an end table or coffeetable, a rug on the floor and a picture on the wall could be a believable living room set.

Shadow box – A box of indeterminate size which has one end open and one end covered with a translucent substance. Customarily these are boxes designed to accept projection from slide projectors. Projection is usually done from behind the screen and is then photographed by video-camera. A mirror is sometimes used in the projection process to avoid the normal reversal that occurs in rear screen projection.

Shot – Applies to picture taking. A scene is shot, we take snapshots, we shoot some film or we refer to the scene that the camera is scanning as a possible shot. A tight shot refers to a close-up and a wide shot means to shoot as much of the total scene as possible.

Sig – Short for "signature."

Signal – Used to describe the intensity strength of audio and video components.

16mm. – Generally applied to film size and projector, camera or other device related to editing, splicing, etc. The "millimeters" refers to film frame areas; the 16 indicates size. The terms 8mm. and 35mm describe other standard sizes.

Sound effects – Any sound which simulates or represents an actual live sound. These may be created manually by a sound effects man or derived from actual recordings of live sounds. The range of available effects is almost endless.

Special effects generator – An electronic device used to create various patterns or images directly on to a video screen. Examples of such would be the effect of having the picture disappear as if it were being "wiped" away from one corner to another.

Splicing – The process of joining ends of audio, video tape or film together. In magnetic tape, the process is done with self-adhesive plastic tape placed upon the shiny side of the tape itself. In film, the process is more complex and is done with an adhesive substance after the emulsion has been removed from the area to be spliced.

Stand by – A phrase signifying get ready, we're about to start. The term is also used for a back up or stand by program in the event the one scheduled fails.

Stand in – One who stands in position for rehearsal for the purpose of checking equipment function, camera angles, shots, lighting, audio, etc. It is generally an individual who is not part of the main body of the video taping.

Stereo – A broadcast or recording system in which sound is recorded on separate tracks, played back through separate amplifying systems, and heard on separate speakers. Stereo ranges from two-track to multi-track systems. It is designed to bring a certain depth perception into sound creating an illusion of space and distance.

Stop-action – Used in motion picture photography in which frames are exposed individually in order to create the illusion of motion in inanimate objects.

300

Story-board — A detailed outline, a step-by-step progression of a production or a word-picture of a format.

Studio — The area in which filming, video-taping or recording is done.

Super — Short for "superimpose." A technique by which a slide or motion picture sequence may be shown simultaneously. A video tape may be made, and after its review the producer may decide it needs to have additional visual material introduced. Insertion of such new material into a new tape by combining it with the old may be considered "supering" the new material upon the previously taped material.

Super-8 — A term designating a specific type of camera, projector and film.

Switcher — A console built to enable equipment used in TV (cameras, film chain, etc.) to be switched into an "on the air" or "in view readiness" position. This is generally done by using a row of buttons or tabs called a "bus."

Sync — Electronic impulse used to stablize and equalize picture quality among all studio components. When the sync signals are all equalized, everything is good—otherwise, distortion and disaster appear.

T

Tag — Generally a musical portion designed to indicate conclusion of an idea or of the show itself.

Take — In motion picture photography and sound recording it indicates an attempt to achieve desired results. A take also indicates the desired portion or completion of a successful attempt.

Talent — Anyone designated to be on mike or camera as part of a production. The word is used loosely in contrast to the term crew.

Talk back — A control room microphone with speaker outlet in the studio for purposes of communicating with the cast and crew.

Tape head — The electro-magnetic area used to re-arrange or interpret molecular patterns to record or playback sound or picture.

Tape recorder (audio, ATR) — A device used to record or play back magnetic tape. There are three types: reel-to-reel, cartridge and cassette. Tape speeds vary from 1 7/8, 3 3/4, 7 1/2 and 15, with 7 1/2 being the most common. There are monaural and stereo machines, some with two, four or eight playing tracks.

Tape recorder (video, VTR) – Video-tape recorders function to provide picture signal on tape either by "helical" or "quadraplex" tape head. They produce lines which are electronically translated into pictures when tape is played back. Tape sizes vary from 1/4 inch to 2 inches. VTRs operate reel-to-reel or in cassettes and cartridges.

Technical director – Sometimes shortened to "TD." The individual who handles or supervises the technical equipment as it relates to control-room operation. He may act as consultant to the director in planning the production and he may determine use of the equipment necessary to achieve the intended results.

Tempo – Signifies the speed or pacing of program content.

Test pattern – A screen-like device used to test camera variants similar in function to test tone or 1000-cycle tone used for testing and equalizing audio components.

Tilt – Moving the camera lens up and down in a vertical plane. "Pan" is the side-to-side motion of lens, "truck" is the side-to-side motion of entire camera and "dolly" refers to moving the camera up and back.

Tracking – In order to get maximum quality in picture and sound recording the tape must pass smoothly and evenly past the heads. It must stay in exact position, or track exactly.

Transistor – A non-vacuum electronic device similar in use to the electron tube. "Solid state" refers to the use of transistors instead of vacuum tubes, allowing for miniturization of electronic circuitry.

Traveler curtain – A curtain which opens either from the middle toward the sides or one pulled from side to side.

Turntable – A circular plate which is used to hold recordings. These are geared to turn at specified speeds ranging from 16, 33 1/3, 45, 78 RPM (revolutions per minute). Variable speed turntables are also available. A turntable is also a device used in the studio upon which objects may be placed to revolve at a designated speed in order that all sides may be photographed. These may be either operated manually or with a variable speed motor.

U

UHF – Ultra high frequency.

Upstage – In theater it means away from the apron (footlights). In TV it means away from the camera.

V

VHF – Very high frequency.

Video – That which pertains to picture.

Video engineer – A technician who operates the equipment during a video-taping session. He makes certain that all meters read "go," and he constantly checks and maintains picture and sound quality.

Video tape – Magnetic tape used in recording picture and sound. Video tape generally comes in half-inch, one-inch and two-inch widths. It does not have the durability of audio tape in that repeated playings decrease its quality. Tapes made on one recording system will not universally play on other systems. Video tapes deteriorate rapidly unless stored and placed under ideal conditions of dust-free and low humidity conditions.

Voice over – Normally applies to adding voice over previously recorded music or sound. In the case of movies it refers to adding voice over silent picture sequences. For whatever reason it is used, it is an addition to previously prepared materials.

VTR – Abbreviation for video tape recorder.

VU meter – Volume unit meter. A meter measuring the volume of intensity of sound frequencies in live or recorded audio performance. Sometimes called "VI" or volume indicator meter.

W

Wipe – Electronic effect designed to produce the feeling that the old picture on the screen is being pushed aside by a new picture entering. There are a variety of such wipes, some beginning in the center, some wiping from corner to corner, etc.

Word card – An information source used either on 35mm. slides or photographed directly from the original which has been placed on an easel or stand. Such a card may be of indeterminate size and may contain almost any information desired, such as graphs, charts, maps, words, line drawings, etc. It is, in fact, a graphic rather than a photograph of a real object.

303

Wow — Wobbly sound or uneven pitch generally caused by malfunction of equipment.

Z

Zoom — An illusion of drawing nearer to or going further away from the subject being photographed. The zoom mechanism may be electronically, mechanically or manually controlled. It is an effective photographic technique.

APPENDIX II

RESOURCES IN MEDIA INSTRUCTION

One of the very first questions asked when the subject of media arises is "Where do you buy it?" The "it" does not refer to hardware generally, for most people seem to know where to buy tape recorders, phonographs, overhead projectors and the many other devices used in media production. Rather, it refers to software. Unless you are a complete do-it-yourself person or have a well-developed staff of production experts at your command, you need to know where such software, great volumes of it already available, can be obtained.

Where to get it is our objective in this Appendix. It is a quick-reference section in which you will find answers to questions from how to procure already-available "telecourses," to how to obtain free films and filmstrips. A list of books on media, transparencies, magazines, guides to maps, tapes and phonograph records and much more are included. It should help you find what you want when you want it.

One last word: consult your local public librarian. You may save yourself much time and postage by looking at materials she already has on hand. And, if she doesn't—well, maybe she would like to borrow your copy of this book.

Carol Ann Mills
Library Staff
The University of Texas
at Dallas

I. Multi-Media Source Guides

Audio Visual Market Place: A Multimedia Guide. New York: Bowker, 1969–.

An annual directory of the audio-visual industry listing producers and distributors, equipment, services and organizations, conventions, film festivals and publications concerned with the new media—films, filmstrips, slides, film loops, tapes, transparenceis, maps and globes.

AV Index. Detroit: Audio Visual Research Institute, 1961–.

An annual selected list of materials covering approximately 1800 entries. It gives information on audio-visual tools, materials and procedures. The entries on films, filmstrips, recordings, etc., are arranged under broad subject classifications. This work is limited in that entries in one edition are not repeated in the following annual publications.

Blue Book of Audio-Visual Materials. Chicago: Educational Screen, 1922–.

A guide to films, filmstrips, recordings and slides updated by *Educational Screen and Audio-Visual Guide.*

Educational Media Council. *Educational Media Index,* 14 vols. New York: McGraw-Hill, 1964.

This index to films, kinescopes, filmstrips, slides, transparencies, maps, charts, graphs, flat pictures, videotapes, phonotapes, records, programmed instruction materials and models indicates the source, content and cost of non-book materials over a wide range of subject fields and age levels.

Frankle, Edna and Frankle, Charles. *Guide to Educational Technology.* Westport, Conn.: Technomic Publishing Co., 1971.

Includes a select list of companies distributing and producing various types of media.

Landers, Bertha, ed. *Foreign Language Audiovisual Guide.* Landers Association, 1961.

Learning Directory. 7 vols. New York: Westinghouse Learning Corp.

A comprehensive listing of over 200,000 items of print and non-print materials, arranged in columns by key word subject indexing. It appears to be a combination of *Books in Print* and indexes prepared by the National Information Center for Educational Media.

Markham, Louis. *New Educational Materials.* New York: Scholastic Magazines, Inc., 1970.

A classified compilation of reviews and evaluations by teachers of over five hundred books, films, recordings, multi-media kits, filmstrips, transparencies, film loops, teaching-learning games and professional references. It is arranged by grade and subject areas.

McClusky, Frederick Dean. *The A-V Bibliography.* 2nd ed. Dubuque, Iowa: W. C. Brown Co., 1955.

An old but comprehensive bibliography of literature on A-V instruction including a special section listing doctoral dissertations in the field from 1921-1954.

McDaniel, Roderick, ed. *Resources for Learning: A Core Media Collection for Elementary Schools.* New York: R. R. Bowker Co., 1971.

This guide lists over 4,000 films, filmstrips, slides, transparencies and recordings by subject, author and title. All titles included have been recommended by one of thirty-four basic sources such as *The Elementary School Library Collection.*

Moldstad, John A. *Sources of Information on Educational Media.* Washington, D. C.: Government Printing Office, 1963.

This annotated collection of published lists of new educational media gives information about equipment, bibliographies and graduate programs in the audio-visual field.

Rufsvold, Margaret Irene, and Guss, Carolyn. *Guides to Newer Educational Media.* 3rd ed. Chicago: American Library Association, 1970.

An excellent annotated bibliography of sources for 16mm. motion pictures, 35mm. filmstrips, 2 by 2 inch slides, 3½ by 4 inch slides, kinescopes, videotapes, phonodisks, tapes and programmed instruction materials, including a list of professional audio-visual organizations and periodicals.

Williams, Catharine M. *Sources of Teaching Materials.* Columbus, Ohio: Teachers Aid Laboratory, Bureau of Educational Research, Ohio State University.

This pamphlet is revised regularly and covers sources and utilization of free and inexpensive teaching aids, such as films, filmstrips, slides, radio, television and recordings.

II. Guides to Pamphlets and Free Teaching Materials

American Library Association. *The Vertical File.* (Supplement C to pamphlet no. 9) Chicago: American Library Association.

Aubrey, Ruth. *Selected Free Materials for Classroom Teachers.* Palo Alto, Calif.: Fearon, 1965

A bi-annually revised guide of sources arranged by subject.

Educators Guide to Free Teaching Aids, 1955–. Randolph, Wisc.: Educators Progress Service, 1955–.

This annual publication contains an annotated list of free maps, bulletins, pamphlets, exhibits, charts and books, arranged under broad subject headings.

Educators Index to Free Materials. J. G. Fowlkes and P. T. Cody (eds.). Randolph, Wisc.: Educators Progress Service.

Free and Inexpensive Learning Materials. 15th Biennial ed. Division of Surveys and Field Services, George Peabody College for Teachers, 1970

Miller, Shirley. *The Vertical File and Its Sattelites: A Handbook for Acquisition, Processing, and Organization.* Littleton, Colo.: Libraries Unlimited, 1971.

This book contains excellent source lists, criteria for material selection and information on the preparation of pamphlets, clippings, vocational material and pictures.

Monthly Catalog of United States Government Publications. Washington, D. C.: Government Printing Office.

A current bibliography of publications issued by all branches of the government. This catalog is arranged by the department or bureau and lists documents published during the month, including title, date, pagination and price.

O'Hara, Frederic J., compiler. *Over 2000 Free Publications: Yours for the Asking.* New York: New American Library, 1968.

This guide to United States Government publications lists depository libraries by subject.

Pepe, Thomas J. *Free and Inexpensive Educational Aids.* New York: Dover, 1967.

Over 1500 materials are listed, 94 percent of which are free.

Salisbury, Gordon and Sheridan, Robert. *Catalog of Free Teaching Aids.* Riverside, Calif.

Schain, Robert L. and Polner, Murray. *Where to Get and How to Use Free and Inexpensive Teaching Aids.* Englewood Cliffs, N. J.: Prentice-Hall, 1963.

Weisinger, Mort. *1001 Valuable Things Free.* New York: Bantam Books.

A regularly-revised book listing free products, services, samples, maps, films and photographs.

Williams, Catharine M. *Sources of Teaching Materials.* Columbus, Ohio: Ohio State University.

A regularly-revised pamphlet covering sources and utilization of films, filmstrips, slides, radio, television, recordings and other free and inexpensive teaching aids.

III. Guides to Picture Sources

Bartran, M. *Guide to Color Reproductions.* New York: Scarecrow Press, 1966.

Catalog of Colour Reproductions of Paintings: 1860 to 1965. 8th ed. Paris: UNESCO, 1966. New York: Columbia University Press, 1966.

Fine Art Reproductions of Old and Modern Masters. Greenwich, Conn.: New York Graphic Society, 1965.

Frankenberg, Celestine G. (ed.). *Picture Sources.* 2nd ed. New York: Picture Division, Special Libraries Association, 1964.

This bibliography lists over 700 sources of pictures including name, address, description, size, subject and price.

McGraw-Hill Dictionary of Art. 5 vols. New York: McGraw-Hill, 1969.

Myers, B. S. (ed.). *Encyclopedia of Painting.* New York: Crown, 1955.

This one-volume encyclopedia contains 1,000 color plates of painters and paintings from prehistoric times to the twentieth century.

The National Geogrphic Index. Washington, D. C.: National Geographic Society.

Osborn, M. B. and Miller, B. *Sources of Free Pictures.* Rev. ed. Riverside, Calif.: Bruce Miller Publications, 1963.

Praeger Picture Encyclopedia of Art. New York: Praeger, 1958.

Vance, Lucie. *Illustration Index.* 2nd ed. Metuchen, N. J.: Scarecrow Press, 1966.

An index to pictures printed in popular magazines.

IV. Guides to Film Sources

The American Educational and Historical Film Center. *American Film Review: Films of America.* St. Davids, Pa.: Eastern Baptist College.

A small guide to films endorsed by the American Educational and Historical Film Center, containing descriptive annotations.

American Film Festival Guide. New York: Educational Film Library Association, Inc., 1959.

This annual publication includes alphabetically arranged descriptions of 35mm., 16mm. and 8mm. films shown at the annual festival sponsored by the Educational Library Association.

Dimmitt, R. D. *A Title Guide to the Talkies.* New York: Scarecrow Press, 1965, 2 vols.

Over 16,000 feature length films released between 1927 and 1963 are arranged alphabetically by title in this guide.

Educational Film Guide. New York: H. W. Wilson Co., 1936-1962.

This basic film bibliography is published in three quarterly issues with an annual volume published in August. The alphabetical subject and title list, classified according to the Dewey Decimal System, includes descriptive notes, evaluations and age-level notations. The last cumulation covered 1954-1958 and annual supplements were published through 1962. Supersedes *Educational Media Index.*

Educational Film Library Association. *Film Evaluation Guide, 1946-1964.* New Haven, Conn.: Reader's Press, 1965.

A cummulated list of film evaluations, 1946-1964, including basic information.

Educational Films. University of Michigan, Audio-visual Education Center, and Michigan State University, Instructional Media Center, 1969. Supplements: September, 1969 and September, 1970.

One of the most complete catalogs for a university media center.

Fawcett, M. *An Index to Films in Review, 1960-1964.* New York: National Board of Review of Modern Pictures, 1966.

Film Evaluation Guide, 1946-1964. New York: Educational Film Library Association, Inc. 1965.

A comprehensive listing and evaluation of over 4500 motion picture films and filmstrips.

Films for Children. New York: Educational Film Library Association, 1961.

A guide to children's entertainment films issued bi-monthly and kept current by *Film Review Digest.*

Films for Libraries. Chicago: Audio-Visual Committee, American Library Association, 1962.

An annotated list of over 400 selected films judged valuable for library collections, including documentary, experimental and avant-garde films arranged alphabetically by title and indexed by subject.

Jones, Emily S. *Manual on Film Evaluation.* New York: Educational Film Library Association, Inc., 1967.

Limbacher, James L. *Feature Films on 8mm. and 16mm.* 3rd ed. Ann Arbor, Mich.: R. R. Bowker Co., 1971.

An alphabetical list of over 10,000 8mm. and 16mm. films from the early silent pictures to the present.

Limbacher, James L. (ed.). *Feature Films on 16: A Directory of 16mm. Sound Feature Films Available for Rental in the U.S.* New York: Educational Film Library Association, 1966.

An alphabetical compilation of feature films from over 40 large rental libraries in the U.S. It includes documentaries and animated cartoons, but no subject index.

National Information Center for Educational Media. *Index to 8mm. Motion Cartridges.* New York: Bowker, 1969.

National Information Center for Educational Media. *Index to 16mm. Educational Films.* New York: Bowker, 1969.

A resource guide to 16mm. educational films recorded in the Master Data Bank at the University of Southern California. It is divided into three sections: subject, title description and film distributor list.

National Information Center for Educational Media. *Index to 35mm. Educational Filmstrips.* New York: Bowker, 1970.

New York Library Association. *Films for Children: A Selected List.* New York: New York Public Library, 1966.

New York Library Association. *Films for Young Adults: A Selected List.* New York: New York Public Library, 1966.

Reid, Seerley and Grubbs, Eloyse. *U. S. Government Films for Public Educational Use.* Washington, D. C.: Office of Education. U. S. Department of Health, Education, and Welfare, 1963.

An alphabetical list of over 6000 films and filmstrips available for public education.

16mm. Films Available for Renting or Purchase. New York: NBC Educational Enterprises, 1969.

NBC specials and documentaries available to libraries for rental or purchase are listed in this catalog.

Solomon, Albert E. *Teacher Evaluation of New Classroom Films, 1964-1965.* Albany, N. Y.: 1965.

Technicolor Corporation. *Directory.* Cosa Mesa, Calif.

A source directory of available 8mm. films.

United World Free Film Catalog. New York: United World Films, 1971.

U. S. Copyright Office. *Motion Pictures, 1912-1939, 1940-1949, 1950-1959.* Washington, D. C.: Library of Congress, 1951–.

Copyright entries for motion picture films are listed in the catalog by the U. S. Copyright Office.

U. S. Government Films: A Catalog of Motion Pictures and Filmstrips for Sale by the National Audio-Visual Center. Washington, D. C.: National Archives and Records Services, General Services Administration, 1969.

Films in this catalog are arranged in broad subject categories with a title index.

U. S. Library of Congress. *Library of Congress Catalog – Motion Pictures and Filmstrips, 1953-1957, 1958-1962.* Ann Arbor, Mich.: Edwards, 1958-1963.

This title is published quarterly, collected annually and cummulated quinquennially in the National Union Catalog. It attempts to cover all educational motion pictures and filmstrips released in the U. S. and Canada.

U. S. Office of Education. *A Directory of 16mm. Film Libraries.* Washington, D. C.: Government Printing Office.

This is a complete biennial directory of film libraries.

U. S. Office of Education. *United States Government Films for Public Use.* Washington, D. C.: Government Printing Office, 1940–.

This regularly-issued guide is a circular of the U. S. Office of Education.

World Film Directory. Paris: Mass Communication Techniques Division Division. UNESCO, 1962.

A list of sources of worldwide agencies concerned with educational, scientific and cultural films.

V. Guides to Filmstrips

Educators Guide to Free Filmstrips. Randolph, Wisc.: Educators Progress Service, 1949–.

An annotated list of filmstrips giving source, availability, terms of loan, price, etc., arranged by subject with subject and title index.

Film Evaluation Guide, 1946-1964. New York: Educational Film Library Association, Inc., 1965.

4500 motion picture films and filmstrips evaluated by the Educational Film Library Association are listed.

Index to 35mm. Educational Filmstrips. National Information Center for Educational Media, University of Southern California. 2nd ed. New York: R. R. Bowker Co., 1970.

This most comprehensive listing of filmstrips is divided into three principal sections. The Subject Guide to 35mm. Filmstrips is arranged under subject headings. The Alphabetical Guide to 35mm. Filmstrips provides complete information for each filmstrip. The third section is a Directory of Producers and Distributors.

U. S. Government Films. *A Catalog of Motion Pictures and Filmstrips for Sale by the National Audio-Visual Center.* Washington, D. C.: National Archives and Records Services, General Services Administration, 1969.

U. S. Library of Congress. *Library of Congress Catalog – Motion Pictures and Filmstrips, 1953-1957, 1958-1962.* Ann Arbor, Mich.: Edwards, 1958-1963.

VI. Guides to Transparencies

Educators Guide to Free Tapes, Scripts and Transparencies. Randolph, Wisc.: Educators Progress Service, 1955–.

This annual publication lists tapes, scripts and transparencies with source, availability, terms of loan, etc. It is arranged by subject, with subject and title index.

National Information Center for Educational Media. *Index to Overhead Transparencies.* New York: R. R. Bowker, Co., 1970.

VII. Guides to Maps

Kingsbury, Robert G. *Sources of Information and Materials: Maps and Aerial Photographs.* Prepared by the Committee on Maps and Aerial Photographs, Provisional Education Association of American Geographers, 1970.

Lists agencies and dealers of maps, atlases, aerial photographs, filmstrips, slides, films, globes, transparencies and raised relief models. It is not a multi-media index, but its special features include a list of atlases for classroom use, a bibliography of non-technical literature on maps and a list of pertinent government agencies.

VIII. Guides to Microforms

Ballou, Hubbard Walter, ed. *The Guide to Microreproduction Equipment.* Annapolis, Md.: National Microfilm Association, 1965.

An annual list of books, journals and other microforms materials in alphabetical order.

Guide to Microforms in Print. Washington, D. C.: 1960–.

An annual list of books, journals and other microforms materials in alphabetical order.

Subject Guide to Microforms in Print. Washington, D. C.

A biennial guide to materials available on microfilm and other microforms from U. S. publishers.

IX. Guides to Phonorecords

Annotated List of Phonograph Records. Brooklyn, N. Y.: Record Division, Children's Reading Service.

Bildersee, Max U. *Audio Cardalog.* New York.

A monthly review of disc and tape recordings of educational value. The information is distributed in a card format and over 400 titles are indexed each year.

Blue Book of Audio-Visual Materials. Chicago: Trade Periodicals, Inc.

This guide includes reviews of disc and tape recordings at all grade levels.

Cohn, Arthur. *The Collectors 20th Century Music and Phonorecords.*

Coover, James B. and Colvig, Richard. *Medieval and Renaissance Music on Long Playing Records.* Detroit: Information Service, Inc., 1964.

Folk Music: A Selection of Folk Songs, Ballads, Dances, Instrumental Pieces, and Folk Tales of the U. S. and Latin America. Washington, D. C.: Music Division, Recording Laboratory, Reference Department, U. S. Library of Congress.

Haggin, B. H. *The New Listener's Companion and Record Guide.* 3rd ed. New York: Horizon Press, 1970.

A guide to composers, musicians, recorded performances, musical forms and meanings, criticisms and critics, this work may be used to determine which release of a particular musical work is judged the best.

Hurst, P. G. *The Golden Age Recorded.* 2nd ed. Lingfield, England: The Oakwood Press, 1963.

Music Trade Directory and Guide. 2nd ed. London: Trafts and Woolf, 1966.

Myers, Kurtz. *The Index of Record Reviews.* In "Notes," 1943—. Harold E. Samuel, editor. Ann Arbor, Mich.: Musical Library Association, School of Music, University of Michigan.

Over 2500 reviews per quarterly issue are indexed from over 20 American and English periodicals.

New York Library Association. *Recordings for Children: A Selected List.* 2nd ed. New York: Children's and Young Adult Section, New York Library Association, 1964.

An alphabetical listing of over 500 entries by title under broad subject headings of records best suited for home and recreation collections.

Records in Review, 1970. New York: Scribner's, 1970.

The 15th annual collection of record reviews from *High Fidelity* is arranged in one alphabetical listing under composer, with performer index included.

Roach, Helen. *Spoken Records.* 3rd ed. Metuchen, N. J.: Scarecrow Press, 1970.

Covers over 500 entries of spoken records including documentaries, lectures, interviews, readings by authors, etc. Arranged by category and then by title, it includes a discography of Shakespeare's plays on record as well as a list of addresses for the major record companies.

Rust, Brian. *Jazz Records A-Z, 1897-1963.* 2nd ed. Hatch End, Middlesex, England: 1965.

Rust, Brian. *Jazz Records A-Z, 1932-1942.* Hatch End, Middlesex, England: 1965.

Schwann Long Playing Record Catalog. Boston: W. Schwann, 1949–.

A monthly guide to monoral and stereo records, this catalog is the *Books in Print* of the record industry.

U. S. Library of Congress. *Library of Congress Catalog–Music and Phonorecords.* Washington, D. C.: 1953–.

A semiannual publication with annual and quinquennial cummulations, this catalog contains entries for music scores and musical and non-musical sound recordings.

Van de Voorde, Ronald A. *A Basic Record Repertoire for Small Libraries.* Tucson, Ariz.: Bureau of Educational Research and Service, College of Education, University of Arizona, 1970.

A listing of major concert compositions with a recommended recording for each composition listed.

X. Guides to Audiotapes

Educators Guide to Free Tapes, Scripts, and Transparencies. Randolph, Wisc.: Educators Progress Service, 1955–.

An annual publication arranging available tapes, scripts and transparencies under broad subject categories. Complete information is included about each.

National Center for Audio Tapes Catalog. Boulder, Colo.: National Center for Audio Tapes, University of Colorado, 1969.

National Tape Recording Catalog, 1962-63. 3rd ed. Washington, D. C.: Department of Audio-Visual Instruction, National Education Association, 1963. Supplement I, 1965.

Lists over 500 tapes available from the National Tape Repository. It contains a description, subject classification and grade level for each tape. This is also a basic source for tape-recorded education programs for radio, covering the major curriculum areas on the elementary and secondary levels.

World Tapes for Education, Dallas.

XI. Guides to Radio and Television

Instructional Television Materials. New York: National Instructional Television Library, 1962–.

Lists television programs suitable for elementary and secondary schools and those designed for college and university audiences.

McKune, Lawrence E. *National Compendium of Telecourses for Credit.* East Lansing, Mich.: Continuing Education Service, University of the Air, Michigan State University, 1962.

A catalog of telecourses which have been produced in the U. S., arranged alphabetically by the college responsible for production. A note on the availability of a recording of the course is included, as well as a brief description of the course, written by the course professor. Appendix A is a list of addresses for the various State Departments of Public Instruction. Appendix B is an alphabetical list of teachers, subject taught, and school where the course was offered.

McKune, Lawrence E. *National Compendium of Television Education.* East Lansing, Mich.: Michigan State University, 1953–.

An annual publication listing videotape recordings by subject and title.

National Education Television Film Service. *Catalog.* Bloomington, Ind.: Audio-Visual Center, Indiana University.

Witherspoon, John P. and Kessler, William J. *Instructional Television Facilities: A Planning Guide.* Washington, D. C.: Office of Education, U. S. Department of Health, Education, and Welfare, 1969.

WRTA Index. San Francisco: Western Radio and Television Association, 1967.

XII. Guides to Programmed Instruction

The Center for Programmed Instruction. Institute of Educational Technology. *Programmed Instruction Materials, 1964-1965.* New York: Teachers College Press, 1965.

A guide to programmed instruction designed for teachers which includes over 500 selections for a wide variety of subjects.

Hendershot, Carl H. *Programmed Learning, a Bibliography of Programs and Presentation Devices.* 4th ed. Bay City, Mich.: 1967. 2 volume Supplement, 1968.

Volume 1 is a subject arrangement of programs. Volume 2 includes the ordering information and descriptive notes.

Lumsdaine, A. A., and Glaser, Robert. *Teaching Machines and Programmed Learning: A Source Book.* Washington, D. C.: Department of Audio-Visual Instruction, National Education Association, 1960.

XIII. Resources in Professional and Popular Periodicals

American Film Institute, Education Membership Newsletter. Washington, D. C.: American Film Institute.

American Record Guide. New York.

American Cinematographer. Los Angeles: American Society of Cinematographers Agency, Inc.

American Recorder. New York: American Recorder Society, Inc.

American School and University. New York: Buttenhein Publishing Corp.

Aspen. New York: Aspen Communications, Inc.

Audio. Philadelphia: North American Publishing Co.

Audio Visual Communications. New York: United Business Publications, Inc.

Audio Visual Journal. Minneapolis, Minn.: University of Minnesota.

Audiovisual Instruction. Washington, D. C.: National Education Association, Association for Educational Communications and Technology.

AV Communication Review. Washington, D. C.: Association for Educational Communication and Technology.

Back Stage. New York: Back Stage Publications, Inc.

318

Better Radio and Television. Los Angeles: National Association for Better Radio and Television.

Billboard. New York: Billboard Publishing Co.

BM/E; Broadcast Management/Engineering. New York: Mactier Publishing Co.

Broadcasting; the Business Weekly of Television and Radio. Washington, D. C.: Broadcasting Publications, Inc.

Business Screen. Wheaton, Ill.: Harcourt Brace Jovanovich, Inc.

Cablecasting. Ridgefield, Conn.: Tepfer Publishing Co., Inc.

CEFP Journal. Columbus, Ohio: Council of Educational Facilities Planners.

Church Music. Nashville, Tenn.: Sunday School Board of the Southern Baptist Convention.

Cinema. Beverly Hills, Calif.: Spectator-International.

Classical Recordaid. Philadelphia: Recordaid, Inc.

College and University Business. Chicago: McGraw-Hill Publications.

Communication Arts Magazine. Palo Alto, Calif.: Coyne and Blanchard, Inc.

Communications News. Wheaton, Ill.: Brookhill Publishing Co.

Computers and Automation. Newtonville, Mass.: Berkley Enterprises, Inc.

Discographer. Venice, Calif.

Down Beat. Chicago: Maher Publications, Inc.

Educational Broadcasting Review. Columbus, Ohio: National Association of Educational Broadcasters.

Educational/Instructional Broadcasting. Los Angeles: Technology Publishers Corporation.

Educational Media. Fort Worth, Tex.: Educational Media Publishing Co.

Educational Product Report. New York: Educational Products Information Exchange.

Educational Screen and Audio-Visual Guide. Chicago: Trade Periodicals.

Educational Technology. Englewood Cliffs, N. J.: Educational Technology Publications, Inc.

319

Educational Television. Ridgefield, Conn.: C. S. Tepfer Publishing Co.

Educators Guide to Media and Methods. New York.

ERIC/CLIS: Eric Clearinghouse on Library and Information Sciences. Washington, D. C.

ETV Newsletter. Ridgefield, Conn.: ETV Newsletter Co.

Film and Television Technician. London: Association of Cinematography, Television, and Allied Technicians.

Film Bulletin. Philadelphia: Wax Publications, Inc.

Film Information. New York: Broadcasting and Film Commission, National Council of Churches.

Film Library Quarterly. New York: FLIC.

Filmlist. New York: Educational Film Library Association.

Film News. New York.

Film Quarterly. Berkeley, Calif.: University of California Press.

Filmmakers' Newsletter. New York: Filmmakers' Newsletter Co.

Films in Review. New York: National Board of Review of Motion Pictures, Inc.

Fine Arts. Cleveland, Ohio: Fine Arts, Inc.

FM Music Program Guide. New York.

Gramaphone. Kenton, Middlesex, England: General Gramaphone Publications, Ltd.

Graphics: U. S. A. New York: Kaye Publishing Corporation.

Great Plains National Instructional Television Library Newsletter. Lincoln, Neb.: Great Plains National Instructional Television Library, University of Nebraska.

Hi-Fi News and Record Review. Croydon, Surrey, England: Link House Publications, Ltd.

Hi-Fi Stereo Buyers' Guide. New York: David Publications, Inc.

High Fidelity. New York: Billboard Publications, Inc.

High Fidelity/Musical America. New York: Billboard Publications, Inc.

Industrial Photography. New York: United Business Publications, Inc.

Jazz and Pop. New York: United Business Publications, Inc.

Jazz Hot. Paris.

Journal of Broadcasting. Philadelphia: Association for Professional Broadcasting Education, Temple University.

Journal of Church Music. Philadelphia: Fortress Press.

Journal of College Radio. Norman, Okla.: Intercollegiate Broadcasting System, Inc., University of Oklahoma.

Journal of Communication. Athens, Ohio: International Communication Association, Ohio University.

Landers Film Reviews. Los Angeles: Landers Associates.

Library Journal. New York: R. R. Bowker Co.

Listen. Philadelphia: Rittenhouse Corp.

List-O-Tapes. Los Angeles: Phono-log Publishing.

Media and Methods. Philadelphia: North American Publishing Co.

Media Decision. New York: Norman Glenn Publications, Inc.

Media: Library Services Journal. Nashville, Tenn.: Sunday School Board of the Southern Baptist Convention.

Micropublisher: A National Newsletter of Microfilming for Libraries. Wooster, Ohio: Micro Photo Division, Bell & Howell Co.

Modern Media Teacher. Dayton, Ohio: George A. Pflaum.

Modern Photography. New York: Herbert Keppler.

Music in Education. London: Novello and Co., Ltd.

Music Library Association, Notes. Ann Arbor, Mich.: University of Michigan.

Music Ministry: for all with Music Responsibilities in Church and Church School. Nashville, Tenn.: Graded Press.

National Association of Educational Broadcasters Newsletter. Washington, D. C.: National Association of Educational Broadcasters.

New Cinema Review. New York.

Newsreel. New York: McGraw-Hill Films.

NSPI Journal. San Antonio, Tex.: National Society for Programmed Instruction, Trinity University.

Opera News. New York: Metropolitan Opera Guild, Inc.

Perspectives of New Music. Princeton, N. J.: Princeton University Press.

Photo Methods for Industry. New York: Gellert Publishing Co.

Picturescope. New York: New York Public Library, Picture Collection.

Popular Photography. New York: Ziff-Davis Publishing Co.

Popular Recordaid. Philadelphia: Recordaid, Inc.

Preview. Bloomington, Ind.: Audio Visual Center Field Services, Indiana University.

Programmed Learning and Educational Technology. London: Sweet and Maxwell, Ltd.

Record Collector. Ipswich, Suffolk, England: James F. E. Dennis.

Recorded Sound. London: British Institute of Recorded Sound.

Recording Engineer/Producer. Hollywood, Calif.

Religious Broadcasting. Madison, N. J.: National Religious Broadcasters, Inc.

Research in Education. Washington, D. C.: U. S. Government Printing Office.

RPM Weekly. Toronto: RPM Music Publications.

School Musician Director and Teacher. Joliet, Ill.: F. L. McAllister.

Schwann Record and Tape Guide. Boston: W. Schwann, Inc.

Sound and Communications. New York: Jerome J. Brookman.

Spin. Wallasey, Cherhire, England: Spin Publications.

Stereo Review. New York: Ziff-Davis Publishing Co.

Teachers College Record; a Professional Journal of Ideas, Research, and Informed Opinion. New York: Columbia University.

Telecommunications. Dedham, Mass.: Horizon House.

Television Quarterly. New York: National Academy of Television Arts and Sciences.

Training in Business and Industry. New York: Gellert Publishing Co.

TV Communications. Englewood, Colo.: Communications Publishing Corp.

TV Film Filebook. East Scarbourough, Ontario: TV Film Filebooks.

University Film Association Journal. Columbus, Ohio: University Film Association, Ohio State University.

U. S. Government Publications. Monthly Catalog. Washington, D. C.: Government Printing Office.

U. S. Library of Congress Catalog – Music and Phonorecords. Washington, D. C.: Library of Congress.

U. S. Library of Congress Catalog – Motion Pictures and Filmstrips. Washington, D. C.: Library of Congress.

U. S. Library of Congress Catalog of Copyright Entries. Third Series, Parts 7-11: Works of Art. Washington, D. C.: Library of Congress.

Visual Education. London: National Committee for Audio-Visual Aids in Education.

Wilson Library Bulletin. New York: H. W. Wilson Co.